PRE-INTERMEDIATE

John Hughes

Helen Stephenson
Paul Dummett

Contents

Listening	Reading	Critical thinking	Speaking	Writing
someone talking about two elderly ballroom dancers a health expert analyses sleep a radio interview about long life	a quiz about how well you sleep an article about centenarians an article about measuring health and happiness	the main argument	a quiz your current life measuring happiness	text type: online advice writing skill: conjunctions (*and*, *or*, *so*, *because*, *but*)
someone describing an Ironman competition three people talking about sport a reporter describing the rules of a competition	quotes by famous sports people an article about crazy competitions an article about female wrestlers in Bolivia	reading between the lines	guess the ambition explaining the rules of a competition your opinions about sport	text type: an advert or notice writing skill: checking your writing
someone describing a photo of a girl travelling by train in India two people discussing the pros and cons of electric cars two documentaries about using animals for transporting	an article about transport in the future an article about dog sledging an article about the fate of the rickshaw in Kolkata	reading between the lines	transport you use attitudes to using animals for transporting arguing for and against keeping rickshaws in Kolkata	a report about how people travel around town text type: notes and messages writing skill: writing in note form
a caver describing Rumbling Falls Cave an interview with a survival expert	an article about adventurers an article about a climbing accident	identifying opinion	asking about your past qualities needed for an expedition events you remember retelling a story	text type: a true story writing skill: using *-ly* adverbs in stories
extract from a documentary about the artist George Sabra a radio phone-in show about recycling	an article about e-rubbish an article about the Greendex an article about a boat made of plastic bottles, the *Plastiki* an online order	close reading	opinions on recycling presenting a report an interview with an environmentalist	a report of a survey text type: emails writing skill: formal language
an explanation to a riddle three people talking about their plans and intentions a news item about Mardis Gras	an article about how a couple changed their life an article about how Mardis Gras is celebrated around the world an article about a Masai rite of passage	identifying the key information	life-changing decisions your favourite festival describing annual events	text type: a description writing skill: descriptive adjectives

Listening	Reading	Critical thinking	Speaking	Writing
someone talking about triplet police officers a documentary about working as a photographer an interview with an engineer	workplace messages with instructions an article about the cost of new jobs to an area an article about modern-day cowboys	the author's opinion	giving directions describing past experiences your opinion of a job	text type: a CV writing skill: action verbs for CVs
a documentary about the importance of technology a science programme about a new invention	an explorer's blog an article about biomimetics	supporting the main argument	problems that inventions solved inventing a new robot planning an expedition using nature to improve designs	text type: a paragraph writing skills: connecting words; topic and supporting sentences
an English teacher talking about working in Japan a radio documentary about learning Kung Fu in China	an article about the history of writing an article about saving languages	fact or opinion	adult education a general knowledge quiz the author's opinion	a general knowledge quiz text type: forms writing skill: providing the correct information
an interview with a herpetologist two conversations about problems whilst on holiday an interview with a *National Geographic* tour guide	an article about tipping in other countries an article about the tunnels in Paris	reading between the lines	a holiday or journey you remember planning the holiday of a lifetime a tourist website	a tourist webpage text type: a formal letter writing skill: formal expressions
an historian talking about Scott's hut at the Antarctic an interview with an archaeologist	an article about moments in space history a biography of Jane Goodall	relevance	items for a time capsule how we used to live moments in history reporting an interview an interview for a biography	text type: a biography writing skill: punctuation in direct speech
a nature expert talking about how animals camouflage themselves a documentary about a photographer	an article about storm chasers a profile on Greenland	close reading	promoting your region planning for every possibility predicting your country's future	text type: a press release writing skill: using bullet points

Life around the world

Unit 4 Alaskan ice climbing

How to climb a wall of ice.

Unit 5 Coastal clean-up

A global effort to clean up the world's beaches.

Unit 8 Wind power

How the wind turbines of Spirit Lake save the schools energy and money.

Unit 6 Steel drums

Steelband music, or pan, is an important part of this Caribbean island's culture.

Unit 11 The lost city of Machu Picchu

The impact of tourism on the Inca city of Machu Picchu.

USA

UK

Trinidad & Tobago

Peru

Unit 2 Cheese rolling

The ancient tradition of cheese rolling in a village in England.

Unit 7 Butler school

Find out how to become a butler.

Unit 1 Slow food

A city that is enjoying itself – taking life slowly.

Unit 10 Living in Venice

Learn what it's like to live in Venice.

Unit 3 Indian railways

Learn more about the Indian railway system.

Unit 12 Cambodia Animal Rescue

Rescuing victims of illegal animal poaching in Cambodia.

Unit 9 Disappearing voices

A project to record the last speakers of disappearing languages.

Italy

India

Cambodia

Australia

**UNIT 1
HEALTH**

**UNIT 2
COMPETITIONS**

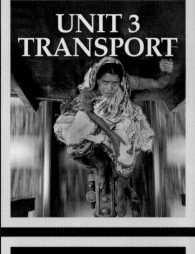

**UNIT 3
TRANSPORT**

**UNIT 4
ADVENTURE**

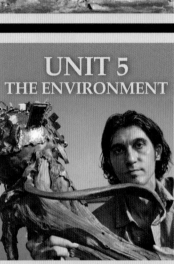

**UNIT 5
THE ENVIRONMENT**

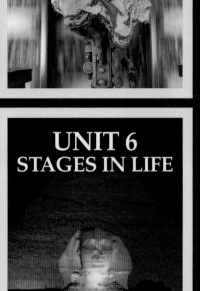

**UNIT 6
STAGES IN LIFE**

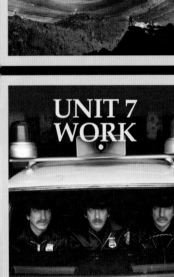

**UNIT 7
WORK**

**UNIT 8
TECHNOLOGY**

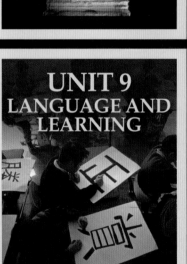

**UNIT 9
LANGUAGE AND
LEARNING**

**UNIT 10
TRAVEL AND
HOLIDAYS**

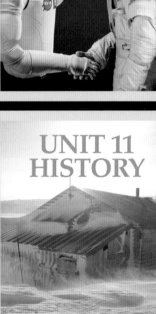

**UNIT 11
HISTORY**

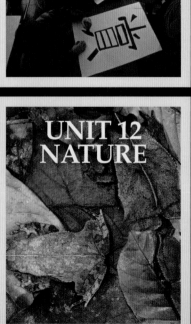

**UNIT 12
NATURE**

Dance practice, Australia
Photo by Brendan McCarthy

FEATURES

1 Look at the two people in the photo. Why do you think they are happy?

2 🔊 **1.1** Listen to someone talking about the people in the photo. Answer the questions.

1 Who are they?
2 How often do they practise dancing?
3 Why do they think dancing is good for their physical and mental health?

3 Work in pairs. Look at these activities. Tell your partner which activities you often do. Why do you do them?

> cycle through the countryside   do crosswords
> go for a long walk   work long hours   read a book
> play computer games   run marathons   watch TV

> I often cycle through the countryside because it's good for my health.

4 Think about other activities you do in your free time that are good for your physical or mental health. Tell your partner.

1a How well do you sleep?

Reading and speaking

1 Do you feel tired today? Why? / Why not?

2 Do the quiz below about sleep. Make a note of your answers.

Listening

3 **1.2** Listen to a health expert talking about the quiz. Tick the characteristics which are true for each answer.

People with mostly A answers:
1 You have regular routines.
2 You are hardly ever tired.

People with mostly B answers:
3 You wake up once or twice a night.
4 You need more sleep than other people.

People with mostly C answers:
5 You regularly work in the evening.
6 You don't like sport.

4 Work in pairs. Compare your answers in the quiz. Which type of person are you? Do you need to change your lifestyle?

Grammar **present simple and adverbs of frequency**

5 Match the sentences from the quiz (1–2) with the uses of the present simple tense (a–b).

1 Before bedtime, I often do some work.
2 I'm never tired at work.

a to talk about things that are always true
b to talk about habits and routines

> **▶ PRESENT SIMPLE**
>
> I/you/we/they sleep
> he/she/it sleeps
>
> I/you/we/they don't sleep
> he/she/it doesn't sleep
>
> Do you sleep ...?
> Does he sleep ...?
>
> For further information and practice, see page 156.

How well do you sleep?

Question: 1 2 3 4 5 6

Q: Do you often feel tired?

A No, I don't often feel tired.
B I sometimes feel tired after a long day at work.
C All the time! I'm always ready for bed.

Question: 1 **2** 3 4 5 6

Q: How many hours a night do you sleep?

A Between seven and eight hours.
B More than nine. I rarely stay up late.
C Fewer than six.

Question: 1 2 **3** 4 5 6

Q: Before bedtime, I often ...

A watch TV or read a book.
B do some exercise.
C do some work.

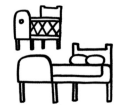

Question: 1 2 3 **4** 5 6

Q: At the weekend, I ...

A usually sleep the same amount as any other day.
B sometimes sleep for an hour or two extra.
C always sleep until midday! I never get up early.

Question: 1 2 3 4 **5** 6

Q: How often do you wake up in the middle of the night?

A I never wake up before morning.
B I rarely wake up more than once, and I usually fall asleep again quite quickly.
C Two or three times a night.

Question: 1 2 3 4 5 **6**

Q: Are you often sleepy during the day?

A No, I'm never tired at work.
B Sometimes, so I take a nap after lunch. After that I'm ready for work again.
C Always! That's because I work long hours and get home late.

> **fall asleep** /fɔːl əˈsliːp/ start sleeping
> **take a nap** /teɪk ə næp/ a short sleep that you have during the day

6 Look at the grammar box. Then complete the article about sleep with the present simple form of the verbs.

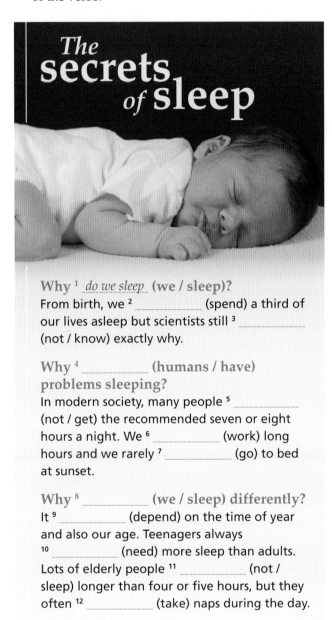

The secrets of sleep

Why ¹ *do we sleep* (we / sleep)?
From birth, we ² _____ (spend) a third of our lives asleep but scientists still ³ _____ (not / know) exactly why.

Why ⁴ _____ (humans / have) problems sleeping?
In modern society, many people ⁵ _____ (not / get) the recommended seven or eight hours a night. We ⁶ _____ (work) long hours and we rarely ⁷ _____ (go) to bed at sunset.

Why ⁸ _____ (we / sleep) differently?
It ⁹ _____ (depend) on the time of year and also our age. Teenagers always ¹⁰ _____ (need) more sleep than adults. Lots of elderly people ¹¹ _____ (not / sleep) longer than four or five hours, but they often ¹² _____ (take) naps during the day.

7 Pronunciation /s/, /z/ or /ɪz/

🔊 **1.3** Listen to the ending of these verbs. Write /s/, /z/ or /ɪz/. Then listen again and repeat.

1 feels /z/
2 needs
3 watches
4 sleeps
5 goes
6 dances
7 does
8 works

8 Discuss the questions.

1 What time do people normally get up in your country? How late do they stay up? Do they ever take a nap in the afternoon?
2 How does this change during the year? Do people sleep longer in the summer or in the winter?

9 Complete this table with adverbs of frequency from the quiz in Exercise 2.

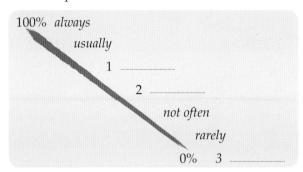

100% *always*
     usually
  1 _____
   2 _____
     not often
       rarely
0%   3 _____

10 Look at the position of the adverbs and expressions of frequency in the example sentences in the grammar box. Then choose the correct options to complete the rules (1–2).

> ▶ **ADVERBS and EXPRESSIONS OF FREQUENCY**
>
> She's **usually** late for work.
> I **often wake up** at seven.
> How **often** do you wake up in the night?
> She wakes up **two or three times a night**.
> **In the winter**, we sleep longer.
>
> For further information and practice, see page 156.

1 An adverb of frequency goes *after / before* the verb *to be* but it normally goes *after / before* the main verb.
2 An expression of frequency usually goes *at the beginning / in the middle* or at the end of a sentence.

11 Work in pairs. Ask and answer questions about these things. Use an adverb or expression of frequency in your answers.

do exercise	be late for work
take public transport	read a novel in the bath
eat out in restaurants	be in a bad mood
do gardening	go on holiday
play board games	be busy at weekends
check your emails	be stressed at work

How often do you do exercise?

Two or three times a week.

Speaking and writing

12 Work in groups. Prepare a *How healthy are you?* quiz for another group. Start each question with *How often …? Are you often …?* or *Do you ever …?* and offer three choices of answer (A, B or C).

13 When you are ready, join another group and ask the questions in your quiz. Afterwards, tell the class about their answers. Do you think the other group is very healthy?

1b The secrets of long life

Reading

1 Who is the oldest person you know? How old are they? How healthy is their lifestyle?

2 Read the article below. Answer the questions.

1 Why are the people of Okinawa famous?
2 What are the reasons for their good health?

3 Which of the reasons for good health in the article are true for your life? Tell your partner.

Vocabulary *do, go* or *play*

4 Complete the table with activities from the article in Exercise 2.

do	go	play
	fishing	

5 Add these activities to the table in Exercise 4. Use your dictionary to help you, if necessary. Then think of one more activity for each verb.

cards   hiking   homework   nothing   running   shopping
tennis   the piano   yoga   football   karate   surfing

▶ **WORDBUILDING verb + noun collocations**

We can only use certain nouns with certain verbs. These are called collocations. For example, *go fishing* but not ~~do fishing~~ or ~~play fishing~~.

For further information and practice, see Workbook page 11.

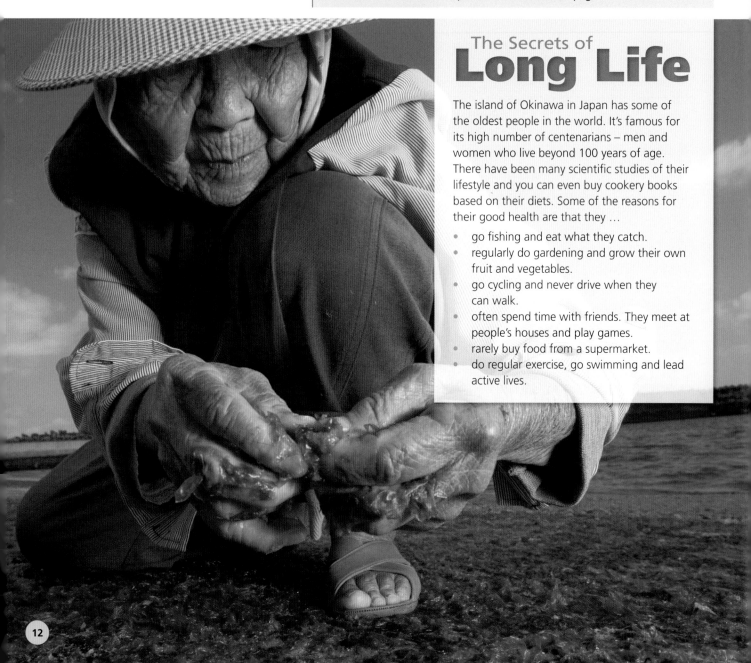

The Secrets of
Long Life

The island of Okinawa in Japan has some of the oldest people in the world. It's famous for its high number of centenarians – men and women who live beyond 100 years of age. There have been many scientific studies of their lifestyle and you can even buy cookery books based on their diets. Some of the reasons for their good health are that they …

- go fishing and eat what they catch.
- regularly do gardening and grow their own fruit and vegetables.
- go cycling and never drive when they can walk.
- often spend time with friends. They meet at people's houses and play games.
- rarely buy food from a supermarket.
- do regular exercise, go swimming and lead active lives.

Listening

6 🔊 **1.4** Listen to a radio interview with David McLain, an explorer and journalist. Answer the questions.

1 What does David want to know?
2 Why is he in Sardinia?

7 🔊 **1.4** Listen again. Are the sentences true (T) or false (F)?

1 David McLain is travelling to different countries.
2 He's talking to the radio presenter in the studio.
3 Men don't live the same number of years as women on Sardinia.
4 Sardinian families often eat together.
5 David thinks Sardinia is less stressful than other countries.
6 Younger people are eating more unhealthy food and they aren't getting much exercise.

Grammar present simple and present continuous

8 Look at the five sentences from the interview in Exercise 6. Which two sentences use the present simple tense? Why?

1 He's currently travelling to places and regions.
2 He's speaking to us right now on the phone.
3 Men live the same amount of time as women.
4 Every Sunday the whole family meets and they eat a huge meal together.
5 Young people are moving to the city so they are doing less exercise because of their lifestyle.

9 The three other sentences in Exercise 8 use the present continuous tense. How do you form the tense? Match the three sentences to the uses (a–c).

a to talk about things happening at the moment of speaking
b to talk about things happening around now but not necessarily at the moment of speaking
c to talk about current trends and changing situations

> ▶ **PRESENT CONTINUOUS**
>
> I am speaking
> you/we/they are speaking
> he/she/it is speaking
>
> I'm not travelling
> you/we/they aren't travelling
> he/she/it isn't travelling
>
> Am I moving?
> Are you/we/they moving?
> Is he/she/it moving?
>
> For further information and practice, see page 156.

10 Complete the sentences with the present simple or present continuous form of these verbs.

check	not / do	not / eat	go	~~learn~~	play
read	spend				

1 We *'re learning* a new language at the moment.
2 My friends and I often ＿＿＿ time at each other's houses.
3 One moment! I ＿＿＿ my emails and then I'm ready to go.
4 How often ＿＿＿ you ＿＿＿ to the gym?
5 I ＿＿＿ a really interesting book at the moment.
6 Currently, a friend of mine ＿＿＿ any sweets and he says he feels healthier.
7 I'm nearly eighty but I ＿＿＿ any exercise!
8 Which computer game ＿＿＿ you ＿＿＿? It looks fun.

Speaking

11 Work in pairs. Take turns to ask and answer the questions. Use the present simple and present continuous tense in your answers.

1 What's your typical working day? Are you working on anything new at the moment?
2 How do you spend your free time? Are you getting much exercise?
3 Do you often read novels? Are you reading anything interesting at the moment?
4 Where do you normally go on holiday? Are you planning your holidays for this year?
5 Do you speak any other languages? Are you learning any new languages?

1c Health and happiness

Speaking

1 Which of these things make you feel happy? Order them from 1 to 5 (1 = most happy). Compare with your partner.

- Sleeping for a long time
- Having money
- Relaxing on holiday
- Going out with friends
- Doing exercise

Critical thinking the main argument

2 Read the article on page 15. Which of the sentences (1–3) is the best summary of the main argument?

1 Happiness improves our health.
2 Denmark is the happiest country in the world.
3 There are different ways to measure happiness.

Reading

3 Choose the correct answer (a–c) for the questions, according to the information in the article.

1 How did the King of Bhutan measure the country's development?
   a by money   b by health
   c by happiness

2 Which is easier to measure?
   a happiness   b health
   c sickness and ill health

3 Why was Iceland number one in a survey?
   a for its money   b for its health
   c for its happiness

4 How did researchers measure happiness in 155 countries?
   a with answers to questions
   b by looking at people's faces
   c by measuring the number of sick people

5 What do visitors to Krikortz's website click on?
   a questions   b faces   c numbers

6 How many categories does Krikortz have for measuring happiness?
   a three   b five   c seven

7 What colour are the lights on the building when Stockholm is happy?
   a red   b green   c purple

Word focus *feel*

4 Look at the sentences (1–4) from the article. Match *feel* in each sentence with the uses (a–d).

1 It's also easy to measure how many people feel ill or unhealthy in a country.
2 Denmark feels happier than other countries.
3 Krikortz feels that there are other ways of measuring happiness.
4 The coloured lights are also useful if you feel like visiting the city.

a to give an opinion
b to talk about an emotion
c to talk about physical illness
d to talk about wanting something or wanting to do something

5 Match the questions (1–3) to the responses (a–c).

1 How do you feel today?
2 What do you feel about Krikortz's project?
3 Do you feel like going for a coffee after the class?

a Fine, thanks. How about you?
b Yes, I'd like to.
c I'm not sure. It's quite interesting I suppose.

6 Work in pairs. Take turns to ask the questions in Exercise 5. Answer with your own words.

Speaking

7 Work in groups. Discuss the questions.

1 In paragraph 1, the King of Bhutan talks about 'Gross National Happiness'. How happy do you think your country is? Give reasons for your answer.
2 In paragraph 2, a doctor said, 'Happy people generally don't get sick.' How much do you agree with this opinion?
3 In paragraph 3 and 4, there are different questions and categories for measuring happiness. Which do you think are useful for measuring happiness? Which are not very useful?

8 Work in the same group. Make a list of five categories for measuring happiness (e.g. money, sleep). Then everyone in the group gives a score for each of the categories (1 = very happy, 2 = happy, 3 = OK, 4 = not very happy). How happy is your group? Present your categories and result to the class.

measuring
HEALTH
AND
HAPPINESS

The small country of Bhutan in the Himalayan mountains is over one thousand years old. In the past it was a poor country and not many people visited it. But nowadays, it is becoming more and more popular with tourists. Medicine and health is improving and its economy is growing. King Jigme Singye Wangchuck, the king of Bhutan until 2006, talked about his country's 'Gross National Happiness'. In other words, he thought happiness is the way to measure the country's development.

But how do you measure happiness? Perhaps health is the best way because a famous doctor once said, 'Happy people generally don't get sick.' It's also easy to measure how many people feel ill or unhealthy in a country. For example, one survey says Iceland is the 'healthiest country in the world' because men and women live a long time there, the air is very clean and there are more doctors available per person than anywhere else in the world.

However, there was another survey of the happiest countries in the world and Iceland was not near the top. The questions on this survey included: How much do you earn? How healthy are you? How safe do you feel? After visiting 155 different countries, the researchers decided that Denmark feels happier than other countries.

So does happiness equal money and good health? Not according to the artist Erik Krikortz. He feels that there are other ways of measuring happiness. Krikortz has a website and visitors click on different happy or sad faces to comment on how well they sleep, their family and friends, their level of stress, their inspiration and their physical activity. When you finish, his website adds the results for each area and it gives you a final result for your happiness.

In his home city of Stockholm, Krikortz also shows the results of his survey as different coloured lights on the side of a large building in the city. For example, red means the people of Stockholm are very happy, green is OK and purple means many people are sad. 'A lot of people look at the building every day and see how "we" are,' Krikortz says. The coloured lights are also useful if you feel like visiting the city. For example, if the lights are red, you know the locals are feeling happy!

inspiration (n) /ˌɪnspəˈreɪʃn/ a feeling that makes you want to do something or gives you exciting new ideas

1d At the doctor's

Vocabulary **medical problems**

1 Look at the pictures. Match the people (1–8) with the medical problems (a–h).

a I've got a headache.
b I've got back ache.
c I've got a runny nose.
d I've got earache.
e I've got stomach ache.
f I've got a temperature.
g I've got a sore throat.
h I've got a bad cough.

2 Pronunciation **sound and spelling**

a Many English words have the same vowel sounds but different spellings. Match the words with the same vowel sounds.

1	head	wake
2	sore	saw
3	throat	off
4	cough	note
5	ache	here
6	ear	bed

b 🔊 **1.5** Listen and check your answers. Then listen again and repeat.

3 What do you do when you have the medical problems in Exercise 1? Categorise them into the three groups. Then compare with your partner.

1 I go to bed.
2 I take medicine or pills.
3 I go to the pharmacy or see my doctor.

Real life **talking about illness**

4 🔊 **1.6** Listen to two conversations, one at a pharmacy and the other at a doctor's. Write the number of the conversation (*1* or *2*) next to the person's medical problems and medical advice they receive.

Medical problem	Medical advice
sore throat *1*	take this medicine twice a day *1*
bad cough	go to bed
runny nose	drink hot water with honey
earache	and lemon
feel sick	take one pill twice a day
temperature	buy a box of tissues
	drink lots of water

5 🔊 **1.6** Listen again and complete the sentences. Then match them with the correct section in the box.

1 I ＿＿＿ ＿＿＿ a sore throat.
2 You ＿＿＿ take this medicine.
3 It's ＿＿＿ ＿＿＿ a sore throat.
4 You ＿＿＿ a box of tissues.
5 If you still feel ill in a few days, see a ＿＿＿.
6 Let me have a ＿＿＿.
7 Do you ＿＿＿ sick?
8 Let me check your ＿＿＿.

> ▶ **TALKING ABOUT ILLNESS**
>
> **Asking and talking about illness**
> I don't feel very well.
> I feel sick / ill.
> Have you got a temperature?
> How do you feel?
>
> **Giving advice**
> Try drinking hot water with lemon.
> You need to take one of these.
> Drink lots of water.

6 Work in pairs. Practise this conversation. Then change roles and repeat the conversation.

Student A: You have a medical problem. (Choose one from Exercise 1.)

Student B: You are a pharmacist. Ask how Student A feels and give advice.

1e Medical advice online

Writing online advice

1 Many people look for medical advice on the internet before they visit their doctor. Do you think this is a good idea? Why? / Why not?

2 Look at the advice forum on a website. Answer the questions.

1 What medical problem has each person got?
2 Do you think the doctor gives them good advice?
3 Can you think of any more advice for each person?

www.askdoctorjoe.com

| Home | Symptom checker | Advice forum |

 Petra: I returned from a walking holiday in the Himalayas a week ago and now I feel sick. Do you think it's from the trip?

 Dr Joe: It could be from the holiday or it could be something you ate at home. But you should visit your doctor or hospital immediately!

 Seth: Hi! I often have problems sleeping at night so I'm tired all the time. Have you got any advice?

 Dr Joe: Sorry to hear this. Do you drink coffee before bed? It has caffeine and this often stops people sleeping. Try drinking herbal tea or a glass of warm milk because these drinks don't have any caffeine.

 Sabine: I'm worried about my health. I like doing exercise, but I spend all day working in front of a computer. What can I do?

 Dr Joe: How do you travel to work? You could go by bicycle. It's good for your health AND it saves you money.

> Accidents an
> Diet and nutr
> Eyes
> Health and w
> Common illne
> News
> Sports and fit
> Travel and im

> **MORE F**

Services
Case studies
Partnership
Research
About
Latest news
Board
Members
Statistics
Careers
Contact us

www.askdoctorjoe.com
FREE advice, 24 hrs

3 Writing skill conjunctions (*and, or, so, because, but*)

a Look at the highlighted conjunctions in the forum in Exercise 2. Then complete the rules with those words.

1 We use *and* to connect two words or parts of a sentence.
2 We use _____ to introduce an idea that is different.
3 We use _____ to say 'with the result that.'
4 We use _____ to explain the reason.
5 We use _____ to connect an alternative word or idea.

b Complete the sentences with the conjunctions in Exercise 3a.

1 You need to do more exercise _____ eat healthy food.
2 Jogging is healthy, _____ eating chocolate is nicer!
3 You could try cycling _____ go walking if you don't have a bicycle.
4 Fruit and vegetables are good for you _____ they are full of vitamins.
5 Fruit and vegetables are full of vitamins, _____ they are good for you.

4 Imagine you want advice from the forum. Choose a medical problem. Then write a message to Doctor Joe and ask for advice.

5 Exchange your message with your partner. Imagine you are Doctor Joe. Write a reply with two or three pieces of good advice. Remember to use conjunctions.

1f Slow food

A place where time is slower.

Before you watch

1 Work in groups. Look at the title of the video and the photo. Discuss the questions.

1 What do you think 'slow food' is?
2 How do you think the people in the photo feel?
3 What do you think the photo caption means?
4 What do you think the video is about?

2 Tick the things you think will be in this video.

> countryside
> farmers and people making food
> fast food restaurants
> lots of cars
> a modern city
> relaxed people enjoying food

While you watch

3 Watch the video and check your ideas from Exercise 2.

4 Watch the video again. Are these sentences true (T) or false (F)?

1 Chianti is a region in Spain.
2 Four thousand people live in Greve.
3 Greve is part of the Slow Cities League.
4 Salvatore Toscano runs an American-style restaurant.
5 His restaurant is in Greve.
6 Farmers make pecorino cheese from cows' milk.
7 Pecorino cheese is not very popular nowadays.
8 Greve wants to escape from the modern world.

5 Watch the video again. Answer these questions.

1 What is Greve famous for?

2 How many cities are in the Slow Cities League?

3 What is the purpose of the Slow Cities League?

4 How many members does the slow food movement have?

5 Why is pecorino cheese popular again?

6 What can you find everywhere in the world?

After you watch

6 Match the people (1–4) with what they say (a–d).

1 the narrator
2 Salvatore Toscano
3 Greve's mayor
4 the cheese maker

a Our aim is to keep Greve the same. We want to keep Greve and all the other slow cities special.
b It's about taking more time so you are more calm and relaxed.
c In the mountains of Pistoia, in northern Tuscany, farmers produce pecorino cheese.
d Not everyone knows about our product. But now the slow food movement means people know about us.

7 Roleplay a conversation with Salvatore Toscano

Work in pairs.

Student A: You are Salvatore Toscano. Read the questions below and make notes about yourself. Then ask your customer about his life.

- Why do you like Greve?
- What is it like living in Greve?
- Do you enjoy your job?

Student B: You are a customer in Salvatore Toscano's restaurant. You come from a large busy city. Read the questions below and make notes about yourself. Then ask Salvatore about his life in Greve.

- What's your name?
- What's your job?
- Do you like visiting Greve? Why?
- Do you want to live somewhere like Greve?

Act out the conversation. Compare your lives. Then change roles and repeat the conversation.

8 Read what the man says at the end of the video. Answer the questions.

From Singapore to Macao, in New York, in Rome, you always find the same pizza, the same hamburgers. Slow food doesn't want this.

1 Do you agree?
2 Do you think slow food is a good idea?

9 Work in pairs. Discuss these questions.

1 Would you like to live in Greve? Why? / Why not?
2 Do you live a quiet life or do you live in the fast lane? In what ways?

---

die out (v) /daɪ ˈaʊt/ disappear
mayor (n) /ˈmeɪə/ the head of the administration of a town
vineyard (n) /ˈvɪnjɑːd/ a place where grapes grow
worldwide (adv) /wɜːldˈwaɪd/ all over the world

UNIT 1 REVIEW

Grammar

1 Work in pairs. Look at the photo. Where are the man and the elephant? What are they doing?

2 Choose the correct forms to complete the text about the man in Exercise 1.

Every day, Nazroo ¹ *drives / is driving* elephants for a living, but, as you can see here, ² *he takes / he's taking* his favourite elephant, Rajan, for a swim. In this photo ³ *they swim / they're swimming* in the sea around Andaman Island. Sometimes they ⁴ *like / are liking* to relax this way after a hard day. I was surprised because Rajan ⁵ *doesn't seem / isn't seeming* worried about being under the water. I guess it feels good after a long, hot day at work.

3 Work in pairs. How often do Nazroo and Rajan go swimming? How often do you go swimming? How do you like to relax?

I CAN	
talk about regular actions and events using the present simple	
describe actions in progress (now or around now) using the present continuous	
ask and answer questions with *How often …?*	

Vocabulary

4 Which words can follow the verb in CAPITAL letters? Delete the incorrect word.

1 FEEL — tired, happy, ~~ache~~, sick
2 DO — exercise, housework, relaxing, yoga
3 PLAY — golf, swimming, games, tennis
4 GO — marathon, racing, hiking, driving

5 Work in pairs. How do you feel about your new English course? Do you feel worried about anything? (Tell your teacher if you are.)

I CAN	
talk about leisure activities	
say how I feel	

Real life

6 Choose the correct words to complete the conversation between two friends.

A: ¹ *How do / Do* you feel?
B: Not very ² *well / ill*. I've got a ³ *pain / sore* throat.
A: ⁴ *Do you feel / Have you got* a high temperature?
B: I don't know. I feel a bit hot.
A: ⁵ *Try / You need* drinking some honey and lemon in hot water.
B: Good idea.
A: But ⁶ *you should / it's a good idea* also see your doctor.

7 Work in pairs. Practise two similar conversations.

Conversation 1:
Student A has got a headache. Student B gives advice.

Conversation 2:
Student B has got stomach ache. Student A gives advice.

I CAN	
talk about feeling ill	
give advice	

Speaking

8 Complete these questions to ask someone about their everyday habits and interests.

1 Do you often play …?
2 How often do you go …?
3 Do you ever …?
4 What are you *-ing* …?
5 Why do you …?

9 Work in pairs. Ask and answer your questions from Exercise 8.

Unit 2 Competitions

Ironman competition
Photo by Patrick McFeeley

FEATURES

1 Look at the photo. What kind of competition is it? Do you like this kind of sport?

2 🔊 **1.7** Listen to someone talking about the photo. Answer the questions.

1 What are the three different types of sport in an Ironman competition?
2 Where is the annual championship?
3 Why do thousands of spectators watch the championship?

3 Work in groups. Discuss the questions.

1 Are you normally a competitor or a spectator? Which do you prefer?
2 Are you competitive? What kinds of competition do you compete in?

> ▶ **WORDBUILDING** word forms

When you learn a new word, try to learn its other forms.
For example:
compete (verb) – competitive (adjective) – competition (noun) – competitor (noun/person)

For further information and practice, see Workbook page 19.

TALK ABOUT ▶ AMBITIONS ▶ COMPETITION RULES ▶ SPORTS ▶ INTERESTS   WRITE ▶ AN ADVERT

2a Competitive sports

Reading and speaking

1 Read the quotes by famous sports people (1–6).
Then discuss the questions.

   1 How are the six quotes similar?
   2 Are all these sports popular in your country?
      What other sports are popular?

1 *'Winning isn't everything,
but wanting it is.'*
Arnold Palmer, winner of 92 golf tournaments

2 *'I never thought of losing.'*
**Muhammad Ali, three times boxing
World Heavyweight Champion**

3 *'I just love winning.'*
**Ayrton Senna, racing driver and
three times Formula One World Champion**

4 *'Swimming isn't everything,
winning is.'*
**Mark Spitz, swimmer and winner of seven
gold medals at the 1972 Munich Olympics**

5 *'A champion is afraid of losing. Everyone
else is afraid of winning.'*
**Billie Jean King, tennis player, won 129 major
tournaments**

6 *'I hate losing.'*
**Sachin Tendulkar, often called
the greatest batsman in the
history of cricket**

Muhammad Ali
taunting Sonny Liston

Grammar verb + *-ing* forms

2 Underline the verb + *-ing* forms in the quotes in
Exercise 1. Which of the underlined forms are:

   1 the subject of the sentence?
   2 after verbs (e.g. *like, dislike*) as an object?
   3 after a preposition?

> ▶ **VERB + *-ING* FORMS**
>
> • Subject of the sentence: ***Swimming*** *is good for you.*
> • After verbs (often *like, love, enjoy, prefer, don't like,
>   hate, can't stand*) as an object: *I like **playing** tennis.*
> • After a preposition: *I'm good **at learning** languages.*
>
> For further information and practice, see page 156.

3 Look at the grammar box. Then correct the
conversation between two friends. Change eight
verbs into the *-ing* form.

A: The *Tour de France* is on TV tonight! I love
   ~~watch~~ it. *watching*

B: Oh no! Cycle is so boring.

A: I really enjoy see the cyclists on the mountains.

B: But it lasts for days! I hate wait for the end.

A: Today is the final day. It's exciting.

B: Sit in front of the TV is not exciting. I prefer do
   something. Hey! Are you good at play tennis?
   We could play this afternoon.

A: But I want to watch this.

B: I see. Are you afraid of lose against me
   or something?

4 Pronunciation /ŋ/

a 🔘 **1.8** Listen to the words and underline the part
of the word with the /ŋ/ sound. What is the most
common spelling with the /ŋ/ sound? Listen again
and repeat.

1	watching	6	losing
2	language	7	winning
3	waiting	8	English
4	thinks	9	competing
5	cycling	10	thanks

b Read the conversation in Exercise 3 aloud.
Pay attention to the /ŋ/ sound in the verb
+ *-ing* forms.

5 Work in pairs. Ask questions to complete the sentences for both of you with the names of any sports or leisure activities.

1 I love watching _____ but my partner doesn't.
2 My partner likes _____ but I prefer _____.
3 I think _____ is boring but my partner loves it!
4 We both enjoy _____ but we can't stand _____.
5 I'm good at _____ but my partner isn't.

> Do you like -ing?

> What do you like -ing?

> Are you good at ...?

Vocabulary and listening
talking about sports

6 Write about the six sports in Exercise 1. Use these words to say where you play each sport and what you need. Then think of two other sports you like and describe them in a similar way.

where you play	what you need
court course pitch pool ring track	ball bat car club gloves goggles net racquet

Example:
You play golf on a golf course. You need a golf club and a ball.

7 Work in pairs. Take turns to describe a sport for your partner to guess.

> The two teams play on a pitch. They use a bat and a ball.

> Cricket.

> Correct!

8 🔊 1.9 Listen to three people talking about sport. Make notes in the table.

	Which sport are they talking about?	Do they like or dislike doing the sport?	Why do they do the sport?
Meg			
Paul			
Kirsty			

> **coach** (n) /kəʊtʃ/ a person who trains sports people

Grammar *like + -ing / 'd like to*

9 🔊 1.10 Listen to Kirsty again and complete the sentences (a–b). Then answer the questions (1–2).

a I _____ tennis so much that currently I'm working with a tennis coach.
b One day I _____ to become a professional player.

1 Which sentence describes a future ambition?
2 Which sentence is true now and talks about a general feeling?

> ▶ **'D LIKE TO**
>
> **would ('d) like + to + infinitive**
> *She'd like to play tennis later.*
> *He'd love to become a boxer one day.*
> *They wouldn't like to judge the competition.*
>
> For further information and practice, see page 157.

10 Make sentences about each pair of pictures using these words. Use *like + -ing* and *'d like to*.

1 love / drive / formula one cars

2 like / play golf

3 not like / lose

Speaking

11 Write down three ambitions for the future, one true and two false. Take turns to read them to your partner. Can he/she guess which of your ambitions are false?

> I'd like to become a rock star.

> No, you wouldn't.

> I'd like to jump from an aeroplane with a parachute.

> Yes, you would.

2b Crazy competitions!

Reading

1 Look at the photos of competitions (A–C) in the article. Which do you think is a fight, a match and a race?

2 Read about the competitions. Check your predictions in Exercise 1.

3 Read the article again. Match the sentences (1–8) with the competitions (A–C).

1 Competitors run from one place to another. ....
2 You can win money. ....
3 It's for individual competitors. ....
4 The competition is once a year. .... , ...
5 You use a type of transport. .... , ...
6 The rules are the same as another real sport. ....
7 It's for teams. .... , ...
8 There is a time limit. ....

4 Which of these sports would you like to play or watch? Do you have any similar competitions in your country?

Crazy competitions!

Ross McDermott and Andrew Owen travel round the United States going to different festivals and write about their experiences on the blog *The American Festivals Project*. Many of these festivals are also competitions.

A The Idiotarod

The Idiotarod is an annual race in New York City. Each team must have five people and a shopping cart. They can decorate their carts but they can't change the wheels. All the teams have to start and finish at the same place but they don't have to run on the same roads. The teams can choose their route but the members of each team must arrive at the finish line together. And they mustn't finish without the cart!

B Mud Bowl Championship

Mud Bowl football is similar to normal American football. The match is shorter but there are two teams and a referee. The winner is the team with the most goals at the end of sixty minutes. The only real difference is that the players have to play in half a metre of mud!

C Combine Harvester Fight

Combine harvesters are normally on farms but, for one day every summer, in the small town of Hillsdale in Michigan, farmers compete against each other for a prize of $1,500. For three hours, the giant machines have to fight until only one combine harvester is still moving.

Grammar modal verbs for rules

5 Look at the sentence from the article about the Idiotarod. What does the highlighted modal verb mean? Choose the correct answer (1–4).

Each team must have five people and a shopping cart.

1 It is necessary and an obligation.
2 It is allowed according to the rules.
3 It is not necessary (but allowed).
4 It is not allowed.

6 Find five more modal verbs in the article about the Idiotarod. Match them to the meanings (1–4) in Exercise 5.

> ▶ **MODAL VERBS FOR RULES**
>
> • Necessary and an obligation: *must, have to*
> • Allowed: *can*
> • Not necessary (but allowed): *don't have to*
> • Not allowed: *mustn't, can't*
>
> For further information and practice, see page 157.

7 Choose the correct options to complete the sentences about different sports.

1 You *have to / don't have to* play cricket with a bat and a ball.
2 Competitors *don't have to / mustn't* argue with the judge's decision.
3 Rugby players *can / can't* throw the ball forwards. It must always go backwards.
4 Competitors *can't / must* run 42 kilometres in a marathon.
5 A referee *can / mustn't* send a player off the pitch.
6 The goalkeeper in football *has to / doesn't have to* stay in the penalty area.
7 A tennis player *has to / doesn't have to* hit the ball inside the white lines.
8 The players *mustn't / don't have to* win every point to win a match.

Listening

8 🎧 **1.11** Listen to a description of another race: The Woolly Worm Race. What does the speaker describe? Choose the correct answer (1–3).

1 why people like racing woolly worms
2 the rules of the competition
3 the history of the competition

9 🎧 **1.11** Listen again. Answer the questions.

1 How often is the competition?
2 How old do you have to be to enter?
3 Do you have to bring your own woolly worm?
4 Can you touch your worm during the race?
5 What is the prize for the winner?

Vocabulary competitions

10 Complete the pairs of sentences with the correct words. Use a dictionary to help you.

1 (win / beat)
   My woolly worm _____ yours!
   Did you _____ the race?
2 (score / win)
   How many matches did you _____?
   How many goals did you _____?
3 (fans / spectators)
   We're your biggest _____! We come to every match.
   There were about 50,000 _____ at the match.
4 (referee / judge)
   The _____ sent the player off.
   One _____ gave the ice skater 10/10.
5 (trophy / prize)
   The President gave the winning team the silver _____.
   The _____ for the winner is $500.

Speaking

11 Work in groups. Imagine that you want to have a new annual competition for your town. Follow these steps.

1 Decide on a crazy competition.
2 Discuss the rules and write a list. Also discuss any other details.
3 Present your new competition to the class and explain the rules.

2c Bolivian wrestlers

Reading

1 Look at the photos on pages 26 and 27. Before you read, do you think the statements (1–3) will be true (T) or false (F)? Read the article and check your predictions.

1   Wrestling is popular in Bolivia.
2   Only men can wrestle in public.
3   People earn a lot of money from wrestling.

2 Read the article again. Which paragraph (1–6) describes:

a   the two wrestlers before the fight? 2
b   the popularity of male and female wrestling in Bolivia?
c   the moments before the wrestlers enter?
d   Yolanda's family life?
e   the reason why a fan watches it?
f   the fight between the two women wrestlers?

3 Find words in the first three paragraphs of the article to match these definitions.

1   three words meaning a large group of people at a performance or sporting event: a_____, s_____, c_____
2   two verbs meaning to speak loudly and make a lot of noise: s_____, s_____
3   to clap your hands together: a_____
4   people who support someone famous: f_____
5   to get away from someone or something: e_____
6   three verbs to describe fast movements: j_____, s_____, t_____
7   the bad person (usually in a story, film or book): b_____
8   the good person (usually in a story, film or book): g_____

Critical thinking reading between the lines

4 An article doesn't always tell us everything about how the people feel, but we can often guess. Match these people from the article (1–3) with the sentences (a–c).

1   Yolanda
2   One of Yolanda's daughters
3   Esperanza

a   I don't like the days when the wrestling is happening.
b   I get a wonderful feeling every time I go out there.
c   Life is very hard for people like me.

Word focus *like*

5 Look at the sentences from the article. Match *like* in each sentence (1–4) with the uses (a–d).

1   Would they **like** to become wrestlers one day?
2   Yolanda and Claudina walk through the crowds **like** pop stars.
3   Esperanza explains why she **likes** watching the wrestling.
4   She also has two daughters who both look **like** her.

a   enjoys in general
b   wants to do in the future
c   similar behaviour to
d   similar appearance to

Speaking

6 Discuss the questions.

1   Do you like watching sports with women in your country? Would you like to watch the type of wrestling in the article?
2   How important are sport and sports people in your country? Do any of them look like or behave like pop or film stars?
3   Do you think most people like watching sport because they want to 'forget their problems' for a few hours? Are there any other reasons?

Bolivian
wrestlers

In El Alto in Bolivia, an audience is sitting around a huge wrestling ring. The spectators are getting impatient and so they start to scream: 'Bring them on! Bring them on!' Suddenly, an announcer speaks into the microphone: 'Ladies and Gentlemen. It's time for Yolanda and Claudina!' The crowd shouts and applauds with excitement.

Two women enter. Yolanda and Claudina walk through the crowd like pop stars. They smile and greet their fans until suddenly the music stops. Both women jump into the wrestling ring and within seconds, Claudina hits Yolanda. Yolanda grabs Claudina. Claudina tries to escape, but Yolanda doesn't let her go. She spins Claudina round and throws her down on the floor. The audience goes crazy!

As Claudina lies on the floor, Yolanda is smiling and waving to the crowd. She doesn't see Claudina get up behind her. Then Claudina pushes Yolanda onto the ropes. The crowd shouts at her. Claudina is the baddie in this competition so when Yolanda – the goodie – gets up and throws Claudina out of the ring, the crowd cheers with happiness. One minute Yolanda is winning. The next minute, Claudina is winning.

Wrestling in Bolivia is incredibly popular and after a hard day's work many people love watching this mixture of sport, drama and entertainment. Usually, the wrestling matches are between men wearing masks and special costumes. But in El Alto you can also see women wrestling where it's especially popular.

The women wrestlers fight here and we laugh and forget our problems for three or four hours.

Yolanda is one of the top women wrestlers. Her father was also a wrestler so it's a family tradition. During the day she makes clothes. She also has two daughters who both look like her. Would they like to become wrestlers one day? Yolanda doesn't think so. 'My daughters ask me why I do this. It's dangerous and they complain that wrestling doesn't bring any money into the house.' But Yolanda loves wrestling because of her fans, and she has lots of them!

One fan called Esperanza Cancina pays $1.50 (a large part of her salary) to sit near the ring. She explains why she likes watching the wrestling: 'It's a distraction. The women wrestlers fight here and we laugh and forget our problems for three or four hours. At home, we're sad.'

2d Joining a club

Speaking

1 Who is a member of a club or local group in your class? Ask them these questions.

   1   Does the club have regular meetings? How often?
   2   Do you pay a membership fee? How much is it?
   3   What are the benefits of being a member?
   4   Does it ever have competitions?

2 Look at the adverts (A–C). Which of the questions in Exercise 1 do they each answer?

A

Would you like to get fit and make new friends?

Our running group meets at 7 p.m. every Wednesday.

There are two groups:
• Beginner's group (for anyone)
• Experienced (you must be able to run twenty or more kilometres)

It's non-competitive and a fun way to get fit!

Call Mike Burgess on 0776 58945.

B

Join us and **WIN** *a new camera!*

The Barton Photography Club welcomes new members. We are a busy club with regular speakers at our club meetings. Join before 1st March and you can also enter our summer photography competition. Three prizes including a brand new camera. The entry fee is 15 euros (including club membership for a year). Visit www.bartonphotoclub.com to download an entry form and for membership details.

C

Theatre group

A local theatre group is looking for actors and actresses to be in a musical comedy this summer. You must be available twice a week starting 2nd April. Enthusiasm is more important than talent!

Contact Mandy Giles on mandy76@dmail.com

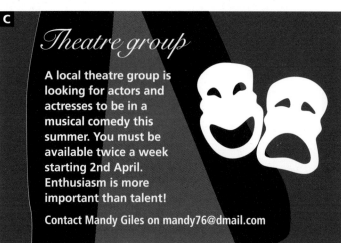

Real life talking about interests

3 🔊 **1.12** Two people are looking at the adverts in their local newspaper. Listen to their conversation and number the adverts in the order they discuss them.

4 🔊 **1.12** Listen again and complete the sentences from the conversation.

   1   You're really _____ doing that.
   2   Well, _____ joining something else?
   3   Are you _____ acting?
   4   I _____ standing up in front of people.
   5   I'm _____ good at singing.
   6   Go _____. I think you'd _____ it.
   7   I think I'd _____ join this on Wednesday evenings.
   8   It _____ fun. _____ you come too?

5 Match the sentences in Exercise 4 with the three categories in the box.

> ▶ **TALKING ABOUT INTERESTS**
>
> **Asking about interests**
> Do you like taking photographs?
>
> **Talking about interests (and likes/dislikes)**
> I'd like/prefer to join a running club.
> I'm good at acting.
> I wouldn't like to do it.
> I'm (not) interested in photography.
>
> **Recommending and encouraging**
> It looks interesting.
> I think you'd enjoy it.
> You should do it with me.

6 **Pronunciation silent letters**

  🔊 **1.13** Some letters are not pronounced in English words. Listen to these words from the conversation in Exercise 3 and cross out the silent letters. Then listen again and repeat.

   1 interested   4 evenings
   2 should   5 something
   3 friends   6 what

7 Work in pairs. Imagine you are interested in joining a club. Talk about each advert in Exercise 2 and each other's interests. Then choose one of the clubs to both join.

TALK ABOUT ▸ AMBITIONS ▸ COMPETITION RULES ▸ SPORTS ▶ INTERESTS   WRITE ▸ AN ADVERT

2e Advertising for members

Writing an advert or notice

1 Read the advice about how to write effective adverts and notices. Then look back at the three adverts on page 28. Answer the questions.

1 Which advert follows most of the advice?
2 How could you improve the other adverts?

> ### *How to* WRITE EFFECTIVE ADVERTS AND NOTICES
>
> • Start with a good headline. You could ask a question or solve a problem.
>
> • The advert should explain the benefits.
>
> • If possible, offer something for free or a prize.
>
> • Include any other important information (dates, times, location, etc.)
>
> • Photos, pictures or images always help.

2 Work in pairs. You are going to plan a new club. Discuss the questions.

1 What type of club is it (e.g. a chess club, a tennis club, a walking group)?
2 Who is the club for?
3 Are there any rules for members?
4 Is there a membership fee? How much is it?
5 How often will it meet?

3 Plan and write an advert for your new club.

4 Writing skill checking your writing

a It's always important to check your writing for mistakes, especially when a lot of people will read it (e.g. in an advert). Read the sentences (1–8) from different adverts and find the mistake in each. Match the sentences with the types of mistake (a–h). Then correct the mistakes.

1 Would you like to learn a musical instrument⌢? *c*

2 *Enter our exciteing competition!*

3 **Are you good at play tennis?**

4 *We meet at Tuesdays and Thursdays.*

5 **It's fun way to get fit.**

6 **Join this club new!**

7 Get healthy and play yoga.

8 Call peter on 077 237 5980.

a	spelling	e	grammar
b	missing word	f	word order
c	punctuation	g	capital letter
d	preposition	h	wrong word

b Read your advert in Exercise 3 again. Are there any mistakes? Correct them.

5 Display your adverts around the classroom. Walk around and read about each other's new clubs. Consider these questions.

• Which clubs would you like to join?
• Which adverts are effective? Why?

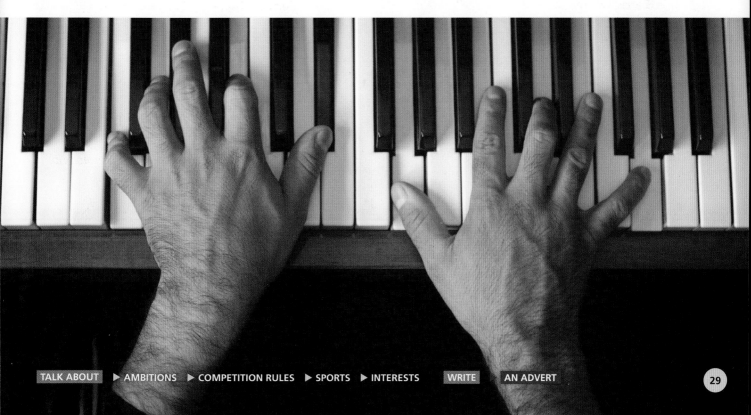

2f Cheese rolling

Cheese rolling has been a tradition in the town of Brockworth since the early 1800s.

Before you watch

1 Work in groups. Look at the photo and discuss the questions. Use the words in the glossary to help you.

1 What are the people doing?
2 Why do you think they are doing this?
3 Do you think they enjoy doing this?

2 Complete the summary with words from the glossary.

Most towns have their own [1]t_____ . However, one town in England has a very unusual one: the annual cheese-rolling [2]r_____ . At the start, the [3]c_____ wait at the [4]t_____ of Cooper's Hill. Then someone pushes a wheel of cheese down the [5]s_____ slope. The competitors run after the cheese. The winner is the first person who gets to the [6]b_____ of the hill. The [7]p_____ is the wheel of cheese. The race can be dangerous, for the competitors and the [8]s_____ . One year a wheel of cheese went into the crowd and thirty people were [9]i_____ . Nowadays there are [10]c_____ to protect the crowd.

While you watch

3 Watch the video and check your answers from Exercise 2.

4 Watch the video again. Put these people and events in the order you see them.

a Doctors helping an injured person.
b People clapping to encourage the competitors.
c Someone carrying a British flag.
d A Japanese man with blond hair talking.
e Craig Brown holding up the cheese.
f The view from the top of Cooper's Hill.

5 Watch the video again. Are these sentences true (T) or false (F)?

1 The race is more than 200 years old.
2 The cheese travels at more than forty miles an hour.
3 Competitors have to catch the cheese before it reaches the bottom of the hill.
4 Craig Brown works in a pub.
5 There is no protection for spectators.
6 The race is dangerous for competitors when the weather is cold.
7 You can only compete once a day.

After you watch

6 Roleplay an interview with Craig Brown

Work in pairs.

Student A: You are a journalist for *National Geographic*. Use the ideas below to prepare questions to ask Craig Brown.

Student B: You are Craig Brown. Look at the ideas below. Think about what you are going to say to the journalist.

- age
- interests
- why you take part in the race
- how many times you have taken part
- if you have ever been injured

Act out the interview. Then change roles and repeat the interview.

7 At the end of the video, the narrator says: 'It's more than just cheese that makes people want to win.' What does she mean?

8 Work in pairs. Discuss these questions.

1 What kind of people do you think take part in the race?
2 Would you like to take part in the race? Why? / Why not?
3 Would you go to watch the race? Why? / Why not?
4 Do you have any unusual traditional races in your country? What are they and why are they popular?

accident (n) /ˈæksɪdənt/ an event where a person is hurt unintentionally
balance (n) /ˈbæləns/ a position in which your body stays in an upright position
bottom (n) /ˈbɒtəm/ the lowest part of a thing or place
competitor (n) /kəmˈpetɪtə/ a person who takes part in a sporting event
crash barrier (n) /ˈkræʃ bæriə/ an obstacle that stops people being hurt
crazy (adj) /ˈkreɪzi/ mad
crowd (n) /kraʊd/ a large group of people
fail (v) /feɪl/ be unsuccessful
ground (n) /graʊnd/ what is under your feet when you are outside
injured (adj) /ˈɪndʒəd/ hurt
protect (v) /prəˈtekt/ keep someone or something safe
prize (n) /praɪz/ something given to a person who is successful in a competition
race (n) /reɪs/ an event to see who can go the fastest
slope (n) /sləʊp/ the side of a mountain or hill
spectator (n) /spekˈteɪtə/ a person who watches a sporting event
steep (adj) /stiːp/ going up or down at a sharp angle
top (n) /tɒp/ the highest part of a thing or place
traditions (n pl) /trəˈdɪʃənz/ things that people have done for a long time
wheel (of cheese) (n) /wiːl/ a round object

Grammar

1 Put the words in order to make sentences and questions.

1 than / losing / winning / is / fun / more
2 I'm / new / good / learning / at / games
3 learning / languages? / you / do / like
4 like / a musical instrument? / learn / would / to / you
5 you / like / who / look / do / in your family?

2 Complete the description of a competition with these verbs.

can   don't have to   have to   mustn't

There's a competition in Alaska where you ¹_____ arrive without facial hair! That's because it's the world's moustache and beard competition. The judges ²_____ choose the winners from the beards and moustaches of over 300 contestants from all over the world. But you ³_____ have the longest moustache or biggest beard because there are many different categories. For example, you ⁴_____ win the prize for 'Best English moustache' and 'Best natural moustache'.

3 Work in pairs. Which sport on TV do you like watching most? Explain the rules to your partner.

I CAN	
talk about likes, dislikes and ambitions	
describe the rules of a competition or sport using modal verbs	

Vocabulary

4 Choose the correct options.

1 My favourite football team *scored / beat* another goal!
2 In ice-skating, the *judges / spectators* give points to the competitors.
3 My grandmother won a *trophy / prize* of a thousand dollars in a competition.
4 My team always loses. We never *win / beat* any matches.
5 Hit the tennis ball with your *racquet / net*!
6 During the fight, the two boxers must not leave the *court / ring*.
7 Wear these *gloves / goggles* over your eyes when you ski.
8 The *track / pitch* is 100 metres long. The fastest runners can complete it in less than ten seconds.

5 Work in pairs. Which sports person would you like to meet one day? Why do you admire this person?

I CAN	
talk about different kinds of sports	
talk about future ambitions	

Real life

6 Complete the conversation. Write one word in each gap.

A: Are you interested ¹_____ painting? There's a new evening course at my college.
B: I'm afraid I'm not very good ²_____ art.
A: I'm not either but I'd like ³_____ learn. Go ⁴_____. You should do it with me.
B: Sorry.
A: ⁵_____ you like taking photos? There's also a course for that.
B: Actually, it looks interesting.

7 Complete these sentences with your own interests.

1 I'm good at …
2 I wouldn't like to …
3 I'm also interested in …
4 I think I'd enjoy learning …

I CAN	
talk about interests	
recommend and encourage people to do things	

Speaking

8 Work in pairs. Take turns to tell each other about your interests in Exercise 7. Then recommend one of your interests to your partner and encourage them to do it in the future.

Unit 3 Transport

Taking the train
Photo by Amy Helene Johansson

FEATURES

1 Look at the photo. Where is the woman? Why do you think she is travelling like this?

2 🎧 **1.14** Listen to someone talking about the photo. Why isn't the woman inside the train?

3 Work in pairs. Which of these modes of transport would you use for the activities (1–10)? Explain your reasons why.

> by bicycle   by bus   in my car   on a ferry   on foot
> by lorry   on a motorbike   on a plane   on a ship
> in a taxi   by train

1 visit relatives
2 move house and furniture
3 get to the airport
4 see the countryside for pleasure
5 cross a river
6 get to the railway station
7 go out in the evening to a party or restaurant
8 take children to school
9 cross the sea
10 go shopping

4 What is your favourite way to travel? Why?
Tell your partner.

3a Transport in the future

Reading

1 Do you travel and use transport every day? How do you commute to work? Are there many travel problems early in the morning?

2 Read the texts in the diagram below about transport in the future. What kind of transport does it describe? How is it different from transport today?

3 Read the texts again. Answer the questions.

Who …
1 commutes to work every morning?
2 knows in advance when there is a problem on the road?
3 don't use electric cars?
4 can't drive a long distance without recharging?
5 always needs to plug in the car before bedtime?
6 has a car which stops you from driving too quickly?
7 doesn't need to commute to his work.
8 works in an office?

Vocabulary transport (1): nouns

4 Find the words in the texts in Exercise 2 for these definitions.

1 machines with engine for transporting people, e.g. car or bus   v_____
2 people who travel to work every day   c_____
3 period in a day when lots of people travel to and from work   r_____ h_____
4 long line of vehicles on the road   t_____ j_____
5 construction or maintenance on part of a road   r_____ w_____
6 place to fill your car with petrol   p_____ s_____
7 the maximum speed you can legally drive   s_____ l_____
8 people on foot in a town or city   p_____

> ▶ **WORDBUILDING compound nouns**
>
> You can join two nouns to make a new noun:
> *rush + hour = rush hour, traffic + jam = traffic jam,*
> *speed + limit = speed limit*
>
> For further information and practice, see Workbook page 27.

5 Do you think the predictions in the texts are true? Are any of the predictions true now? Would you prefer an electric car to a petrol one? Why? / Why not?

TRANSPORT IN THE FUTURE

Meet the Watts. They are a three-car family in the near future which uses electric vehicles.

Bob is similar to most commuters. He charges his car at home overnight so it's ready for the morning rush hour. If he needs more electricity, there's a 'charging station' in the office car park.

Sonia's car travels about 30 kilometres on a full battery so it's good for short trips such as going to the shops or visiting friends nearby. The car also has its own computer which tells her if there are traffic jams or road works on the road ahead.

Justin works from home but enjoys going on a long journey in his sports car at the weekend. Instead of going to a petrol station for petrol, he can change his battery on the motorway or plug into a high-voltage charger. Another device in the car's engine stops him from going over the speed limit.

Their neighbours still use a car with a petrol engine but most cars have electric engines. The roads are quieter and there is less pollution so life is also better for pedestrians and cyclists!

Listening

6 🔊 **1.15** Listen to two people discussing electric cars. What reasons do they give for and against this kind of transport?

7 🔊 **1.15** Listen again. Choose the correct options.

1 Electric cars are much *cleaner / louder* than petrol cars.
2 Electric cars have the *more efficient / most efficient* type of engine.
3 Electric cars are much *cheaper / more expensive* than petrol cars.
4 Eight o'clock in the morning is the *best / worst* time of the day for commuting.
5 The town needs *better / faster* public transport.

Grammar comparatives and superlatives

8 Look at the comparative and superlative adjectives in Exercise 7. Answer the questions.

1 What letters do you add to regular short adjectives to form comparative and superlative adjectives? How do you form the comparative and superlative forms with longer adjectives?
2 Which are examples of irregular comparative and superlative adjectives?
3 Which word usually comes after a comparative adjective? Which word usually comes before a superlative adjective?
4 What word adds emphasis to a comparative adjective?

► COMPARATIVES and SUPERLATIVES		
Regular adjectives		
clean	clean**er**	clean**est**
big	big**ger**	big**gest**
happy	happ**ier**	happ**iest**
expensive	**more** expensive	**most** expensive
Irregular adjectives		
good	better	best
bad	worse	worst
For further information and practice, see page 158.		

9 Pronunciation *than*

🔊 **1.16** Listen to the pronunciation of *than* in sentences 1 and 3 in Exercise 7. Notice how we say /ðən/ not /ðæn/. Practise saying the two sentences.

10 A local town council asked residents for their views on transport. Look at the grammar box in Exercise 8. Then complete this extract from the report with the comparative or superlative form of the adjectives.

◄ ◄ ◄ **REPORT BACK**

Your views on transport

For commuting and daytime travel, the [1] .... (popular) form of public transport is the bus. [2] .... (large) number of people in the survey use buses every day to get to work or school. However, taking the bus isn't [3] .... (fast) form of transport. Everyone said that parking in the town centre is still the [4] .... (big) problem so they don't often drive their car. The situation is much [5] .... (good) in the evenings than during the day. As a result, taxis are [6] .... (popular) than private cars. However, taxis are the [7] .... (expensive) form of transport so many people want buses to run [8] .... (late) in the evenings.

Speaking and writing

11 Look at the questionnaire for the survey in Exercise 10. Use these questions to interview other students about transport where they live. Make a note of their answers.

QUESTIONNAIRE ► ► ►

Resident views on transport

• How do you usually commute to and from work/college? Why?

• How often do you use public transport?

• What types of public transport do you use?

• How do you rate car parking in the town? Excellent ____ Good ____ Poor ____

• How often do you take taxis?

• Do you have any suggestions to improve travel and transport in the town?

12 Work in pairs. Compare your notes and answers from the questionnaire. Then write a short report, similar to the one in Exercise 10.

3b Animal transport

Listening

1 Look at the photos. What is each animal transporting? Do people use animals for transporting in your country?

2 🎵 **1.17** Listen to an extract from two documentaries. What kind of modern transport does the speaker compare each animal to?

3 🎵 **1.17** Listen again. Answer the questions.

Documentary 1
1 What special event is happening?
2 What jobs did the Asian elephant do in the past?
3 What kind of people do they transport nowadays?

Documentary 2
4 Lester Courtney is a 'logger'. What do loggers do?
5 Why does Lester prefer to use horses?

Grammar *as ... as*

4 Look at the sentence from the documentary. Answer the questions (1–2).

Elephants are as heavy as cars but they aren't as fast – and most people also think elephants aren't as comfortable as cars.

1 Are elephants and cars the same weight?
2 Do they travel at the same speed?

> ▶ **AS ... AS**
>
> Use *as* + adjective + *as* to compare something and say they are the same or equal.
> Use *not as* + adjective + *as* to compare two things and say they are different or not equal.
>
> For further information and practice, see page 158.

5 Look at the grammar box. Then complete the second sentence so that it has the same meaning as the first sentence.

1 Most people think cars are more comfortable than elephants.
   Most people think elephants aren't as
   _____.
2 Elephants have the same importance now as they did in the past.
   Elephants are _____ as ever.
3 Lester believes horses are better than modern machines.
   Lester doesn't believe modern machines are as _____ horses.
4 Lorries and trucks are stronger than horses.
   Horses _____ as _____ as lorries and trucks.
5 Trucks are noisier than horses.
   Horses _____ as trucks.

6 Pronunciation sentence stress

🎵 **1.18** Listen to these sentences. Notice the stressed words in each sentence. Then listen again and repeat.

1 **Lorries** are **heavier** than **horses**.
2 **Elephants** are as **heavy** as **trucks**.
3 They **aren't** as **fast** as **cars**.
4 **Horses** are the **fastest**.

7 Work in pairs. Make sentences using the adjective to compare these animals. Use comparative and superlative adjectives and (*not*) as + adjective + *as*.

1 strong: lion, mouse, horse
2 fast: snail, cheetah, elephant
3 comfortable: car, camel, plane
4 heavy: hippopotamus, blue whale, elephant
5 dangerous: shark, alligator, snake

8 Read out your sentences from Exercise 7, stressing the most important words.

Reading

9 Complete the article on the right with these words.

as	best	fast	longest	more	much
than	the				

10 Read the article again. Then discuss the questions.

1 What are the advantages and disadvantages of the huskies in Alaska?
2 Why do you think some people say the *Iditarod* is cruel for the dogs?
3 What sports do you have in your country with animals? Do people think they are cruel for the animals?

Speaking

11 Work in groups. Read and discuss these comments from different people about using animals for transport and sport. What's your opinion? Do you agree or disagree?

It's more natural and cleaner to use animals for work and transportation than engines. We should use them more.

It's wrong to use animals like horses and dogs in sports.

Modern transport is much better. There's no reason to use animals.

We still need animals for certain kinds of work.

> I think it's better because ...

> I don't think it's as bad as ...

> In my opinion, it's worse because ...

> I agree ...

THE BEST WAY TO TRAVEL

In the most northern state of the USA you'll see every type of modern transport. But during the winter months the state of Alaska becomes one of [1] _____ coldest parts of the world. Temperatures fall as low [2] _____ – 50 °C. Car engines can freeze and even if your car starts, the snow and ice on the road can make travel impossible. When the weather is like this, the [3] _____ way to travel is with a team of huskies pulling you. That's according to people like Geoff Roland who prefer travelling by dog sledge. 'Huskies might not be as [4] _____ as a modern snowmobile but they are better for the environment. The journey is also much quieter [5] _____ by snowmobile. It's what makes travel through the wilderness so enjoyable.'

When Geoff was younger he took part in the *Iditarod*. The word *Iditarod* originally comes from an old native American word meaning 'a faraway place' but nowadays it's the name of the world's [6] _____ dog sledge race which takes place in Alaska each spring. The 1,600 kilometre route follows the old roads which the original Indians once used. As years passed, aeroplanes and snowmobiles became [7] _____ common and people started to forget about the old trails. But in 1973 a group of people started the race in order to maintain Alaska's history and its traditional form of transport. Some people criticise the *Iditarod* because they think it's cruel for the dogs but Geoff disagrees: 'Huskies are natural racers. I think they're [8] _____ happier when they're in front of the sledge.'

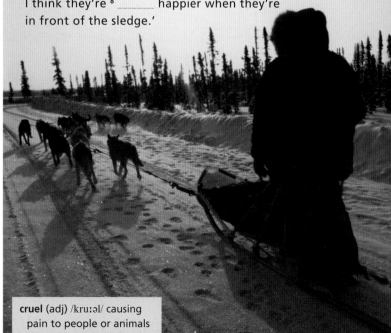

cruel (adj) /kruːəl/ causing pain to people or animals

TALK ABOUT ▶ TRANSPORT IN THE CITY ▶ **ATTITUDES TO ANIMALS** ▶ ARGUMENTS FOR AND AGAINST ▶ GOING ON A JOURNEY
WRITE ▶ NOTES AND MESSAGES

37

3c Last days of the rickshaw

Reading

1 Look at the photo of the rickshaw in the article on page 39. Why do you think people choose this kind of transport? Are there any advantages with a rickshaw compared with other types of transport?

2 Read the first paragraph of the article. Which of these words and expressions describe Kolkata?

> busy   highly-populated   noisy   polluted   quiet
> safe for pedestrians

3 Read the second and third paragraph of the article. Which of these arguments in favour of rickshaws does the article mention?

Rickshaws are useful because ...

1   they are better in traffic jams.
2   they can travel down small streets.
3   they don't produce pollution.
4   they are good for shopping.
5   they are cheaper than other public transport.
6   they always travel during the monsoons.

4 Read the last paragraph. Why don't local officials and politicians ban rickshaws? Choose the correct reason (1–3).

1   There isn't much other employment for the drivers.
2   The tourists want them.
3   The drivers don't want to go back to the countryside.

Vocabulary transport (2): verbs

5 Find these verbs in the article Underline them and the noun which follows.

> catch   take   pick up   miss   drop off
> get on / off   go by

Example:
catch a train

6 Replace the verbs in bold in the sentences with a verb of similar meaning from Exercise 5.

1   Do you want me to **collect** the children from school?
     pick up
2   We need to **leave** the train at the next station.
3   I was late and I nearly didn't **get** my flight.
4   You'd better leave now. You don't want to **not catch** your flight.
5   I should **travel by** a taxi. It's much quicker.
6   Ask the driver to **leave** the children outside their school.

Critical thinking reading between the lines

7 Using the information in the article, which of these statements do you think people in Kolkata often say about the rickshaws in their city?

1   'Rickshaw drivers always blow their horns so loudly.'
2   'They represent our city!'
3   'They should not be on the roads!'
4   'They are very useful for day-to-day life.'
5   'You can never find a rickshaw when you need one.'
6   'Rickshaws are cruel.'

Speaking

8 Work in groups. Make a list of the reasons for and against keeping rickshaws in Kolkata. Use the information in the article and add your own ideas.

Example:
Rickshaws don't have engines so they are quiet and don't pollute the air.

9 You are going to have a debate to decide if Kolkata should ban rickshaws. Each person in the group has a role. Choose one of the roles below and think about if your person wants to ban rickshaws or to keep them in Kolkata. Choose arguments for or against from your list in Exercise 8 and plan your arguments for the debate. When you are all ready, discuss the topic and try to find a solution.

• a rickshaw driver in Kolkata
• a local politician who wants to modernise Kolkata
• a foreign tourist visiting the city
• a local person who uses rickshaws for shopping and sending the children to school
• a taxi driver in the city

> *In my opinion we should ban rickshaws because ...*

> *I think rickshaws are good for the city because ...*

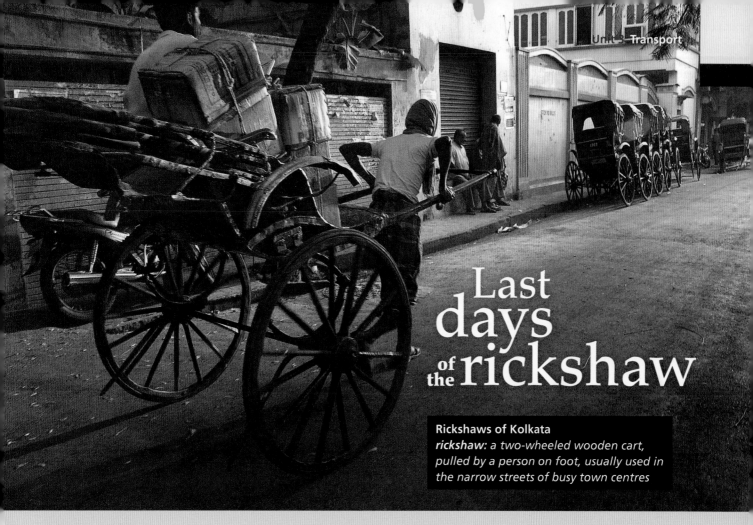

Last days of the rickshaw

Rickshaws of Kolkata
rickshaw: a two-wheeled wooden cart, pulled by a person on foot, usually used in the narrow streets of busy town centres

Kolkata (previously known as Calcutta) is the famous capital of West Bengal in India and the home of nearly 15 million people. The traffic jams and engine fumes begin early in the morning with long lines of private cars, public buses, taxis, three-wheeled scooters and pedicabs. There aren't many alternatives. You can catch a train through the city or take the underground but sooner or later you have to go on foot and walking in Kolkata is a dangerous activity. As the drivers race towards pedestrians, they blow their horns. The sound never stops from morning to night.

So when I crossed a small road on my first day in the city, I was surprised because I heard a bell – not a horn. It was a tiny man pulling a rickshaw. He stopped and picked up two children from the front door of their house and then, with great strength, pulled them to school. For many people, the rickshaw is a symbol of Kolkata and they have many advantages. When the traffic is bad, rickshaws find a way through the traffic. If you miss your bus and there aren't any taxis, you can always find a rickshaw in Kolkata. Rickshaws are also very popular with local shoppers. The driver takes you from your house to the market and waits for you. Then he loads all your purchases, drops you off outside your home and helps you unload. No other type of public transport offers this kind of service.

You also see lots more people getting on and off rickshaws during the monsoon season. That's the period from June to September when Kolkata gets heavy rainfall. Sometimes it rains for 48 hours without a break. In the older parts of the city, the roads flood. The water can rise as high as people's waists in the worst part. When it's this bad, anything with an engine is useless. But the rickshaw drivers never stop working, even with water all around them.

But not everyone thinks rickshaws are a good thing. Some local officials and politicians want to ban rickshaws on 'humanitarian grounds'. They believe it is wrong for one man to pull another person when there is modern transport in the city. However, there is a problem with this plan. Many of the rickshaw drivers come from the countryside with no job and no qualifications. The only job they can find in Kolkata is pulling a rickshaw. If the city bans rickshaws, these men won't have a job or income. So for the moment, the people of Kolkata still go by rickshaw.

fumes (n) /fjuːmz/ smoke and gases from an engine
scooter (n) /ˈskuːtə(r)/ a small motorbike
pedicab (n) /ˈpedekæb/ a type of taxi with no engine. The driver cycles.
monsoon (n) /ˌmɒnˈsuːn/ period from June to September with lots of rain
flood (v) /flʌd/ when water covers an area (e.g. a floor, road, city)
ban (v) /bæn/ to stop or make illegal

TALK ABOUT ▶ TRANSPORT IN THE CITY ▶ ATTITUDES TO ANIMALS ▶ ARGUMENTS FOR AND AGAINST ▶ GOING ON A JOURNEY
WRITE ▶ NOTES AND MESSAGES

39

3d Getting around town

Vocabulary and listening taking transport

1 Look at these pairs of words. Match them with the correct definition (a or b).

1 stop / rank
   a where you can get a taxi
   b where you can get a bus
2 fare / price
   a the money you pay for a journey by bus, train or taxi
   b the amount of money something costs
3 change / receipt
   a the money you receive when you pay more than the price because you don't have the correct amount
   b the piece of paper you receive to show you paid for something
4 gate / platform
   a where you get on a train
   b where you get on a plane
5 book / check in
   a when you buy a ticket in advance
   b when you arrive at the airport and leave your bags

2 🔘 **1.19** Shelley and Javier are going to the airport and they take different transport. Listen to their conversations and answer the questions.

1 At the taxi rank: Where does Javier want to go?
2 In the taxi: How much is the fare? Does Javier want a receipt?
3 At the bus stop: Where does Shelley want to go? What type of ticket does she buy?
4 At the train station: How much is the ticket? Which platform does the train leave from?
5 At the airport: Where did Shelley book her plane ticket? Does she check in any bags?

Real life going on a journey

3 🔘 **1.19** Look at the expressions for going on a journey. Then listen to the conversations again. Tick the sentences you hear.

> ▶ **GOING ON A JOURNEY**
>
> **In a taxi**
> I'd like to go to the station, please.
> You can drop me off here.
> How much is that?
> Do you have change?
> Do you want a receipt?
>
> **On a bus**
> Do you stop at the airport?
> A single or return ticket?
> Please stop at the next one.
> That's two pounds.
>
> **At the train station**
> A return ticket to the airport, please.
> First or second class?
> Can I pay by credit card?
> Which platform is it?
>
> **At the airport**
> Can I see your passport?
> How many bags are you checking in?
> I only have this carry on.
> Window or aisle?
> Can I have a seat next to my friend?

4 Pronunciation intonation

🔘 **1.20** People often ask questions with incomplete sentences, e.g. *Single or return?* instead of *Do you want a single or return ticket?* Listen to these questions. Mark the intonation ↗ or ↘ down on the words. Then listen again and repeat.

1 Single or return?
2 Window or aisle?
3 Credit card or cash?
4 Bus or train?
5 North or south?
6 First or second?

5 Work in pairs. Student A is going to the airport. In each situation, Student B is the driver or the person at the ticket office or check-in desk. Practise the conversations, using the expressions for going on a journey to help you.

In the taxi. A has a $50 note. The fare is $23.50. | On the bus. | At the train station. | At the airport. You have two bags.

6 Change roles and repeat the four conversations in Exercise 5.

TALK ABOUT ▶ TRANSPORT IN THE CITY ▶ ATTITUDES TO ANIMALS ▶ ARGUMENTS FOR AND AGAINST ▶ **GOING ON A JOURNEY**
WRITE ▶ NOTES AND MESSAGES

3e Quick communication

Writing notes and messages

1 Read these notes and messages (1–8). Match them with the reasons for writing (a–e).

a thanking
b apologising
c giving travel information
d suggesting a time and place
e giving a message from someone else

2 Writing skill writing in note form

a People often miss out words in notes and messages. This is called elision. Find examples of these kinds of words missing in the notes and messages in Exercise 1.

- articles
- pronouns (e.g. *I, me*)
- auxiliary verbs
- polite forms (e.g. *Would you like to …? Can we …?*)

Example:
(Can we) Meet outside (the) airport at 2? (Is that) OK?

b Rewrite these transcripts from a telephone voicemail as shorter messages.

1 'I'm sorry but I'm stuck in a traffic jam. I'll see you in half an hour.'
   Sorry. Stuck in traffic. See you in 30 mins.
2 'Thank you for booking the train tickets. I'll pay you when we meet at the station.'
3 'Take the underground to Oxford Street and the Moon café is at the end of platform one.'
4 'Peter wants to come with us in the taxi. Can you call him and tell him where to meet us?'
5 'My flight is an hour late. Meet me at the arrivals terminal at five o'clock.'

3 Work in pairs. Write a short note or message for each situation.

1 You have to work late. Write a short text message to your friend. Say you will arrive at the bus station an hour later.
2 You are meeting tonight in the city centre. Suggest your friend takes a taxi from the taxi rank outside the train station.
3 You cannot travel with your friend on the underground to the airport. Explain you will travel by bus and meet him/her at the check-in desk.

4 Write a short message to your partner. Then, exchange messages. Can you understand your partner's message? Write a reply if necessary!

1
Meet outside airport at 2? OK?

2
Sorry. Bus late. Will be 15 minutes late.

3
Javier called. Call him back. 0770 657 655.

4
Train leaves platform 6.

5
Thanks for getting tickets. Here's the money.

6
Plane at gate 6. Boarding now.

7
Am in taxi. See you outside museum in 5?

8
Afraid I missed meeting. My apologies.

3f Indian railways

In this country, the best
way to travel is by train.

Before you watch

1 Work in groups. Look at the photo and the caption. Discuss the questions.

1 How important are trains in your country?
2 Do many people travel by train? Why? / Why not?

2 Work in pairs. Think about Indian railways and choose the option you think is correct.

1 Every day approximately *two hundred thousand / two million* passengers pass through Mumbai train station.
2 There are over *two billion / one billion* people in India.
3 The British built the railways in India in the *eighteenth / nineteenth* century.
4 There are over *38,000 / 3,800* miles of railway track in India.
5 The Grand Trunk Express has travelled through India since *1939 / 1929*.
6 India's railways carry *four billion / four million* passengers every year.
7 Indian Railways employs *one hundred thousand / one and half million* staff.

While you watch

3 Watch the video and check your answers from Exercise 2.

4 Watch the video again and answer the questions.

1 When did the first steam train run in India?

2 Is it easy for everybody in India to get to a railway station?

3 What is the key man's job?

4 Who tries to get travellers' attention and money at Indian railway stations?

5 What do passengers do on the train?

5 Complete the sentences with words from the glossary.

1 At the Victoria Terminus, Mumbai, it always seems to be _____ .
2 Many of the trains have _____ names.
3 India's railways are the world's largest _____ .
4 A huge _____ keeps this enormous system running.

After you watch

6 **Roleplay a conversation between passengers**

Work in pairs.

Student A: You are from the city. Use the questions below to make notes about yourself and your journey.

Student B: You are from a small village, a day's walk from the station. Use the questions below to make notes about yourself and your journey.

- What's your name?
- How old are you?
- Who do you live with?
- What's your job?
- What's your daily routine like?
- What's the best moment of your day? And what's the worst?

Act out the conversation. Describe your journey to the station today, your life at home and give your reason for travelling.

7 At the end of the video, the narrator says: 'The Indian railways are their own adventure.' What does she mean?

8 Work in pairs. Discuss these questions.

1 In what way are trains in your country similar to, or different from, trains in India?
2 Is travelling by train a good way to see a country? Why? / Why not?

employer (n) /ɪmˈplɔɪə/ a person or organisation that gives work to other people
impressive (adj) /ɪmˈpresɪv/ something that causes admiration
passenger (n) /ˈpæsɪndʒə/ a person who travels in a vehicle
rural (adj) /ˈrʊrəl/ of the countryside
rush hour (n) /ˈrʌʃ aʊə/ the busiest time of day, when a lot of people are going to or from work
staff (n) /stɑːf/ people who work for an organisation
track (n) /træk/ metal rails that a train runs on
villager (n) /ˈvɪlɪdʒə/ a person who lives in a very small town, often in the countryside
workforce (n) /ˈwɜːkfɔːs/ people who work for an organisation

Grammar

1 Complete the article with the correct form of the adjectives.

The city of **Guangzhou** **wins** transport prize

China has the [1] _____ (large) population in the world and its capital city, Beijing, has some of [2] _____ (bad) traffic problems. A few decades ago, China's streets weren't as [3] _____ (polluted) as they are now because most people rode bicycles. But in modern China, cars are selling [4] _____ (fast) than in the USA.

However, one city in China recently received a prize for its transportation system from the Institute for Transportation and Development Policy (ITDP). The ITDP works with cities to make city life [5] _____ (good). This year it gave the city of Guangzhou a prize because it has one of the [6] _____ (good) public transport systems, not only in China, but worldwide. The system transports 800,000 people a day and runs on time. And bicycles are still as [7] _____ (popular) as ever because of the extensive network of bicycle paths. It all means the air in Guangzhou is much [8] _____ (clean) than in other cities.

2 Work in pairs. Compare your country to its nearest neighbours. Make five sentences using comparatives, superlatives or *as ... as* about these things:

- size (larger / smaller / as big as)
- population
- age
- other?

I CAN	
compare differences between two or more things	
talk about the similarities between things	

Vocabulary

3 Complete the sentences with transport words.

1 I work from home so I don't have to c_____ to and from work every day.
2 You can avoid the r_____ hour if you leave home earlier in the morning and leave work earlier in the afternoon.
3 There's always a bad traffic j_____ on the roads through the centre of the city. You sit in your car and never move.
4 The speed l_____ on a motorway in the UK is 70 miles per hour.
5 Look out! There's a p_____ crossing the road.
6 You can either cross the river by driving south for 30 minutes to the bridge or wait for the f_____ to arrive.

4 Complete the sentences with a preposition.

1 Can you pick _____ my shopping on the way home?
2 Please drop me _____ outside the café on the corner.
3 We both fell asleep on the train and so we didn't get _____ at our station!
4 I think I'll go _____ foot today and save some money.
5 Did you come _____ your car or _____ your motorbike?

I CAN	
talk about transport and travel in the city	

Real life

5 Number the lines of a conversation in the correct order (1–8).

1 Hi. I'd like a ticket to Moscow, please.
__ At ten thirty. Here's your ticket.
__ Single or return?
__ OK. A single ticket is 61 euros. Is that OK?
__ Thanks. Which platform does it go from?
__ Yes, that's fine. What time is the next one?
8 Platform eight.
__ Single, please.

6 Work in pairs. Roleplay this situation.

Student A: You are a tourist in Kolkata, India. Ask a rickshaw driver to take you to your hotel.

Student B: You are rickshaw driver. Talk to the tourist and discuss your price.

I CAN	
ask for and buy a ticket	
go on a journey using different types of transport	

Speaking

7 Work in pairs. What is your favourite way to travel (e.g. by plane, train, bus)? What is your least favourite way to travel? Why?

Unit 4 Adventure

The Rumble Room in Rumbling Falls Cave, Tennessee
Photo by Stephen Alvarez

FEATURES

1 Look at the photo. Where are the people? Do you think it looks exciting or dangerous?

2 🎵 **1.21** Listen to a caver whose favourite cave is the Rumbling Falls. Answer the questions.

1 Why do colleagues at work think Vic is 'a bit crazy'?
2 Why do cavers need to be physically fit?
3 What does Vic say 'The Rumble Room' is like?

3 Match these words from the caver's description (1–3) with the definitions (a–c).

1 risk   2 challenge   3 achievement

a something which is dangerous
b something after a lot of hard work and effort (e.g. passing an examination)
c something new and very difficult to do

4 Work in groups. Discuss the questions.

1 Do you think you are a person who takes risks or are you usually very careful?
2 What is your biggest achievement in life so far?
3 What is your biggest challenge in the future?
4 Is there any kind of adventurous or risky activity you would like to try in the future?

4a Adventurers of the year

Reading

1 Read the article. Complete the diagram with the phrases (1–6).

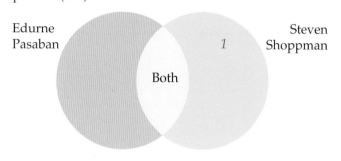

Edurne Pasaban — Both — Steven Shoppman

1

1 born in the USA
2 travelled round the world
3 qualified in engineering
4 is famous
5 finished the adventure
6 loves adventure

2 Read the article again. Answer the questions.

1 What was Edurne's biggest challenge?
2 Why is she famous?
3 What was Steven and Stephen's ambition?
4 What was their biggest risk?

Grammar **past simple**

3 Underline all the verbs in the past tense in *The mountaineer* section of the article. Answer the questions.

1 What do you add to regular verbs in the past simple?
2 What auxiliary verb do you use to make the verb negative?

ADVENTURERS of the YEAR

EVERY YEAR, READERS OF **NATIONAL GEOGRAPHIC MAGAZINE** VOTE FOR THEIR ADVENTURERS OF THE YEAR. HERE ARE TWO OF THEM.

THE MOUNTAINEER

As a child, Edurne Pasaban lived in the mountainous Basque region of Spain and she climbed her first mountain when she was fourteen. At university, she studied engineering but she didn't want a nine-to-five job. In May 2010 she finished her biggest challenge, to climb the world's fourteen tallest mountains. Nowadays she is famous for her many climbing achievements, However, she didn't climb in order to become famous. She says, 'For me, adventure is a way of life.'

THE ROAD TRIPPERS

Steven Shoppman and Stephen Bouey were old friends who grew up together in Denver. But they knew each other a lot better after their adventure. They both had an ambition to go on a road trip round the world. From 2007 to 2010, they drove through 69 different countries during their 122,000-kilometre journey and had many adventures. They took a big risk when they went across a minefield (see photo). They also got help from lots of people and they found that the world wasn't as dangerous as they thought!

road trip (n) /ˈrəʊdtrɪp/
a long journey by road

4 Pronunciation /d/, /t/ or /ɪd/

🎵 **1.22** Listen to the *-ed* ending of these regular verbs. Write /d/, /t/ or /ɪd/. Then listen again and repeat.

1	lived	/d/	5	waited	
2	finished	/t/	6	looked	
3	wanted	/ɪd/	7	decided	
4	studied		8	climbed	

> ▶ **PAST SIMPLE**
>
> He climbed the mountain.
> He didn't climb a mountain.
> Did he climb a mountain?
>
> For further information and practice, see page 159.

5 Find the past tense form of these irregular verbs in *The road trippers* section of the article in Exercise 1.

1	be	*was / were*	6	grow up	
2	drive		7	have	
3	find		8	know	
4	get		9	take	
5	go		10	think	

6 Complete the text about another adventurer with the past simple form of the verbs.

THE PHOTOGRAPHER

Reza ¹ _was born_ (be born) in Tabriz, Iran, in 1952. He ² _____ (study) architecture at the university in Tehran but he ³ _____ (not / become) an architect. When he was a teenager, Reza ⁴ _____ (love) photography and, after university, he ⁵ _____ (get) a job with a local newspaper as a photographer. But he ⁶ _____ (not / want) to take photos of local news and in 1978 he ⁷ _____ (go) abroad and he ⁸ _____ (take) photos of wars. Nowadays he works for *National Geographic* magazine.

7 Read the text in Exercise 6. Answer the questions.

1 When was Reza born?
2 Where did he study architecture?
3 What did he love when he was a teenager?
4 What did he do after university?
5 Did he want to take photos of local news?
6 When did he go abroad?

> ▶ **PAST SIMPLE QUESTIONS**
>
> When were you born? In 1989.
> What did you study at university? Economics.
> Did you go abroad when you were young?
> Yes, I did. / No, I didn't.
>
> For further information and practice, see page 159.

8 🎵 1.23 Work in pairs. Read the article in Exercise 1 again. Write questions for these answers (1–6). Then listen and compare your questions with the recording.

1 In the mountainous Basque region of Spain.
2 When she was fourteen.
3 Engineering.
4 From 2007 to 2010.
5 A minefield.
6 That the world wasn't as dangerous as they thought.

Speaking

9 Write eight to ten questions to ask your partner about their past. Use some of these prompts to help you.

> where / born?   where / live?
> what subjects / like / at school?
> go / university?   what job / want?
> what / do after that?

10 Take turns to interview each other. Make notes about your partner's answers.

11 Swap partners and describe your first partner's life.

> *Chan was born in Hong Kong in 1982 …*

4b The survivors

Vocabulary and speaking personal qualities

1 Look at the photo of an expedition. How dangerous is this situation? What kind of people do this, do you think?

2 Read the sentences and comments (1–8) about this kind of expedition. What kind of personal quality does each describe? Match these adjectives to the sentences.

> ambitious   careful   decisive   determined
> experienced   intelligent   patient   reliable

1 'The leader of our team has climbed in the Himalayas many times before in his thirty years as a mountaineer.'
2 'Whatever the risk, we always achieved our goal. Nothing stopped us.'
3 'Even as a child, I wanted to be the best at everything.'
4 'It's important to plan before any expedition.'
5 'When the weather is really bad, you have to wait. There's no point in taking stupid risks.'
6 'Everyone in the team always has to be there for each other. You won't survive without each other's help and support.'
7 'He has a quick brain and you need that for this kind of expedition.'
8 'The leader is the person who makes the final decision and everyone has to agree.'

> ▶ **WORDBUILDING negative prefixes**
>
> You can make some adjectives for personal qualities negative by adding a prefix: *unambitious*, *indecisive*, *impatient*.
>
> For further information and practice, see Workbook page 35.

3 What personal qualities do these people need? Make sentences with the adjectives in Exercise 2 and explain your reasons.

> a teacher   a close friend   a language learner
> a news photographer   a President
> a sports competitor   a TV presenter

Example:
A teacher is patient because the students need time to learn.

Listening

4 🔊 **1.24** Listen to part of a radio interview with survival expert Doctor Weisz. Match the survivors (1–3) to the situations (a–c).

1 Maria Garza
2 Bethany Hamilton
3 Mr and Mrs Carlson

a lost at sea for thirty-one days
b escaped from a burning aeroplane
c surfing when attacked by a shark

5 🎧 **1.24** Listen again. Choose the correct option (a–c) to complete the sentences.

1 The main aim of the TV programme is to talk about _____.
   a recent survival stories
   b the best survival stories
   c the personal qualities of survivors

2 Doctor Weisz says all survivors _____.
   a are decisive
   b need determination
   c are decisive and need determination

3 The Carlsons' story is different to Bethany's because _____.
   a they were at sea for a long time
   b they were in the water
   c they didn't have experience

4 Most survivors _____.
   a don't take risks
   b often take risks
   c aren't very careful

6 Do you ever need the personal qualities of a survivor? For example, are there other situations when you need to be decisive, experienced or careful?

Grammar **past continuous**

7 Look at the highlighted verbs in the extract from the interview in Exercise 4. Answer the questions.

She was sitting on an aeroplane in Denver airport with her one-year-old child when she saw a fire from the window. While the other passengers were running to the exits, Maria climbed out of the window.

1 Do all the highlighted verbs talk about the past?
2 Which verbs describe a completed action?
3 Which verbs describe actions in progress at a particular time?
4 How do you form the past continuous tense? What is the auxiliary verb? What is the form of the main verbs?

> ▶ **PAST CONTINUOUS**
>
> | I/he/she/it was sitting | you/we/they were sitting |
> |---|---|
> | I/he/she/it wasn't sitting | you/we/they weren't sitting |
> | Was I/he/she/it sitting? | Were you/we/they sitting? |
>
> We often join the past continuous tense with the past simple with the words *when* or *while* to talk about one action happening at the same time as another.
> Maria was sitting on an aeroplane in Denver airport **when** she saw a fire from the window.
> **While** the other passengers were running to the exits, she climbed out of the window.
>
> For further information and practice, see page 159.

8 Look at the grammar box. Then choose the correct options to complete the true life survival stories.

TRUE *life*
SURVIVAL STORIES!

The sun **1** *shone / was shining* when Bethany Hamilton arrived at the beach on a beautiful morning in Hawaii. But hours later, the young teenager **2** *surfed / was surfing* out at sea when a shark attacked her and she lost her left arm. Amazingly, Bethany **3** *swam / was swimming* back to the beach with one arm and, as she was swimming, she told other surfers to get out of the water.

While Steven and Rachel Carlson **4** *sailed / were sailing* around the Canary Islands, their boat sank. They **5** *didn't have / weren't having* much food and water but after 31 days at sea they still survived.

It was a normal afternoon at Denver airport but as Flight 455 was taking off, passengers **6** *saw / was seeing* a fire from the window. Immediately, the plane's captain realised that the engines **7** *didn't work / weren't working* and radioed for help. While passengers **8** *ran / were running* towards the front exits, Maria Garza pulled her daughter through the window exit next to the wing.

9 Which survival story do you think is the most amazing? Why?

10 Pronunciation *was*

🎧 **1.25** Listen to these sentences. Notice how the pronunciation of *was* changes. Then listen again and repeat.

/wəz/
1 She was surfing in Hawaii.

/wɒznt/
2 It wasn't snowing.

/wɒz/
3 Was it raining?

Speaking

11 Work in pairs. Tell your partner which of these events happened to you in the past. Explain:

1 when they happened
2 what you were doing at the time

> broke a bone   got your first job
> first fell in love   fell off your bicycle

> *I was climbing on a wall when I was eight. I fell and broke my arm.*

12 Think of three more real or special events in your life. Tell your partner.

Examples:
While I was working in …, I met …
I was living abroad when I …

4c The right decision?

Reading

1 Work in pairs. What was your best decision in life? What was your worst decision? What happened? Tell your partner.

2 Read the true story on page 51 about two climbers, Simpson and Yates. What decision did Yates make? What decision did Simpson make?

3 Read the story again. Are the sentences true (T) or false (F).

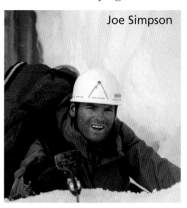

Joe Simpson

Simon Yates

1 The accident happened while Simpson and Yates were climbing up the mountain.
2 They didn't reach the top of Siula Grande.
3 Yates cut the rope because he wanted to survive.
4 Yates didn't look for Simpson afterwards.
5 Simpson managed to get to the base camp on his own.

Vocabulary geographical features

4 Match these words from the story to the picture.

> lake   north face   mountain   cave   summit   ridge
> glacier   cliff   crevasse

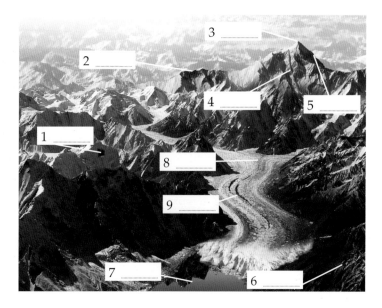

Critical thinking identifying opinion

5 Read the last paragraph again. Do the following people (1–3) think that Yates made the right decision or the wrong decision?

1 some climbers
2 Simpson
3 the author of the article

6 Do you think Yates made the right decision? Why? / Why not?

Vocabulary *in, on* or *at* for time expressions

7 Look at these time expressions from the story. Then complete the rules (1–4) with *in, on* or *at.*

> in May 1985   on Day 1
> three days later   at the last second
> at four o'clock in the afternoon
> in the middle of that night   in 1988

1 We use _____ with months, years, seasons, decades, centuries and parts of the day.
2 We use _____ with days, dates and special days such as *her birthday, New Year's Day.*
3 We use _____ with times and special expressions such as *night, the weekend, the final moment.*
4 We don't use _____ , _____ or _____ with time expressions such as *yesterday, last week, two days later.*

Speaking

8 Work in pairs. Match the time expressions in Exercise 7 to these events from the story. Then tell the main parts of the story using the time expressions.

> stood at the top of the mountain
> cut the rope   wrote a book
> heard his name
> crawled near to base camp
> started climbing Siula Grande

In May 1985 two climbers, Joe Simpson and Simon Yates, left their base camp by a lake and started climbing the north face of a mountain called Siula Grande in the Peruvian Andes. This climb was incredibly dangerous but the two men were experienced climbers and physically fit. On Day 1, the weather was good and the climb began well. At night they made a snow cave and slept on the side of the mountain.

Three days later, after some very difficult climbing and bad weather, the two men stood at the summit. Unfortunately, the weather was getting worse so they didn't stay long. As they were going down a mountain ridge, a disaster happened. Simpson fell and broke his knee. Quickly, Yates tied a rope to himself and then to his friend. He began lowering Simpson down the mountain and, for hours and hours, Yates helped Simpson get down the mountain. They were getting close to the glacier at the bottom of the mountain but suddenly Simpson slipped. This time he went over the edge of a cliff. He was hanging in mid-air. Simpson shouted up to Yates, but the wind was blowing loudly and Yates couldn't hear him.

Yates didn't know it but Simpson was – unbelievably – still alive inside the crevasse.

Yates didn't know what was happening below. He waited for an hour but the rope was too heavy and it was pulling Yates down the mountain towards the cliff. He had two choices: hold the rope but then both of them might die, or cut the rope and survive. It was an impossible decision for Yates but, at the last second, Yates cut the rope and saved himself. Immediately, Simpson fell thirty metres into a crevasse.

The next day, while Yates was desperately looking for Simpson, he found the crevasse. He called for Simpson but he heard nothing. Sadly, he decided that Simpson was dead. Yates didn't know it but Simpson was – unbelievably – still alive inside the crevasse.

Simpson waited for hours but when he realised Yates wasn't coming, he decided to take a risk. He had some rope so he abseiled to the bottom of the crevasse. He managed to find a way out. For three days, Simpson drank water from the snow and ice. He crawled back towards the base camp and at four o'clock in the afternoon of Day 7, Simpson was very near.

In the middle of that night, Yates was sleeping in his tent at base camp when he woke up. He was sure someone was shouting his name. Excitedly, he ran outside and looked around. Finally, after searching and searching he found Simpson. He was lying on the ground, not moving, but he was still breathing.

After a few days, the two men returned home and their story became famous. Unfairly, some climbers criticised Yates for cutting the rope. But, in 1988, Simpson wrote a book about the events and defended Yates. Simpson believed Yates made the right decision.

The RIGHT DECISION?

edge (n) /edʒ/ the place where something stops
abseil (v) /ˈaebseɪl/ to lower yourself down a mountain on a rope
crawl (v) /krɔːl/ to move on your hands and knees

4d A happy ending

Real life **telling a story**

1 💿 **1.26** Listen to a conversation between two friends about a camping trip. Answer the questions.

1 Was the start of the weekend good or bad?
2 When did Mark and the others leave?
3 Where did the car break down? Who fixed it?
4 Why couldn't they find the campsite at first?
5 What happened after they found the campsite?
6 Where did they go instead?

2 💿 **1.26** Listen again and complete the conversation.

A: Hi Mark. How was your camping trip?
B: It was great in the end but we had a terrible time at the beginning.
A: Why?
B: ¹ _____, we left the house early on Saturday morning but after only half an hour the car broke down.
A: Oh no!
B: ² _____, there was a garage nearby and the mechanic fixed the problem. But ³ _____ we arrived at the forest, it was getting dark. ⁴ _____ we drove around for about an hour, we ⁵ _____ found the campsite but it was completely dark by then. ⁶ _____, it started raining so we found a nice hotel down the road!
A: That was lucky!
B: Yes, it was a great hotel and ⁷ _____ _____ _____ we stayed there for the whole weekend.
A: ⁸ _____ _____!

3 Match the words and expressions (1–8) in Exercise 2 with the correct section in the box.

> ▶ **TELLING A STORY**
>
> **Sequencing the story**
> At the beginning ...   Then ...   Next ...
> While ...
>
> **Introducing good and bad news**
> Luckily ...   But ...
>
> **Reacting to good and bad news**
> Why?   That was a good idea!   Oh no!

4 Pronunciation **intonation for responding**

💿 **1.27** Listen to the expressions in 'Reacting to good and bad news' in the box. Notice how the listener uses intonation to show interest. Then listen again and repeat.

5 Work in pairs. Read the conversation in Exercise 2 aloud. Take turns to be person A. Pay attention to your intonation when you are responding.

6 Practise telling another story with your partner. Student A cycled to work and these events happened.

- You had a terrible journey to work.
- You were cycling and it started raining.
- A car hit your bicycle.
- You weren't hurt.
- The driver was very nice. He owns a bicycle shop.
- He gave you a new bike! It's much better than your old bicycle!

Tell your story to Student B. Student B listens and responds. Then change roles and repeat the story.

7 Think of a bad journey you had. Did it have a happy ending? Make a list of the events. Then tell your partner the story.

4e A story of survival

Writing a true story

1 When you read the news, is it always bad news? Are there ever any news stories with good news or happy endings?

2 True stories in the news often include some or all of this information. Read the story and find out which of this information is included.

> the location　　the weather　　the people
> why they were there　　any sudden or unexpected
> events that changed the situation
> how the situation ended　　a happy or sad ending

BOYS SURVIVE
50 DAYS LOST AT SEA

It's an amazing story and it's true! Fifty days ago, three teenage boys suddenly disappeared from the island of Atafu in a small boat. Immediately, rescue boats went to look for them but sadly there was no sign of their boat. Eventually, a fishing boat in the middle of the Pacific Ocean safely pulled them from the sea. The boys were badly sunburned and dehydrated but doctors said they were in surprisingly good health. Now, they are back happily with their families.

3 Writing skill using -*ly* adverbs in stories

Look at the sentence from the story in Exercise 2. We often use -*ly* adverbs to make a story more interesting. Underline the other -*ly* adverbs in the story.

Fifty days ago, three teenage boys <u>suddenly</u> disappeared from the island of Atafu in a small boat.

4 Match the adverbs you underlined in Exercise 3 with the rules (1–3).

> ▶ -*LY* ADVERBS
>
> We often use -*ly* adverbs to:
> 1 comment on the whole clause or sentence.
>   ***Eventually**, they saw another ship in the distance.*
> 2 describe the verb (how someone did something or how it happened).
>   *He **slowly** swam towards the island. (Also He swam towards the island **slowly**.)*
> 3 describe an adjective.
>   *The three survivors were **amazingly** healthy.*
>
> Many adverbs are adjectives + -*ly*, e.g. *sudden – suddenly*.

5 Make these sentences from short stories more interesting using the adverbs.

1 The climb was dangerous. (incredibly)
   The climb was incredibly dangerous.
2 The sun was shining. (brightly)
3 The man jumped into the car. (quickly)
4 They were nearly at the top of the mountain but one of them slipped. (suddenly)
5 It started raining. Gill had an umbrella. (fortunately)
6 The Amazon river was long and they were lost for days. (amazingly)
7 They walked back and looked into each other's eyes. (slowly)
8 They were lost in the forest for hours but they found the road again. (eventually)

6 You are going to write a true story. It can be from your own life or a story you read in the newspaper. Think about these questions and make notes.

- Where did it happen?
- What was the weather like?
- Who was there and what were they doing?
- What unexpected event happened?
- What happened next?
- Did it have a happy or sad ending?

7 Write your story. Use -*ly* adverbs to make it more interesting.

8 Work in pairs. Exchange stories. Use these questions to check your partner's story.

- What information in Exercise 6 does your partner include?
- Does he/she use -*ly* adverbs effectively?

4f Alaskan ice climbing

It's hard work climbing the glacier.

Before you watch

1 Work in pairs. Look at the photo and discuss the questions.

1. Where is the woman?
2. What is she doing?
3. Do you think this is a dangerous activity?
4. How do you think she is feeling?

2 What do you think these words mean? Try to match the words (1–3) with the correct meaning (a–c).

1	serac	a	a narrow, deep hole in ice
2	crevasse	b	an area with many seracs
3	ice fall	c	large piece of glacial ice that sticks up in the air

While you watch

3 Watch the video and check your answers from Exercise 2.

4 Watch the video again and put the events from the climbers' trip in order (1–8).
   a It was a very special feeling for the woman when she got to the top.
   b They drove to the Matanuska glacier.
   c They hiked across the glacier.
   d When they arrived at Talkeetna, the weather was so bad that they couldn't fly to Mount McKinley.
   e A woman slipped, but the rope saved her.
   f After a long walk they reached solid ice at the heart of the glacier.
   g When they arrived at the glacier, the guides explained how to use the equipment.
   h They started climbing the ice wall.

5 Watch the video again and make notes about these topics.

the weather on the trip	
the glacier	
the guides	
the equipment	
the dangers	

After you watch

6 Roleplay **telling a friend about a trip**

Work in pairs.

Student A: You are one of the people who went to the glacier. You are now back at home. Tell a friend about your trip. Use the ideas below to make notes.

Student B: Your friend went on a trip to a glacier in Alaska. Use the ideas below to prepare questions to ask your friend.

- the journey to the glacier
- what the glacier was like
- what the weather was like
- the equipment
- what the climb was like
- how it felt to get to the top

Act out the conversation. Then change roles and have another conversation about a different trip.

7 The narrator says Colby and Caitlin are not usually doubtful when they're in the mountains. What does this tell you about them?

8 Work in pairs. Discuss these questions.

1. What kind of people like ice climbing?
2. Would you like to go ice climbing? Why? / Why not?

---

climb (v) /klaɪm/ go up with a lot of effort
climber (n) /ˈklaɪmə/ a person who climbs
crampons (n) /ˈkræmpɒnz/ spikes that climbers put on the bottom of their boots
doubtful (adj) /ˈdaʊtfl/ not feeling certain about something
glacier (n) /ˈɡlæsiə/ a large mass of ice
guide (n) /ɡaɪd/ a person who shows a place to visitors
heel (n) /hiːl/ the back part of the foot
hike (n) /haɪk/ a walk in a wild place
rope (n) /rəʊp/ a thick string used for tying things
stable (adj) /ˈsteɪbl/ not likely to fall or move in the wrong way
unsafe (adj) /ʌnˈseɪf/ dangerous
weather (n) /ˈweðə/ atmospheric conditions like rain, snow, sun, temperature

Grammar

1 Work in pairs. Look at the photo. What can you see? Where do you think it is?

2 Read about two adventurers and check your ideas in Exercise 1. Then complete the text with the past simple form of the verbs.

Steve O'Meara [1] _____ (meet) Donna in Boston in 1986. On their second date, Steve [2] _____ (take) Donna in a helicopter to Hawaii. That sounds romantic but they [3] _____ (not / fly) to a beach. They [4] _____ (go) to the Kilauea volcano. A year later, they [5] _____ (visit) to the volcano again and this time they [6] _____ (get) married on the volcano. It [7] _____ (not / be) only for romantic reasons. Steve and Donna both [8] _____ (become) volcanologists and they [9] _____ (travel) all over the world to study volcanoes. But they really [10] _____ (want) to spend more time by the Kilauea volcano and some years later they [11] _____ (buy) a house there. Donna explains why: 'This volcano can still kill you but for me to live on the volcano is exciting every day.'

3 Work in pairs. Make questions about Steve and Donna O'Meara using these prompts. Then take turns to ask and answer using information from the text.

Student A: When / meet?
Where / get married? What / want to do?

Student B: Where / take Donna?
What / become? What / buy?

I CAN
talk about past events and important moments in my life
ask questions about the past

Vocabulary

4 Choose the correct option (a–c) to complete the sentences.

1 My biggest _____ at school was passing my mathematics exam. I got an A grade in the end!
   a achievement b challenge c decision
2 Don't get angry when things don't happen as fast as you'd like. Learn to be _____.
   a patient b reliable c experienced
3 Probably the most _____ person in history was Albert Einstein. He had an amazing brain.
   a ambitious b careful c intelligent
4 You dropped water everywhere. Please try to be more _____!
   a ambitious b careful c determined

I CAN
talk about challenge and personal qualities

Real life

5 Look at the pictures (1–5) and write sentences about what happened in each part of the story.

6 Work in pairs. Take turns to tell each other your stories from Exercise 5. The person telling the story has to include the words on the left. The person listening uses the words on the right.

then	next	Why?	Oh no!
while	luckily	Good idea!	

I CAN
sequence the stages of a story
introduce good and bad news in a story
respond to a story

Speaking

7 Write down five years when something important happened in your life. Show the years to your partner. Take turns to guess why each year was important.

Unit 5 The environment

An artist with his sculpture made from recycled parts of old computers
Photo by Peter Essick

FEATURES

1 George Sabra is an artist and sculptor. What do you think
of his sculpture in the photo? Which of these materials
did he use?

cardboard   glass   leather   metal   paper   plastic   wood

2 🔊 1.28 Listen to part of a documentary about George Sabra.
Answer the questions.

1 What everyday objects does the speaker talk about?
2 What does George Sabra do with these objects?
3 What does he want us to think about?

3 Look at the highlighted expressions for talking about objects.
Make sentences about these everyday objects in a similar way.

A dictionary is made of paper. You use it for looking up words.

dictionary   mobile phone   pen   scissors   tin can

4 Work in pairs. Think of other everyday objects. Don't tell your
partner the object but describe what it's made of and what it is
for. Your partner has to guess the object.

5a Recycling

Compost | Glass | Paper and cardboard | Metal | Plastic

Vocabulary **household items**

1 How much do you recycle or reuse items in the house or at work? How easy is it to recycle where you live?

2 You can recycle all these objects. Match each object with the correct recycling bin above.

> aluminium foil   carton
> cereal box   coffee   eggshell
> yoghurt pot   jar   tin can
> envelope   newspaper   bottle
> plastic bag   vegetable peel

3 Look at the grammar box. Which of the nouns in Exercise 2 are countable (C) and which are uncountable (U)?

> ▶ **COUNTABLE and UNCOUNTABLE NOUNS**
>
> **Countable nouns** have singular and plural forms: *a bottle, two bottles*.
> **Uncountable nouns** are singular and have no plural forms. You cannot use them with numbers: *milk*.
>
> For further information and practice, see page 160.

Listening

4 🔊 **1.29** Listen to two callers on a radio phone-in show about recycling. Answer the questions.

1 Which caller (Reg or Sandra) thinks more people need to recycle?
2 Which caller doesn't think recycling helps the environment?

Grammar **quantifiers**

5 🔊 **1.29** Listen to the radio show again. Match the two parts of the sentences.

1	There aren't any	a	people on my street recycle.
2	Are there any	b	bags.
3	There are some	c	recycling bins.
4	They don't recycle much	d	recycling bins there?
5	Not many	e	rubbish every week.
6	They throw away a lot of	f	minutes every day.
7	Some people recycle a little	g	recycling centres in my town.
8	You only need a few	h	stuff.

6 Find these quantifiers in the sentences in Exercise 5. Which of the quantifiers do we use to talk about small quantities?

> any   a few   a little   a lot of   not many   not much   some

> ▶ **QUANTIFIERS**
>
> **Countable nouns**
> We use *some*, *a lot of* and *a few* in affirmative sentences. We use *any* or *many* in negative sentences or questions.
>
> **Uncountable nouns**
> We use *some*, *a lot of* and *a little* in affirmative sentences. We use *any* or *much* in negative sentences or questions.
>
> Note: *a lot of = lots of* (there is no difference in meaning or use)
>
> For further information and practice, see page 160.

7 Work in pairs. Look at the grammar box. Then make sentences about what you recycle and throw away using the table.

I We	(don't)	recycle throw away	a lot of many much any a few a little	metal newspapers plastic glass tin cans cardboard ink cartridges food other?

Reading

8 Read the article about e-rubbish. Answer the questions using quantifiers.

1 How many of us know where our e-rubbish goes?
2 Did Peter Essick follow the rubbish to lots of countries?
3 How many of the computers do sellers resell?
4 How much metal do the parts of the computers contain?
5 Why is the process of recycling these parts so dangerous?
6 How much e-rubbish does Peter Essick think we should export? Why?

> **WORDBUILDING**
> **hyphenated words**
>
> We often join words or parts of other words with a hyphen to make new words: *e-rubbish, out-of-date, eco-friendly.*
>
> For further information and practice, see Workbook page 43.

E-RUBBISH

Nowadays, every household produces electronic rubbish (or e-rubbish) – an old TV or computer printer, or an out-of-date mobile phone we no longer need. But when we throw these everyday items away, not many of us know where these objects go. The journalist and photographer, Peter Essick, decided to follow this e-rubbish to several different countries around the world.

In particular, Essick found a lot of e-rubbish goes to Ghana. There, he saw mountains of old computers in the local markets. The sellers resell some of them but not much equipment works. Instead, they recycle the broken computers by melting the parts inside. These parts contain a little metal such as copper or even gold sometimes. However, this process of recycling is dangerous for the workers because it produces a lot of toxic chemicals.

As a result of his journey, Peter Essick thinks it's important to stop exporting e-rubbish. It's bad for the environment and it's bad for people's health. Instead, he believes manufacturers need to produce more eco-friendly electronics in the future; in other words, electronic products which you can recycle cheaply, safely and in the country where they were made.

melt (v) /melt/ to heat an object until it turns to liquid
toxic (adj) /ˈtɒksɪk/ poisonous

9 Complete these sentences about the article. Then compare your sentences with the class.

I knew *a little / a lot* about this topic before reading this.

This article *is / isn't* surprising for me because …

I *agree / partly agree / don't agree* with Essick because …

Speaking

10 Work in pairs. Imagine you are talking on a radio phone-in programme.

Student A: You are the radio presenter. Turn to page 153 and follow the instructions.

Student B: You are a caller. Turn to page 154 and follow the instructions.

5b The Greendex

Reading and speaking

1 We describe people and their behaviour as 'green' when they help the environment. How green are you? Answer the questions.

1 Do you …
- recycle your rubbish?
- ever buy second-hand goods?
- switch computers and TVs off before you go to bed?
- use public transport or share car journeys?

2 Can you think of more ways to be green in your daily life?

2 Work in groups. Read the first paragraph in the article about the 'Greendex'. Then discuss the questions.

1 What is the purpose of the 'Greendex'?
2 Is your country in the survey?
3 What kinds of cost do you think each of the four categories includes (e.g. housing = electricity, gas)?

3 Read the latest results from the 'Greendex'. Label the pie charts (1–5) with the correct country.

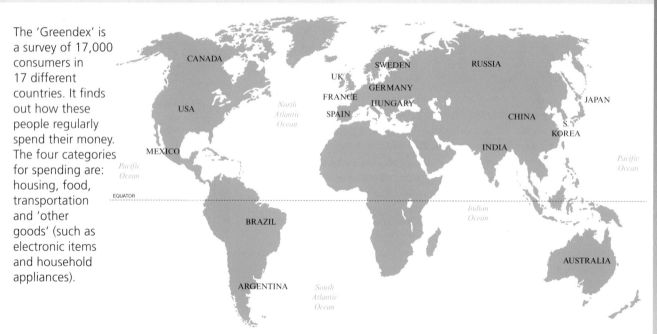

The **Greendex**™

The 'Greendex' is a survey of 17,000 consumers in 17 different countries. It finds out how these people regularly spend their money. The four categories for spending are: housing, food, transportation and 'other goods' (such as electronic items and household appliances).

LATEST RESULTS FROM THE 'GREENDEX':

- About ninety per cent of people in Argentina eat beef nearly every day.
- Exactly half of all Russians use public transport every day or most days.
- Just over two thirds of people in Germany drink a bottle of water daily and most of them also recycle the bottle.
- Consumers in the United States have the most TVs at home. Well over two thirds have four or more.
- Nearly half of all Canadians regularly recycle electronic items.

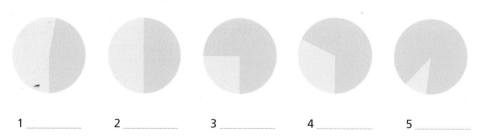

1 .... 2 .... 3 .... 4 .... 5 ....

Vocabulary results and figures

4 Look at these words from the results in Exercise 3. Choose the correct percentage (a–c).

1 about ninety per cent
   a 89%   b 90%   c 99%
2 exactly half
   a 49%   b 50%   c 51%
3 just over two thirds
   a 64%   b 66%   c 69%
4 well over two thirds
   a 66%   b 69%   c 75%
5 nearly half
   a 48%   b 50%   c 52%

5 Approximately, what percentage of your money do you spend on housing, food, transport and 'other goods'? Divide the pie chart to show the percentages.

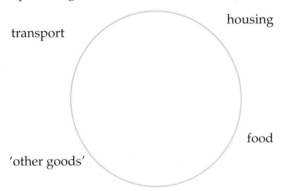

6 Work in pairs. Present your pie chart using words from Exercise 4.

> *I spend about half my money on …*

> *Well over eighty per cent is on …*

Grammar definite article (*the*) or no article

7 Complete the text with *the* or Ø (no article). Then check your answers in the 'Greendex' results in Exercise 3.

- Just over two thirds of people in ¹ _____ Germany drink a bottle of water daily and most of them also recycle ² _____ bottle.
- ³ _____ consumers in ⁴ _____ United States have ⁵ _____ most TVs at ⁶ _____ home.

8 Look at the grammar box. Then match the rules (a–f) with the gaps (1–6) in Exercise 7.

> ▶ **DEFINITE ARTICLE (*THE*) or NO ARTICLE**
>
> Use the **definite article** (*the*):
> a with something or someone you mentioned before.
> b when it is part of the name of something (e.g. *The United Kingdom*).
> c with superlative phrases (e.g. *the best*).
>
> Use **no article**:
> d with most countries.
> e to talk about people and things in a general way.
> f with certain expressions (e.g. *at night, at school*).
>
> For further information and practice, see page 160.

9 Look at these sentences from the 'Greendex' survey. Delete *the* where it isn't necessary.

1 ~~The~~ European houses do not have air conditioning.
2 Countries such as the Brazil are using the electric cars more and more.
3 Many people around the world are trying to use less energy at the home.
4 The fish and seafood is the most common dish in the Japan.
5 The people in the United Kingdom are sharing the cars more and more to save costs.

10 Pronunciation /ðə/ **or** /ðiː/

a 🔘 **1.30** Listen to the difference in the pronunciation of *the* before a consonant sound and a vowel sound.

/ðə/   /ðiː/
the TV   the internet

b 🔘 **1.31** Listen and write /ðə/ or /ðiː/. Then listen again and repeat.

1 the bottle   5 the electricity
2 the phone   6 the gas
3 the fuel   7 the insurance
4 the apple   8 the water

Writing and speaking

11 Work in groups. You are going to prepare a 'Greendex' report about the class. Follow these steps:

1 Write eight to ten questions to find out how 'green' everybody is.
2 Each group member meets students from the other groups and interviews them using the questions.
3 Work with your first group again. Collect the information from your questions and summarise the results.
4 Present your conclusions to the class, using pie charts to help your presentations.

5c A boat made of bottles

Reading

1 Look at these words from the article on page 63. What do you think it is about? Read the article. Were your predictions correct?

> boat   plastic bottles   recycle   sail   San Francisco
> Sydney   the Pacific Ocean

2 Read the article again. Complete the fact file about the Plastiki. Write the information as figures.

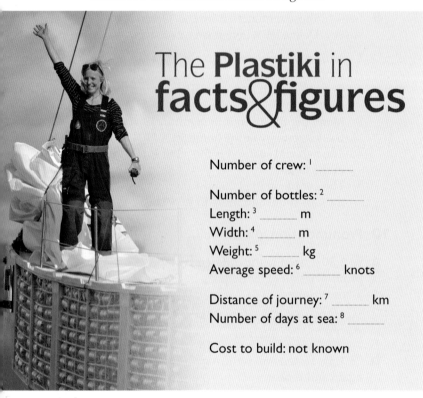

The **Plastiki** in facts&figures

Number of crew: [1] _____

Number of bottles: [2] _____
Length: [3] _____ m
Width: [4] _____ m
Weight: [5] _____ kg
Average speed: [6] _____ knots

Distance of journey: [7] _____ km
Number of days at sea: [8] _____

Cost to build: not known

Critical thinking **close reading**

3 Read sentences 1–8. Write answers A, B or C.

A = The sentence is true. The information is in the text.
B = The sentence is false. The information is in the text.
C = We don't know if it's true or false. The information isn't in the text.

1 The *Plastiki* is made of the same material as other boats.
2 Nowadays, humans recycle most of their plastic bottles.
3 The boat doesn't use renewable energy.
4 The crew only ate vegetables for the whole journey.
5 Plastic in the sea is killing animals.
6 The size of the 'Great Garbage Patch' is growing.
7 Some people criticised De Rothschild and his journey.
8 De Rothschild wants to sail the Plastiki again one day.

4 Do you think the *Plastiki* made a difference to people's attitude to rubbish? Will De Rothschild's journey make people change their behaviour? Why? / Why not?

Word focus *take*

5 Find five expressions with *take* in the article on page 63. Then match them with the correct category (1–4).

> ...to
> ...ation   ...tains that athlete's status as a
>   role model
> ...ours
>
> **take** /teɪk/
> 1 transport: *take a taxi*
> 2 daily routines: *take a walk*
> ...loid   3 lengths of time: *take a few days*
> ...elebrity   4 idioms: *take time (to do*
>   *something)*
>
> ...was a   **takeaway** /teɪkəweɪ/
>   1 food: *we ordered some Chinese*

6 Complete the sentence with *take* and these phrases.

> regular breaks   many days   care
> ~~a plane~~   time

1 Most people _take a plane_ from San Francisco to Sydney so they don't know about the pollution in the ocean.
2 The journey across the Great Garbage Patch _____.
3 The journey was tiring and the crew needed to _____.
4 For this kind of project, it's important to _____ to plan everything.
5 The Pacific Ocean can be dangerous so everyone on the ship had to _____.

Speaking

7 Work in pairs. Imagine you are going to interview David De Rothschild about the *Plastiki*. Prepare six to eight questions using the information in the article and any other questions you would like to ask him.

> *How long did the whole journey take?*

> *How do you think you made a difference?*

8 Change partners with another pair. Take turns to roleplay the interview and ask each other your questions. When you are De Rothschild, use information from the article or create new answers with your own ideas and opinions.

A boat with a difference

The *Plastiki* looks similar to many other boats or yachts in Sydney harbour. It's eighteen metres long, six metres wide and it weighs about twelve thousand kilogrammes. It carries a crew of six people and has an average speed of five knots. However, once you get near to the *Plastiki* you realise there's a big difference. It's made of twelve thousand five hundred reclaimed plastic bottles.

How did the *Plastiki* begin?

One day, the environmentalist David De Rothschild was reading some information about all the plastic in the seas and oceans. He couldn't believe what he was reading. For example, humans throw away four out of every five plastic bottles they use and plastic rubbish causes about eighty per cent of the pollution in the sea. Soon afterwards, Rothschild decided he wanted to help the fight against pollution in the sea. To create publicity for the problem, he started building a boat made of plastic bottles.

Designing the *Plastiki*

As well as building the boat with recycled plastic, it was important for him to make the boat environmentally-friendly and user-friendly. The boat uses renewable energy sources including wind power and solar energy. The crew can make meals with vegetables from the small garden at the back of the boat. They can take a break from work and get some exercise by using the special exercise bicycle. The energy from the bike provides power for the boat's computers. And if anyone needs to take a shower, the boat's shower uses saltwater from the sea.

The journey

De Rothschild sailed the *Plastiki* across the Pacific Ocean from San Francisco to Sydney. That's fifteen thousand three hundred and seventy two nautical kilometres. On the way, De Rothschild took the special boat through the 'Great Garbage Patch'. It is a huge area in the Pacific with 3.5 billion kilogrammes of rubbish. You can see every kind of human rubbish here: shoes, toys, bags, toothbrushes, but the worst problem is the plastic. It kills birds and sea life.

How well did the *Plastiki* survive the journey?

The journey wasn't always easy and De Rothschild and his crew had to take care during storms. There were giant ocean waves and winds of over one hundred kilometres per hour. The whole journey took one hundred and twenty nine days. Originally, De Rothschild thought the boat could only travel once but it survived so well that he is planning to sail it again one day.

A BOAT *made of* BOTTLES

knot (n) /nɒt/ measurement of speed at sea (1 knot = 1.8 km/hr)
garbage (n) /ˈgɑːbɪdʒ/ (US Eng) rubbish (UK Eng)
patch (n) /pætʃ/ area

5d Online shopping

Reading

1 Do you normally go shopping or do you prefer shopping online?

2 Read the website and email order. What did the customer order? What is the problem?

WWW.TECOART.COM

| HOME | MY ACCOUNT | SHOPPING CART | CHECKOUT |

Unusual clocks, Office clocks, Unique Clocks, Computer clocks, Computer art and Vintage clocks all from recycled computers!

Computer Hard Drive Clock with Circuit Board.
£39.00

Apple iPod Hard Drive Clock on a Circuit Board.
£35.00

Order number: 80531A

Order Date: 20 March

Thank you for your order. Unfortunately, the model you ordered is currently not available. We expect delivery in seven days. We apologise for the delay. For further information about this order, speak to a customer service assistant on 555-01754.

Ms Jane Powell
90 North Lane

| Item Number | Description | Quantity | Price |
| HCV1N | Hard drive clock | 1 | £35 |

Real life phoning about an order

3 🎵 **1.32** Jane Powell telephones customer services about her order. Listen to the conversation. Answer the questions.

1 What information does the customer service assistant ask for and check?
2 Why does Jane want the clock quickly?
3 How much does the other clock cost?
4 What does Jane decide to do?
5 What will the customer service assistant email her?

4 🎵 **1.32** Look at the expressions for phoning about an order. Then listen to the conversation again. Tick the sentences the customer service assistant uses.

▶ PHONING ABOUT AN ORDER

Telephone expressions
Good morning. Can I help you?
I'm calling about an order for a clock.
Can I put you on hold for a moment?
Is there anything else I can help you with?

Talking about an order
Do you have the order number?
Would you like to order a different product?
Would you like to cancel the order?
Would you like a refund?
Would you like confirmation by email?

Checking and clarifying
Is that A as in Alpha?
Let me check.
So that's F for Freddie.
That's right.

5 Pronunciation **sounding friendly**

a 🎵 **1.33** Listen to the sentences from a telephone conversation. Does the customer services assistant sound friendly (F) or unfriendly (U)?

1 Good morning. Can I help you?
2 Can I put you on hold?
3 Is that A as in Alpha?
4 I'm calling about an order.
5 Is there anything else I can help you with?
6 Do you have an order number?

b 🎵 **1.34** Listen to the sentences again but now they are all friendly. Listen and repeat with a similar friendly intonation.

6 Work in pairs. Practise two phone conversations similar to the one in Exercise 3.

Student A: Turn to page 153 and follow the instructions.

Student B: Turn to page 155 and follow the instructions.

5e Problem with an order

Writing emails

1 Read the correspondence between a customer and a customer service assistant. Put the emails in order (1–5).

> **A** Dear M Cottrell
>
> I would like to inform you that the e-book reader you ordered is now in stock. I would be delighted to deliver this item immediately. Please reply to confirm you still require this item.
>
> Charlotte Lazarro

> **B** Dear Sir or Madam
>
> I recently ordered an 'e-book reader'. However, I received an email which said this was not currently available. Please refund my money back to the credit card.
>
> Yours sincerely
>
> Mr M Cottrell

> **C** Thanks, but I bought the same product at a shop yesterday. Therefore, please cancel the order and, as requested, send me my refund.
>
> M Cottrell

> **D** As requested here is the order number: 80531A

> **E** Dear M Cottrell
>
> Thank you for your email. I apologise for the difficulties with your order. In order to provide you with the necessary assistance, could you please send the order number?
>
> Best regards
>
> Charlotte Lazarro
>
> Customer Service Assistant

2 Read the emails in Exercise 1 again. Underline any phrases and expressions that request something or give instructions to do something.

3 Writing skill **formal language**

a The language in the emails in Exercise 1 is fairly formal. Match the formal verbs in the emails to these less formal verbs and phrases (1–9).

1 get   *receive*
2 be happy
3 asked for
4 give
5 give back (money)
6 help
7 say sorry
8 tell
9 want

b Work in pairs. Make these sentences more formal.

1 I want my money back.
2 I'm writing to tell you that I didn't get the delivery.
3 Do you want any help?
4 Please give us your credit card details.
5 Sorry, but I can't give you your money back.

4 You ordered a printer but it doesn't work. Write an email to the supplier and request a refund.

5 Work in pairs. Exchange emails with your partner. Write a formal reply from the supplier to your partner's email.

6 Use these questions to check the emails in Exercise 5.

- Did the writer make polite requests and give clear instructions?
- Did the writer use formal language?

5f Coastal clean-up

The aim of this clean-up is to make the coastlines beautiful again.

Before you watch

1 Work in groups. Look at the photo and the title of this video. Discuss the questions.

1 Where are the people?
2 What do you think they are doing? Why?
3 What are they thinking?

While you watch

2 Watch the video and check your ideas from Exercise 1.

3 Watch the video again and number the actions in the order you see them.

a writing information on a form
b getting off a bus
c swimming underwater
d picking up tin cans
e putting bags of rubbish on a boat

4 Watch the video again. Are these sentences true (T) or false (F)?

1 The government pays the people who collect the rubbish.
2 They collect a lot of the rubbish along the coast.
3 The Ocean Conservancy makes a note of every piece of rubbish it collects.
4 Most of the rubbish comes from boats at sea.
5 They cleaned everything up along the river, so there isn't any more to do there.

5 Watch the video again. What do these numbers and dates refer to?

1 half a million

2 3,500,000 kilos

3 35

4 1986

5 1,000 kilos

6 Complete what the people say with these words.

| amazing | disgusting | litter | shocked | trash |
| twice |

'It's ¹ _____ all this stuff that's out here. I was so ² _____ when I came out here. I thought 'oh, you know people don't ³ _____ that much.' You see stuff on the side of the road, but when you come here it's just everywhere.'

'Yeah it is pretty ⁴ _____ , actually. We can pick a lot of it up one day and the next day we come back and there's ⁵ _____ as much as the day before. So it seems like there is no end to the ⁶ _____ .'

7 According to the narrator, what two reasons are there for doing the clean-up?

After you watch

8 Roleplay a conversation between a coastal clean-up volunteer and a member of the public

Work in pairs.

Student A: You are a coastal clean-up volunteer. You want to get more volunteers. Make a list of reasons for helping with the coastal clean-up.

Student B: You live near the coast but you enjoy your free time and don't want to help with the coastal clean-up. Make a list of reasons why you are busy and can't volunteer.

Act out the interview. Student A must convince Student B to volunteer. Then change roles and repeat the conversation.

9 Jay says: 'we are getting there.' What does he mean?

10 Work in pairs. Discuss these questions.

1 Are there places in your country where there is a lot of rubbish?
2 Would you do voluntary work like this?
3 How can you stop people littering?

---

amazing (adj) /ə'meɪzɪŋ/ very surprising
cigarette end (n) /sɪgə'ret end/ the part of the cigarette people throw away after they finish smoking it
coast (n) /kəʊst/ the place where the sea meets the land
clean-up (n) /'kliːn ʌp/ the process of making something clean
collect (v) /kə'lekt/ pick up
disgusting (adj) /dɪs'gʌstɪŋ/ very unpleasant
litter (v) /'lɪtə/ leave things like paper and plastic bags in public places after you finish using them

rubbish (n) /'rʌbɪʃ/ things people throw away when they don't need them (British English)
search (v) /sɜːtʃ/ look for
shocked (adj) /ʃɒkt/ surprised in a negative way
trash (n) /træʃ/ things people throw away when they don't need them (American English)
twice (adv) /twaɪs/ two times
volun'teer (n) /vɒlʌntɪə/ a person who does something without being paid

Grammar

1 Choose the correct options to complete the article about recycling. (Ø = no article)

Recycling around the World

New statistics give a view of recycling around the world. Here are three of the countries in the report.

Switzerland

[1] *A / The* Swiss score well at recycling. With so many different types of recycling bins, local people only have to throw away [2] *a little / a few* household items. For example, they recycle 80% of their plastic bottles. That's much higher than other countries in [3] *Ø / the* Europe with plastic recycling levels of only between 24–40%.

United States of America

Overall [4] *Ø / the* USA doesn't recycle as [5] *many / much* rubbish as a country like Switzerland but it's introduced [6] *a lot of / any* new projects in recent years and so its record is really improving quickly. This year it recycled 48% of its paper, 40% of its plastic bottles and 55% of its cans.

Senegal

Senegal only recycles [7] *a few / a little* of its waste industrially. However, people don't throw away [8] *any / much* items that they can use for something else. For example, you can buy shoes made from old plastic bags and drinking cups from tin cans. Here, everything has another purpose.

2 Work in pairs. Discuss these questions about the countries in the article.

1 Which country recycles the most?
2 Which country reuses items the most?
3 Which country do you think your country is most similar to?

3 Complete the questions with *many, much* or *any*. Then ask your partner the questions.

1 How _____ of your rubbish do you recycle? 70% or more? Between 30 to 69%? 29% or less?
2 How _____ newspapers and magazines do you buy a week?
3 Do you reuse _____ of your household items for something else? For example, glass jars to put other items in, or vegetable peel for compost?

4 Can you name three different countries in each of these regions?

South America	Europe	Asia	Africa
The Middle East			

I CAN
talk and ask about quantities
talk about countries and different regions in the world

Vocabulary

5 Match the percentages from the article in Exercise 1 with the definitions (1–5).

1 just over half   4 two fifths
2 four fifths   5 nearly half
3 about a quarter

6 Work in pairs. Make two sentences about your weekly life using percentages. Talk about:

- the amount of time you spend at work a week.
- the percentage of your money you spend on food.

Then say the same sentences using descriptions (e.g. a quarter, over a half).

I CAN
talk about results and figures

Real life

7 Work in pairs. Practise making a telephone call.

Student A: You want to speak to the Customer Service Manager at an online shop. You bought a TV but it doesn't work. You want the company to collect and replace it. Telephone the customer helpline and explain your problem.

Student B: You work on the customer helpline for an online company. Your manager is not available so take the caller's name, number and write down the details of the complaint.

I CAN
make a telephone call and leave a message
answer a telephone call and take a message

Speaking

8 Write three sentences about your country or another in the world. Two sentences are true facts and one sentence is false.

Example:

1 *The United Kingdom has a population of well over sixty million people.*
2 *The average person in the UK works about forty hours a week.*
3 *70% of the population in the UK is below the age of 30.*
(Sentence 3 is false)

9 Work in pairs. Take turns to say your three sentences and guess which of your partner's sentences is false.

Unit 6 Stages in life

The Egyptian Sphinx
Photo by Bill Ellzey

FEATURES

1 The Sphinx is from ancient Greek and Egyptian mythology. The Sphinx in the photo is the most famous sphinx in the world. Where is it? What else do you know about it?

2 Read this story about the Sphinx. Do you know the answer to the Sphinx's question?

> In Greek history, the Sphinx was a giant monster with the body of a lion, the wings of a bird and a human head. When travellers wanted to enter the city of Thebes, the Sphinx asked them a question: 'What goes on four legs in the morning, on two legs at noon, and on three legs in the evening?' The Sphinx killed any traveller who didn't answer correctly.

3 🔴 **1.35** Listen to an explanation of the story and find out the answer. Did you guess correctly?

4 Look at these different life events. Answer the questions.

> get a pension   get engaged   get married
> get your driving licence   go to college or university
> learn to ride a bicycle   leave home   start a family
> start your career   take a career break

1 At what age do people in your country do these things?
2 Do you think it's important to do each one at a particular age?

6a Changing your life

Vocabulary **stages in life**

1 Put these stages of life into the correct order (1–7) from youngest to oldest.

> adolescent   child   infant   middle aged
> pensioner   teenager   young adult

2 What age do you think these stages begin and end? What is your current stage of life?

Reading

3 Read the article on page 70 about Rich and Amanda. What was their stage of life? Why did they decide to leave their jobs?

4 Read the article again. Underline the answers to these questions.

1 What did they intend to do at the weekend?
2 What did they realise they wanted to do?
3 Why did they buy a campervan?
4 Where did they plan to travel to by container ship?
5 What did colleagues at work find difficult?
6 What did friends think they were crazy to do?
7 What did Rich and Amanda start to do after they left home?

5 Who do you think you are most similar to in the article: Rich and Amanda, or their work colleagues and friends? Explain your answer.

Grammar and listening **verb patterns with** *to* **+ infinitive**

6 Look at the sentences (a–c). Match the sentences to the verb patterns (1–3).

a We intend to leave our jobs.
b Let's buy a camper to travel in.
c It's difficult to understand your decision.

1 a verb followed by the *to* + infinitive
2 an adjective followed by the *to* + infinitive
3 the *to*-infinitive explains the purpose of the main verb

> ▶ **VERB PATTERNS WITH *TO* + INFINITIVE**
>
> **1 verb + *to* + infinitive**: *We intend/plan/want/hope/'d like to travel across Africa.*
> **2 adjective + *to* + infinitive**: *It isn't easy to learn. That's good to know.*
> **3 infinitive of purpose**: *Save your money to buy something special.* (= in order to do something)
>
> For further information and practice, see page 161.

7 🔊 **1.36** Listen to three people talking about their plans and intentions. What is their stage in life? Match the two parts of the sentences.

1 One day I plan to
2 I want to take a year off to
3 I'd like to travel to
4 I intend to
5 I'll be happy to
6 These days, it's really difficult to
7 It's hard not to

a get some work experience abroad.
b do all the things I wanted to do but never had time.
c buy a house.
d go to university.
e leave my job.
f feel sad about it.
g somewhere like Australia.

CHANGING your life

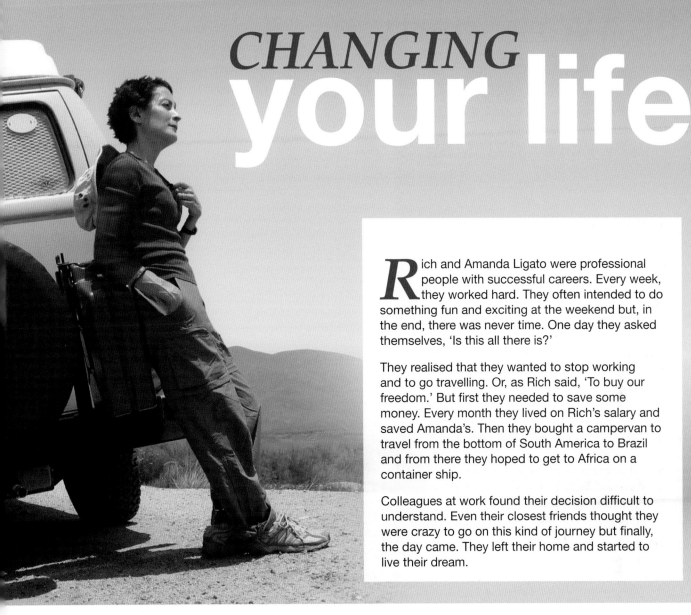

Rich and Amanda Ligato were professional people with successful careers. Every week, they worked hard. They often intended to do something fun and exciting at the weekend but, in the end, there was never time. One day they asked themselves, 'Is this all there is?'

They realised that they wanted to stop working and to go travelling. Or, as Rich said, 'To buy our freedom.' But first they needed to save some money. Every month they lived on Rich's salary and saved Amanda's. Then they bought a campervan to travel from the bottom of South America to Brazil and from there they hoped to get to Africa on a container ship.

Colleagues at work found their decision difficult to understand. Even their closest friends thought they were crazy to go on this kind of journey but finally, the day came. They left their home and started to live their dream.

8 Pronunciation /tə/

🎵 **1.37** Listen to the sentences in Exercise 7. Notice how *to* is not stressed /tuː/ but pronounced /tə/. Listen again and repeat.

9 Write your own sentences using the sentence beginnings (1–7) in Exercise 7. Then compare your sentences with your partner.

Speaking

10 Work in groups of three or four. Imagine you are one of the people on the right. Read about your current situation and make plans for the future. Is there anything you need to do or buy in order to change your life?

11 Present your plans and intentions to your group. Do they think it's a good idea to do these things or do they find them difficult to understand?

Marie (45) and Javier (43)
This couple are both accountants and they own a small apartment in a city. They love skiing but they never have time because the mountains are so far away.

Ahmed (25)
When he was young, he wanted to star in films but his parents said it was difficult to be an actor. So he studied engineering at university and he got a good job. However, sometimes he still dreams about being in films.

Lucy (68)
She's a retired teacher and gets a good pension, but life at home is boring. She never travelled when she was younger but she likes watching travel programmes on TV.

6b World party

VENICE
(ITALY)

NEW ORLEANS
(USA)

PORT-OF-SPAIN
(TRINIDAD AND TOBAGO)

RIO DE JANEIRO
(BRAZIL)

WORLD PARTY

People in different countries celebrate
Mardi Gras with live music, costumes,
fireworks, parades and lots of good food.
The most famous celebrations are in New Orleans, Venice,
Rio de Janeiro and Port-of-Spain.

New Orleans, USA
Small parties for Mardi Gras began in the 1700s. By the 1800s
they were huge events with masks, costumes and jazz bands.
Visitors also have to try 'King Cake' with its gold, purple and
green decorations.

Venice, Italy
Mardi Gras is called *Carnevale* in this beautiful city. The first
celebrations were in the 11th century and you can still enjoy
the costumes, candles and fireworks at night from a gondola
in Venice's canals.

Rio de Janeiro, Brazil
The world famous parades started in the mid-1800s with
decorated floats and thousands of people dancing to samba.
There is also the famous meat and bean stew called *Feijoda*.

Port-of-Spain, Trinidad
The French landed here in the 18th century and brought Mardi
Gras with them. Nowadays, everyone enjoys the parties and
concerts with the famous steel drums from morning to midnight.

Reading and vocabulary celebrations

1 Which events do you celebrate in
your country? When do you have
parties?

> *When a child is born, everyone in
> the family has a party.*

2 Look at the first paragraph of the
article. Why is it called 'World party'?

3 Read the article. Match the sentences
(1–6) to the place described.

1 There were no Mardi Gras
celebrations here before the
mid-1800s.
2 It has the oldest celebration.
3 One type of food is decorated with
different colours.
4 One type of musical instrument is
especially important.
5 One type of music is especially
important.
6 People can travel to the party on a
type of boat.

4 Find words in the article for these pictures.

1 .... 2 .... 3 ....

4 .... 5 .... 6 .... 7 ....

5 Work in groups. Describe your favourite festival or celebration
in your country. Think about these things.

• History: When and why did it begin?
• Traditional food: Is there any special food like cakes with
candles?
• Clothes: Do people wear special costumes or masks?
• Parades: Do people walk round the streets or ride on floats?
Do you have fireworks in the evenings?
• Live music: Is music important? What kind of music do
people play?

Listening

6 🔊 **1.38** Listen to a news item about Mardi Gras. At which celebration in the *World party* article is the presenter?

7 🔊 **1.38** Listen again. Answer the questions with *Yes, No* or *Don't know.*

1 Are a lot of people going to come?
2 Is the woman riding on the float on her own?
3 Is she wearing her mask when the interview starts?
4 Does she think she'll have a good time?

Grammar future forms

8 Look at the sentences (a–c) from the interview in Exercise 6. Answer the questions (1–3).

a Are you going to be in the parade this afternoon?
b I'm meeting everyone at the float in a few minutes.
c Interviewer: And do you have a mask?
  Lorette: Sure. Here it is. I'll put it on.

1 Which sentence is about a plan or future intention? (It was decided before the conversation.)
2 Which sentence is a decision during the conversation?
3 Which sentence is about an arrangement with other people at a certain time in the future?

> ▶ **FUTURE FORMS**
>
> **going to**
> I'm
> he's/she's/it's   *going to* + verb
> you're/we're/they're
>
> **'ll (will)**
> I/he/she/it/you/we/they   *'ll* + verb
>
> **Present continuous for future**
> She's leaving next Friday.
> When are they arriving?
>
> For further information and practice, see page 161.

9 Look at the grammar box. Then choose the correct options to complete the sentences.

1 A: Did Geoff email the times of the parade?
   B: I don't know. *I'll check / I'm checking* my inbox right away.
2 *You'll go / You're going* to visit New Orleans! When did you decide that?
3 A: Hey, this costume would look great on you.
   B: Maybe. *I'm trying / I'll try* it on.
4 A: I forgot to tell you. I'm travelling back home today.
   B: Oh, so *I won't see / I'm not seeing* you later?
5 One day when I'm older, *I'm visiting / I'm going to visit* Venice.
6 A: What time *will we meet / are we meeting* everyone for the parade?
   B: At two in the main square.
7 A: *Are we going to give / Will we give* Mark the present tonight?
   B: No, because his birthday isn't until tomorrow.
8 A: What time *will you leave / are you leaving*?
   B: Straight after the firework display.

10 Pronunciation contracted forms

🔊 **1.39** Listen to sentences 1–5 in Exercise 9. Notice how the contracted forms are pronounced. Listen again and repeat.

Speaking

11 Work in groups. Next year, your town is five hundred years old. Have a town meeting to plan and prepare a celebration. Discuss this list. Decide what you need and who is in charge of organising each thing.

- type of celebration? (e.g. a party, floats, parade, fireworks)
- type of food?
- music?
- where? (e.g. indoors, outdoors)
- date and time?
- items to buy? who will buy them?
- anything else?

> *We're celebrating the town's birthday next year ...*

> *I'll buy the food!*

12 Present your final plans to the whole class. Explain what you are going to do.

> *We're going to ...*

TALK ABOUT ▶ A LIFE-CHANGING DECISION ▶ **PLANNING A CELEBRATION** ▶ EVENTS IN THE YEAR ▶ AN INVITATION
WRITE ▶ A DESCRIPTION

73

6c Masai rite of passage

Reading

1 Discuss these questions.

1 At what age can people legally do these things?

> drive a car   get married   buy cigarettes
> leave home   buy fireworks
> open a bank account

2 At what age do you think teenagers become adults?

3 Do you have special celebrations in your country for young people as they become adults?

2 Look at the photo and the title of the article on page 75. What do you think the expression 'rite of passage' means? Choose the correct option (a or b). Then read the article and check.

a a long journey from one place to another
b a traditional celebration where you move from one stage of life to the next

3 There are six paragraphs in the article. Each paragraph answers one of these questions. Read the article again and number the questions 1 to 6. Then answer the questions.

a How is hair important in Masai culture?
b Where do the Masai live? *1*
c Why are the Masai more famous than other tribes?
d What is the 'Osingira'?
e Who are the warriors?
f How does 'Eunoto' end?

Critical thinking identifying the key information

4 Write notes about the 'Eunoto'. Use these headings and only write down the most important information from the article.

- Location
- Purpose
- Special clothing or appearance
- Special places
- Responsibilities of older men and women

5 Work in pairs. Compare your notes from Exercise 4. How similar are they? Did you include the same information?

Word focus *get*

6 *Get* has different meanings. Underline examples of *get* in the article with these meanings.

> arrive   become   receive

7 Read the description of a wedding. Notice the different ways we can use *get*. Replace the bold words with these words.

> ~~become~~   catch   meet and socialise   prepare
> receive   return   wakes up and gets out of bed

> Once the couple ¹ **get** ___become___ engaged, people start to ² **get ready** _____ for the big day! On the morning of the wedding, everyone ³ **gets up** _____ early. Family and friends sometimes have to travel long distances but it's always a great chance for everyone to ⁴ **get together** _____ again. After the main ceremony, the couple ⁵ **get** _____ a lot of presents. Nowadays, many couples go abroad on their honeymoon so they leave to ⁶ **get** _____ their plane. When they ⁷ **get back** _____, they move into their new home.

Speaking

8 Work in pairs. Choose one of these events. Describe it to your partner and try to use the word *get* three times in your description.

> a birthday   a religious day or period
> New Year's day   your country's national day
> Valentine's day   another special occasion

The Masai are an African tribe of about half a million people. Most of them live in the country of Kenya, but they are also nomadic. Groups of Masai also live in other parts of east Africa, including north Tanzania and they move their animals (cows, sheep and goats) to different areas of the region.

There are many other African tribes but, for many people, the Masai are the most well-known. They are famous for their bright red clothing and their ceremonies that include lots of music and dancing. Probably, one of the most colourful ceremonies is the festival of 'Eunoto'. This is a rite of passage when the teenage boys of the Masai become men.

'Eunoto' lasts for many days and Masai people travel across the region to get to a special place near the border between Kenya and Tanzania. The teenage boys who travel with them are called 'warriors'. This is a traditional name from the past when young men fought with other tribes. Nowadays, these warriors spend most of their time looking after their cattle.

MASAI
RITE OF
PASSAGE

At the beginning of the ceremony, the teenagers paint their bodies. Meanwhile, their mothers start to build a place called the 'Osingira'. It is a sacred room in the middle of the celebrations. Later, the older men from different tribes will sit inside this place and, at different times, the boys go inside to meet them. Later in the day, the boys run around the 'Osingira', going faster and faster each time. It is another important part of the ritual.

The teenagers also have to change their appearance at 'Eunoto'. Masai boys' hair is very long before the ritual but they have to cut it off. In Masai culture, hair is an important symbol. For example, when a baby grows into an infant, the mother cuts the child's hair and gives the child a name. At a Masai wedding, the hair of the bride is also cut off as she becomes a woman. And so, at Eunoto, the teenage boy's mother cuts his hair off at sunrise.

On the final day, the teenagers meet the senior elders one more time. They get this advice: 'Now you are men, use your heads and knowledge.' Then, people start to travel back to their homes and lands. The teenagers are no longer 'warriors'. They are adult men and now they will get married, have children and buy cattle. Later in life, they will be the leaders of their communities.

tribe (n) /traɪb/ large group of families living in the same area
nomadic (adj) /nəʊ'maedɪk/ moving from one place to another and not staying in one place
warrior (n) /'wɒriə(r)/ soldier or someone who fights for the tribe
ritual (n) /'rɪtʃuəl/ formal ceremony with different stages
sunrise (n) /'sʌnraɪz/ when the sun comes up and the day starts
elder (n) /'eldə(r)/ older and experienced person in a tribe or community

6d An invitation

Speaking

1 Which of these events are very formal? Which are less formal?

> an end-of-course party
> an engagement party
> a barbecue with family and friends
> a leaving party for a work colleague
> your grandfather's ninetieth birthday party
> going out for dinner with a work client

Real life inviting, accepting and declining

2 🔊 **1.40** Listen to two conversations. Answer the questions.

Conversation 1
1   What event does Ian invite Abdullah to?
2   Why does Abdullah decline the invitation at first?
3   How does Ian convince Abdullah to come?
4   Does Abdullah need to get anything?

Conversation 2
5   When is Sally leaving?
6   Where does Joanna invite Sally?
7   Does Sally accept the invitation?
8   Do you think this conversation is more or less formal than conversation 1? Why?

3 🔊 **1.40** Look at the expressions for inviting, accepting and declining. Listen to the conversations again. Tick the expressions the speakers use.

▶ GOING ON A JOURNEY		
	Less formal	**More formal**
Inviting	Do you want to …? How about -ing? Why don't you …?	Would you like to come to …? I'd like to take you to …
Accepting	It sounds great/nice. Thanks, that would be great. Yes, OK.	I'd like that very much. That would be wonderful. I'd love to.
Declining	Thanks, but … Sorry, I can't. I'm …	I'd like/love to, but I'm afraid I … It's very nice of you to ask, but I …

4 Pronunciation emphasising words

a 🔊 **1.41** Listen to these sentences from the box in Exercise 3. Underline the word with the main stress.

1   I'd love to.
2   That would be wonderful.
3   It's very nice of you to ask.
4   I'd like to, but I'm afraid I'm busy.

b 🔊 **1.41** Listen again and repeat with the same sentence stress.

5 Work in pairs. Take turns to invite each other to different events. (Think about how formal you need to be.) Practise accepting and declining.

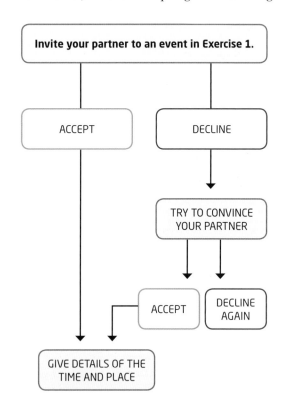

> **Invite your partner to an event in Exercise 1.**
>
> ACCEPT   DECLINE
>
> TRY TO CONVINCE YOUR PARTNER
>
> ACCEPT   DECLINE AGAIN
>
> GIVE DETAILS OF THE TIME AND PLACE

6e A wedding in Madagascar

Writing a description

1 On the website *Glimpse,* people write descriptions of their experiences abroad. Read this post. Which of the things in the box does the writer describe?

> food and meals   clothes   festivals and ceremonies
> nature and geographic features   people
> towns, cities and buildings   transport

glimpse YOUR STORIES FROM ABROAD

I was staying in Madagascar with a family and they invited me to their daughter's wedding. On the big day, I arrived outside an enormous tent. There was a zebu at the entrance and it looked miserable. Inside the tent, there were beautiful decorations and over 300 excited relatives and guests were waiting for the bride and groom to arrive. The women wore colourful dresses. The older men wore smart suits but the younger men were less formally dressed. I even saw jeans and T-shirts. Finally, the ceremony began with some very long and sometimes dull speeches. But the crowd listened politely and sometimes they laughed and applauded. Finally, it was dinner and I suddenly realised what the zebu was for. We ate from massive plates of meat. I felt sorry for the zebu but the meat was the best part of the ceremony! It was delicious!

2 Writing skill descriptive adjectives

a In the description, the writer uses interesting adjectives. Match the highlighted adjectives to these less descriptive adjectives (1–4).

1 big   *enormous*, ...
2 unhappy   ....
3 nice   *beautiful*, ..., ..., ...
4 boring   ....

> ▶ **WORDBUILDING synonyms**
>
> Some words have the same meaning as another word. These are called synonyms: *historic* = old, *big* = huge, *boring* = dull.
>
> For further information and practice, see Workbook page 51.

b Work in pairs. Improve the sentences with more descriptive adjectives. You can use words from the description in Exercise 2 or your own ideas.

      beautiful   *historic*
1 Venice is a ~~nice~~ city with lots of ~~old~~ buildings.
2 In the USA, you can buy big burgers.
3 The parade was a bit boring after a while.
4 The crowd was happy because the nice fireworks started.
5 All the costumes were nice.
6 I was very sad to leave Paris.
7 I tried sushi for the first time and it was really good.
8 The view of the mountains was nice.

c Work in pairs. Look back at the list of subjects in Exercise 1. Think of two or three interesting adjectives to describe each one. Use a dictionary to help you. Then join another pair and compare your adjectives.

Example:
food and meals – delicious, tasty, disgusting

3 Choose one of these topics and write a short description (one paragraph) for the *Glimpse* website.

• a day you remember from a holiday
• your favourite place in the world
• a special occasion in your life
• a festival or celebration

4 Work in pairs. Read your partner's descriptions. Does he/she use interesting adjectives?

Steel drums

Steelband music is a popular part of life here.

Before you watch

1 Work in groups. Look at the photo and discuss the questions.

1 Where do you think these people are from?
2 What kind of musical instrument are they playing?
3 Why do you think this music is important for them?

While you watch

2 Watch the video and check your answers from Exercise 1.

3 Watch the video again. Put these actions in the order you see them.

a Beverley and Dove learn to play the drums.
b A steel band with children and adults play together.
c A person runs into the sea.
d Honey Boy tunes a drum.
e A man makes an oil drum into a steel drum.
f People sell food in a market.

4 Watch the video again and answer the questions.

1 What are the islands of the Caribbean region famous for?

2 Is the 'steelband' or 'pan' native to all the islands?

3 When did people invent this musical instrument?

4 Why did Trinidad have many oil drums?

5 Is the music of the island old? Where did it come from?

6 Do most people play by reading music?

7 What is the name of a person who tunes the drums?

8 Who do you find in a 'panyard'?

5 Match the people (1–4) with the comments (a–d).

1 Beverly
2 woman in market
3 Tony Poyer
4 Dove

a You got that!
b It's part of our culture.
c It's the music of my country so I should learn it.
d This is ours. We made it. We created it.

6 Complete the summary with words from the glossary.

Everywhere you go on the island of Trinidad and Tobago, you can't [1] _____ the sound of the steel drum. It's [2] _____ to the island. It was the only new musical instrument of the twentieth century. Because the county produces oil, it has lots of [3] _____ . During the Second World War, people made them into steel drums or '[4] _____'. However, the music of the region is much older and originally it came over with the African people. Today, the drums still give pleasure to children and adults. Most people play the drums by [5] _____ and every night places call '[6] _____' are full of musicians, learning to play and enjoying part of their country's culture.

After you watch

7 Roleplay a conversation with Tony Poyer

Work in pairs.

Student A: You are Tony Poyer, the expert on steel drums in the video. A journalist is going to interview you. Look at the information below and think about what you are going to say to the journalist about the drums.

Student B: You are a journalist. You are making a documentary about steel drums in Trinidad and Tobago. Use the information below to prepare questions about the drums.

- its history
- how it's made
- how people learn to play it
- the importance of the drum in local culture

8 Work in groups. Discuss these questions for each of your countries.

1 What is the most important or popular musical instrument in your country?
2 What is the most common musical instrument that people play in your country?
3 What is an important symbol of your culture? Does it have a special type of music?
4 Do you think symbols are important for a country or culture? Why? / Why not?

---

escape (v) /ˈɪskeɪp/ run away from
be native to (v) /biː neɪtiv tuː/ be from somewhere originally
oil drums (n) /ɔɪl drʌmz/ round metal containers for oil
play by ear (expression) /pleɪ baɪ iːə/ play musical instrument by listening and not by reading music
pans (n) /pænz/ local word in Trinidad and Tobago meaning 'steel drums'
panyards (npl) /pænjɑːdz/ local word in Trinidad and Tobago meaning place to play steel drums

UNIT 6 REVIEW

Grammar

1 Add the word *to* in six of these sentences. One sentence is correct.

1   I intend $\land^{to}$ find a new job.

2   It's difficult learn a musical instrument.

3   Save your money have a nice holiday this year.

4   We're going meet everyone later.

5   Do you want join us for a drink?

6   I'll see you at the parade.

7   Would you like come for dinner?

2 Choose the correct option (a–c) to complete the sentences.

1   We ——— visit my family this weekend but we aren't sure yet.
   a   hope to
   b   're going to
   c   'll

2   A: I need someone to carry these books for me.
    B: I ——— you!
   a   'm going to help
   b   'm helping
   c   'll help

3   It isn't easy ——— the lottery.
   a   win
   b   to win
   c   will win

4   A: When ——— bring the cake?
    B: In a few minutes.
   a   are you going to
   b   will you
   c   are you

5   Rachel ——— a party tonight. She arranged it months ago.
   a   will have
   b   plans to have
   c   is having

3 Work in pairs. Tell each other:

- your plans for this weekend.
- your future career intentions.

I CAN	
talk about my future plans and intentions	
talk about decisions and arrangements	

Vocabulary

4 Complete the text about the Notting Hill Carnival with these words.

costumes   decorations   drums   floats   parades

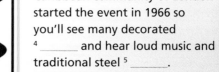

Every year at the end of August, the London neighbourhood of Notting Hill is full of colourful ¹ *parades* for the biggest carnival in Europe. Over 40,000 volunteers help by putting up ² ——— along the streets of west London and welcoming over one million visitors to the party. Many of them make and wear their own ³ ———. The Caribbean community of London started the event in 1966 so you'll see many decorated ⁴ ——— and hear loud music and traditional steel ⁵ ———.

5 Match the verbs (1–6) with the nouns (a–f).

1	start	a	home
2	get	b	a pension
3	leave	c	a mask
4	take	d	a career break
5	wear	e	a family
6	ride	f	on a float

I CAN	
talk about stages and events in life	
talk about parties and celebrations	

Real life

6 Replace the words in bold with these phrases.

I'd like you to   I'd like to   that sounds   would you like

1   **Do you want** to go for a coffee?
2   **Why don't you** come with me to the cinema?
3   **It's nice of you to ask** but I'm out this evening.
4   Thanks. **That'd be** great.

7 Work in groups. Invite each other to do something this week. Accept or decline the invitations.

I CAN	
invite people	
accept and decline invitations	

Speaking

8 Work in groups. You are halfway through this course. Discuss and plan a mid-course party for your class.

Three brothers
Photo by Michael S. Yamashita

FEATURES

1 Look at the photo. What is their occupation? Why is the photo surprising?

2 🔊 **2.1** Listen to someone talking about the photo. Answer the questions.

1 When did the three brothers (or triplets) become police officers?
2 Which police force do they work for?
3 What do they deal with?

3 We sometimes make job titles with two words. Make six jobs.

A	computer	electrical	fashion	~~police~~	security	shop

B	assistant	designer	engineer	guard	~~officer~~	programmer

Example:
police + officer = police officer

> ▶ **WORDBUILDING suffixes**

You can make many verbs into job titles by adding a suffix:
assist – assistant, design – designer, represent – representative.

For further information and practice, see Workbook page 59.

4 What is your current job title? Which company do you work for? What do you deal with?

7a X-ray photographer

Listening

1 Look at the photo. Where is it? In what way is it different from normal photos?

2 🔊 **2.2** Listen to a documentary about the photographer, Nick Veasey. Answer the questions.

1 What types of people, places and things does he take photos of?
2 Where does he take the photos?
3 Where can you see his photos?

3 🔊 **2.2** Listen again. Choose the correct options (a–c) to complete the sentences about Nick's job.

1 The job is _____.
  a creative   b unskilled   c highly-qualified
2 He works in _____.
  a an office   b a factory   c a studio
3 The workplace is _____.
  a old-fashioned   b well-equipped   c spacious
4 The job involves _____.
  a lots of meetings   b travelling
  c working very long hours
5 He spends a lot of the time _____.
  a answering the phone   b sending emails
  c working on his computer

4 Work in pairs. Think about your current job (or a job you want in the future) and complete the sentences in Exercise 3 for you. Use the options (a–c) or your own ideas.

Vocabulary office equipment

5 Look at the photo on page 82 again and find these items. How many of them have you got in your workplace?

> bookshelf   coffee area   desktop lamp
> filing cabinet   newspaper   notice board
> photocopier   swivel chair   water cooler

Reading

6 Read two emails from people working in the office building in the photo. Follow the instructions and find the location of:

1 the broken photocopier
2 the drawer with the report

> **Subject: Broken photocopier**
>
> Hi
>
> My office is on the ground floor. When your technician comes into the building, tell him my door is on the right. Go through the first office and into the next room. The broken photocopier is opposite the door.
>
> Regards
>
> Jennie Clark
>
> Office Administration Manager

> Sahi – I'm away this week so go up to my office and the report is in the filing cabinet behind my assistant's desk.

Grammar prepositions of place and movement

7 Look at the highlighted words in the sentence from the email in Exercise 6. Which words describe the location or place of an object or person? Which describe the direction of movement?

When your technician comes into the building, tell him the lift is on the left.

▶ **PREPOSITIONS OF PLACE and MOVEMENT**

Prepositions of place
It's opposite the door. / It's on the third floor. / It's at the top of the building. / It's next to the photocopier.

Prepositions of movement
Prepositions of movement follow a verb of movement, e.g. *go down, walk into, climb up, run across.*

For further information and practice, see page 162.

8 Look at the grammar box. Then underline the other prepositions of place and movement in the emails in Exercise 6. Which are prepositions of place? Which are prepositions of movement?

9 Complete the emails with these prepositions.

> at   down   in   into   next   on   through   up

> Let's meet ¹ _____ the coffee area at 11. It's the room ² _____ the top of the building. See you there.

> Can you fix my printer for me? My office is ³ _____ the third floor. The printer is ⁴ _____ to my desk.
>
> Jennie
>
> PS The lift is out of order today so you'll have to go ⁵ _____ the reception area to the fire exit and walk ⁶ _____ the emergency stairs.

> We got ⁷ _____ the lift on the fifth floor and now it won't go ⁸ _____ to reception. Please help!

10 Pronunciation intrusive /w/

🔊 **2.3** Sometimes when a word ends in a vowel and the next verb starts in a vowel, we add the /w/ sound. Listen and repeat these examples with *go* + preposition.

1 go /w/ in   3 go /w/ at   5 go /w/ up
2 go /w/ on   4 go /w/ into   6 go /w/ across

Speaking

11 Work in pairs. Take turns to give directions to your partner from where you are now to these different parts of the building. Your partner says the place.

> the lifts or stairs   your favourite café
> the toilets   another classroom
> the reception area

7b The cost of new jobs

Reading

1 Work in pairs. Think of one big change in your life (e.g. moving to a new place, changing jobs). Use these questions to tell your partner about the change.

- Was it recently or long ago?
- Why did the change happen?
- Were you happy about the change, or did you want to stop it?

2 Read the extract from an article about the state of Pennsylvania in the USA and the people living there. Answer the questions.

1 When did the energy companies discover natural gas in Pennsylvania?
2 What are two changes in the State because of the discovery?
3 Why does Donald Roessler think the discovery is good?
4 Why do Chris and Stephanie Hallowich think the discovery is bad?

Grammar **present perfect simple**

3 Look at the sentences (a–c) from the article. Answer the questions (1–3).

a In 2004, an energy company discovered natural gas under the ground.
b Donald Roessler has lived on his farm for most of his life.
c Many people have found new jobs.

1 Which sentence describes a finished action at a definite time in the past?
2 Which sentence describes an action that happened sometime in the past but we don't know the exact time?
3 Which sentence describes an action that started in the past and is still true today?

4 Sentences b and c in Exercise 3 are in the present perfect. How do you form this tense? Underline more examples in the article.

▶ PRESENT PERFECT SIMPLE		
	have	past participle
I/you/we/they	have (haven't)	found
he/she/it	has (hasn't)	found
Have they found gas?		
Has he found a new job?		

For further information and practice, see page 162.

The *cost* of new jobs

The State of Pennsylvania in the northeast of the USA is famous for its beautiful countryside. However, in 2004, an energy company discovered natural gas under the ground. Since then, this discovery has changed many people's lives – in good and bad ways. Many people have found new jobs but it has also changed the environment. Here are the opinions of some of the local people ...

The farmer

Donald Roessler has lived on his farm for most of his life. He hasn't earned much money from farming but two years ago an energy company wanted the gas under his farm. They offered Donald a regular monthly income and he signed the contract immediately.

The teacher and the accountant

Chris and Stephanie Hallowich built their 'dream house' in the middle of the Pennsylvania countryside in 2007. But at the same time, gas companies moved into the area. Since then, Chris and Stephanie have found chemicals in their drinking water and pollution in the air. They want to move but they haven't sold their house yet.

5 Complete the text below about two more people in Pennsylvania. Use the past simple or present perfect form of the verbs.

The businessman

Paul Battista [1] _has run_ (run) a tool supply business for thirty years. In the beginning, it [2] _____ (be) very successful but around the year 2000 his sales [3] _____ (start) to decrease because of Pennsylvania's bad economy. Fortunately Paul's profits [4] _____ (increase) again since the new energy industries came to the region.

The trainee driver

In 2009, Lee Zavistak [5] _____ (lose) her job at a bottle factory. At that time, there [6] _____ (not / be) many other jobs for Lee. However, since 2009, the new energy companies [7] _____ (employ) lots of new people, especially truck drivers. Lee [8] _____ (not / find) a new job yet but she's now learning to drive trucks so she's confident about the future.

6 Pronunciation irregular past participles

🎵 2.4 Write the past participle form of these irregular verbs. Then listen, check and repeat.

1 find _____
2 sell _____
3 buy _____
4 fly _____
5 think _____
6 do _____
7 win _____
8 teach _____
9 grow _____
10 run _____
11 lose _____
12 fall _____

7 Do you think the discovery of natural gas has been a good or bad thing for the State of Pennsylvania? Why? / Why not?

Listening

8 🎵 2.5 A radio journalist in Pennsylvania is making a programme about the changes in the region. Listen to her interview with an engineer from one of the gas companies. Are the sentences true (T) or false (F)?

1 The engineer has always worked for the same company.
2 He's always lived in Pennsylvania.
3 He moved to Pennsylvania before they found gas.
4 Everyone has been friendly.

9 🎵 2.5 Write the interviewer's questions using the prompts in the past simple or present perfect form. Then listen to the interview again and check.

1 how long / work / for your company?
2 when / you / study / engineering?
3 have / always / live / in Pennsylvania?
4 when / you / move here?
5 how many different places / you / live in?
6 have / ever / live / abroad?
7 it / be / easy living here?
8 the local people / be / friendly?

Vocabulary *for* or *since*

10 Look at the two ways the engineer answers the question from the interview. Then complete the rules with *since* and *for*.

Journalist: How long have you worked for your company?
Engineer: For twenty-five years. Since I left college.

We use [1] _____ to talk about a point in time. We use [2] _____ to talk about a length of time.

11 Complete the phrases with *for* or *since*.

1 _____ 2008
2 _____ two weeks
3 _____ six days
4 _____ one o'clock
5 _____ I started work
6 _____ 1st January
7 _____ 24 hours
8 _____ I was ten

Speaking

12 Work in pairs. Practise asking and answering questions on these topics using the present perfect and past simple.

| current job/studies | where you live | travel |
| languages | people you know | interests/hobbies |

Example:
A: Have you ever studied Chinese?
B: No, I haven't, but I study Arabic.
A: Really? How long have you studied it?
B: For about three years ago.
A: Why did you start learning Arabic?

7c Twenty-first century cowboys

Vocabulary job satisfaction

1 Work in groups. What is important in a job? Put these items in order of importance (1 = most important).

> colleagues and teamwork   independence
> number of days' holidays   pension   promotion
> salary   training   working hours

2 Look at the cowboys in the photo on page 87. What do you think is important in their job?

Reading

3 Read the article on page 87. Which of these headings (1–3) best summarises the text?

1 How modern cowboys really live and work.
2 The truth about Hollywood cowboys.
3 Why people don't want to be cowboys anymore.

4 Read the article again. Choose the correct option (a–c) to complete the sentences.

1 The writer explains that life as a cowboy is ....
  a similar to life as a Hollywood actor
  b adventurous and romantic
  c hard work
2 The cattle industry ....
  a hasn't changed for three hundred years
  b is very different from the past
  c doesn't need cowboys anymore
3 People like Pat Criswell become cowboys for ....
  a job security
  b the salary
  c job satisfaction
4 Tyrel Tucker enjoyed the job because it involved ....
  a making decisions
  b working in teams
  c being independent

5 Find these sentences in the article. Who or what do the bold words refer to?

1 **It** was a classic symbol of the United States of America. (paragraph 1)
2 People come and stay for a holiday and live the cowboy's life (or a Hollywood version of **it**). (paragraph 2)
3 And so cowboys ride on horses to bring **them** home. (paragraph 3)
4 **They** all thought Pat was crazy. (paragraph 4)
5 ... and Tyrel is growing **his**. (paragraph 6)

Word focus *make* or *do*

6 Complete these phrases with *make* or *do*. Then find the verb + noun combinations in the article and check your answers.

1 .... business   4 .... a call
2 .... money   5 .... breakfast
3 .... a job

7 Complete these phrases with *make* or *do*. Use a dictionary to help you, if necessary.

1 .... your homework
2 .... a mistake
3 .... a decision
4 .... someone a favour
5 .... well at work/school
6 .... your bed
7 .... a noise
8 .... work

8 Work in pairs. Ask your partner three questions using verb + noun combinations with *make* and *do*.

> *What kind of job do you do?*

> *What do you normally make for breakfast?*

Critical thinking the author's opinion

9 What kind of image does the author give of twenty-first century cowboys? Choose a word from the box and underline any sentences in the article to support your choice.

> hard-working   romantic   sad   unskilled

Speaking

10 Discuss as a class. Which comments are similar to your own opinions? Explain why or give a new opinion.

> I admire the modern day cowboy because I admire people who work hard.

> I think these cowboys are strange because they don't want to be part of the modern world.

> It's better to be a Hollywood cowboy than a modern cowboy.

> I'm more like Pat Criswell than his colleagues: job satisfaction is much more important than money.

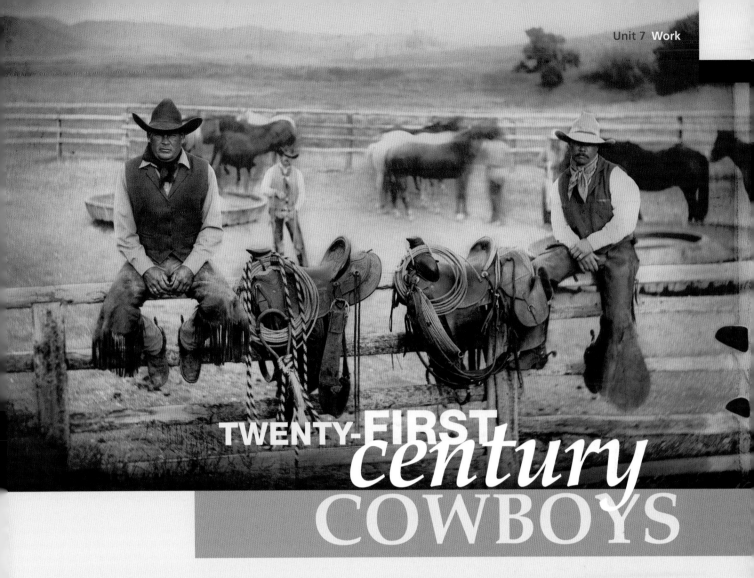

TWENTY-FIRST century COWBOYS

Cowboys have always had a romantic image. When people first watched Hollywood films, being a cowboy wasn't a job. It was a life of adventure, freedom, horses. It was a classic symbol of the United States of America. In reality, the real American cowboys have lived and worked here in the west and south-west of the United States for over three centuries, long before Hollywood. The adventure and romance have disappeared but the hard work and long hours are the same as they've always been.

No one knows how many cowboys are still working. Maybe between ten and fifty thousand. It's also difficult to define a twenty-first century cowboy. Surely it can't be the big cattle owners who do business with a seventy-billion dollar beef industry? These modern ranches use the latest technology and employ accountants. But even some of the old traditional cattle ranches make more money nowadays by offering holidays to tourists; people come and stay for a holiday and live the cowboy's life (or a Hollywood version of it).

But even with technology and Hollywood romance, real cowboys still do the same job they have done for years. The cattle still need to walk across huge plains and eat grass many miles from the ranch. And so cowboys ride on horses to bring them home. Cowboys work in the middle of nowhere, in a place where you can't make a phone call because mobile phones don't work. Like the cowboys of the past, twenty-first century cowboys still get up early on freezing cold mornings and make breakfast over an open fire. There is no Monday to Friday, weekends off or paid holidays.

So why do men – because it is usually men – choose this life? Pat Crisswell had a good job with the government. He made good money but he didn't like the city. He wanted to do something different. So one day, he gave up his job and moved to a ranch in Texas, earning much less as a cowboy. He remembers his work colleagues in the city on the day he left. They all thought Pat was crazy. But he wanted job satisfaction more than money.

Two brothers – Tyrel and Blaine Tucker – have lived on ranches and worked with cows since they were children. Their mother had a ranch in Wyoming. Last winter, they looked after 2,300 cows. Every day from December until April, they rode across nearly 100,000 acres of land with only the cattle, the horses, and each other for company. Eighteen-year-old Tyrel Tucker says, 'It was fun. You get to be by yourself.'

Blaine has a large moustache and Tyrel is growing his. They wear traditional cowboy clothes with the famous hat and boots. You could do the same job in a baseball cap and a truck but Tyrel and Blaine prefer the traditional cowboy culture: 'It's a real life about you, your horse and the open country.'

symbol (n) /ˈsɪmbl/ something that represents a society, country or type of life
cattle (n) /ˈkaetl/ cows
ranch (n) /rɑːntʃ/ large farm for cattle, horses or sheep
plain (n) /pleɪn/ grassy areas of open land
good money /gʊd ˈmʌni/ expression meaning 'a lot of money' or 'well-paid'
acre (n) /ˈeɪkə(r)/ measurement of land

7d A job interview

Vocabulary job adverts

1 Look at the job advert. Would you apply for this kind of job? Why? / Why not?

Sales Assistant required

E.I. Books is a large national bookshop. We are opening our latest bookshop and so we are recruiting sales staff for full and part-time positions (flexible hours).

CLICK HERE for a full job description and contact details. All applicants must send their application and CV.

Salary is according to previous experience.

2 Match words in the advert with the definitions (1–8).

1 people applying for the job
2 a letter or email to say you'd like to apply for the job
3 the amount of money you will make a year
4 looking for people to work for a company (formal word for 'employing')
5 a more formal word for 'jobs' with a company
6 abbreviation meaning Curriculum Vitae (with information about you, your qualifications and experience)
7 information about what you will need to do in the job
8 information including name, number and address

Real life a job interview

3 🔊 **2.6** Ruby applied for the job in the advert in Exercise 1 and was invited for an interview. Listen to extracts from the interview. Are the sentences true (T) or false (F)?

1 The interviewer has received her letter of application and CV.
2 Ruby has already left her last job.
3 She wants to leave Raystone's bookshop because she doesn't like the job.
4 The interviewer is pleased Ruby has found out about E.I. Books.
5 Ruby doesn't have any questions for the interviewer.
6 They discuss something in the job description.

4 Do you think Ruby is the right person for the job? Why? / Why not?

5 🔊 **2.6** Listen again and complete these questions from the interview. Then match them with the correct category in the box.

1 _____ long have you _____ there?
2 _____ have you _____ for this position?
3 _____ you _____ yourself as ambitious?
4 _____ are some of your main strengths?
5 _____ you _____ any questions for me?
6 _____ you _____ me more about that?

▶ **A JOB INTERVIEW**

Your current situation and job
Tell me about your current job.
Why do you want to leave your current job?

Reasons for applying
Why do you think you'd like to do this job?

Strengths, weaknesses and personal qualities
Do you have any weaknesses?
How would other people describe you?

Questions for the interviewer
What questions do you have about the job?
Can you give me some information about (the salary, the hours, the benefits, etc.)?

6 Work in pairs. Look at the job advert. You are going to roleplay a job interview for this position.

Displaying **1–12** of **84** jobs   Page: **1** 2 3

Office Assistant required

MFR industries is recruiting an assistant to help in our new Sales offices. You will be responsible for helping six staff including answering calls, doing filing, answering enquiries and helping customers. Previous experience of office work is helpful but not essential. The ability to work in a team and an enthusiastic personality is more important. Some knowledge of English is also useful. Click here for full job description and contact details. All applicants must email their application and CV. Salary is according to previous experience.

Student A: You are the interviewer. Prepare your questions for five minutes.

Student B: You are the applicant. Think about answers for any questions the interviewer might ask you.

When you are both ready, begin the interview.

7 Change roles in Exercise 6 and repeat the roleplay.

7e Applying for a job

Writing a CV

1 Complete the CV (curriculum vitae) with these headings.

> Address Date of birth Education Home telephone Interests
> References Skills Work experience

Curriculum Vitae

Aldo Peterson

Nationality	Swiss and British
1	17 September, 1987
2	Flat 3A, 85 Cadogan Gardens, London SW1
Email	a_peterson@swisstel.com
3	0207 685 74653
Mobile	07759 856 746

4 ....

2008–2009	MA in Events Management, London College of Catering and Hotel Management
2005–2008	BSc in Geography and Economics, London University

5 ....

2011–present	Assistant manager: Managed a medium-sized hotel, supervised staff, assisted the general manager in all areas of hotel activities
2009–2011	Hotel receptionist: Received international guests, collaborated as team member, translated hotel correspondence in French, German and English.
Summer 2010	Camp counsellor on summer camp in USA: Co-ordinated groups of teenagers and planned events.

6 ....

Languages: English and German (bilingual), French (fluent)
Computing: Word, Excel, web design

7 ....

Captain of local hockey team, most winter sports, theatre

8 ....

Dr Miles Keeping, Dept of Hotel Management, 15 Gower Street, London
Alessandra Delfs, Mattenstrsse 7, Reinach, 4153, Switzerland

2 How similar is the layout to a CV in your country? Would you advise Aldo to add any other information?

3 Writing skill action verbs for CVs

We often give a short description of our work experience in CVs using 'action' verbs in the past simple without the pronoun *I*. Find eight examples of action verbs in Aldo's CV in Exercise 1.

Example:
Managed a medium-sized hotel.

4 Look at the spoken sentences (1–6). Replace the words in italics with these action verbs to make them suitable for a CV.

> advised ~~assisted~~ designed
> planned and organised
> represented supervised

1 *I often had to help* the manager with office duties.
   Assisted the manager with office duties.
2 *As a student counsellor, one of my roles was to talk to students and help* students on future career paths.
3 *Because I'd made some websites at home, I was put in charge of making* a new website for the company.
4 *The company had lots of staff who travelled so had to book plane tickets and hotels – anything to do with* travel arrangements.
5 *The company did lots of trade fairs so sometimes I had to be there for* the company at trade fair events.
6 *I was never officially the team leader but my job included managing* a team of four.

5 Think of a job you have done in the past. Write sentences that summarise the main parts of the job using action verbs. Use the verbs from the CV and Exercise 4 to help you.

6 Write your complete CV.

7 Work in pairs. Exchange CVs. Use these questions to check your partner's CV.

- Does it have clear headings?
- Has he/she used action verbs effectively?

7F Butler school

There are lots of secrets to being a good butler.

Before you watch

1 Work in groups. Look at the photo and discuss the questions. Use as many of the words and phrases in the glossary as you can.

1 Who are the people?
2 What are they doing? Why?
3 What do you think the caption means?

2 Tick the things and people you think you might see in the video.

> glasses   hats   a London taxi   a newspaper
> the Queen   shoes   suits

While you watch

3 Watch the video and check your answers from Exercise 2.

4 Watch the first part of the video (to 02.31). Are these sentences true (T) or false (F)?

1 There are not many butlers in England today.
2 On the first day of class, the students learn how to make tea correctly.
3 There were about 200 butlers seventy years ago.
4 All the students come from England.
5 Butlers from the school sometimes work for important leaders and kings.
6 The course lasts thirteen weeks.
7 There are 86 lessons during the course.
8 The first two days are very easy for everybody.

5 Watch the second part of the video (02.31–05.01). Complete the sentences with the missing word(s).

1 Students have to _____ a lot.
2 The word 'butler' comes from a French word which means '_____'.
3 David Marceau starts to show some _____.
4 David talked to his _____ last night.
5 Ivor Spencer irons a _____.
6 Butlers may have to deal with _____ guests.

6 Watch the final part of the video (05.01 to the end). Answer the questions.

1 What three things are mentioned as 'the finer things in life'? _____ _____ _____

2 What jobs did the people do before the course? _____

7 Match the people (1–6) with what they say (a–f).

1 Ivor Spencer
2 the man in the pipe shop
3 the narrator
4 David Marceau
5 the taxi driver
6 David Suter

a Long ago, England was a land of country houses, palaces, gardens and afternoon tea.
b I haven't seen a butler for a long time.
c On every course there are about two people that don't make it past the first two days.
d Practice makes perfect, so hopefully, with a lot of practice, I'll be just as good as any other butler out there.
e I just hope I'm going to be right for the job and hope I can do it!
f It's not just a piece of wood, it's a piece of art.

After you watch

8 Roleplay a conversation with David Marceau

Work in pairs.

Student A: You are David Marceau. A friend phones you. Look at the ideas below. Think about what you are going to tell him or her about your experiences on the course.

Student B: You are a friend of David's. Phone him and ask him about the course and his stay in England. Use the ideas below to prepare questions to ask David.

- the length of the course
- how many hours they studied every day
- how hard the course was
- what he found difficult
- what they had to do
- what job he wants to get now

9 Work in groups. Discuss these questions.

1 Would you like to be a butler? Why? / Why not?
2 Would you employ a butler? Why? / Why not?
3 Do you agree that you need to 'practise, practise, practise' if you want to succeed?

---

burnt (adj) /bɜːnt/ marked by fire or heat
butler (n) /ˈbʌtlə/ the head servant in a house
deal with (v) /ˈdiːl wɪð/ solve a problem
fetch (v) /fetʃ/ go and bring
guest (n) /gest/ a person who is invited to a house or party
improvement (n) /ɪmˈpruːvmənt/ getting better
iron (v) /ˈaɪən/ move a hot electrical apparatus across something to make it smooth
make it (v) /ˈmeɪk ɪt/ be successful
miss (v) /mɪs/ feel sad because you are not with a person
palace (n) /ˈpæləs/ place where a king or queen lives
servant (n) /ˈsɜːvənt/ a person who is paid to work in a house
unwelcome (adj) /ʌnˈwelkəm/ not invited and not wanted

Grammar

1 Complete the sentences with these prepositions.

> across   at   in   on   opposite
> through

1   Walk _____ to the other side of the car park and the factory is there.
2   Can you pass me that book _____ the shelf?
3   There's lots of water _____ the water cooler so help yourself to a drink.
4   Go _____ those doors at the end and the photocopier is there.
5   The cafeteria is _____ the top of the building on the fifth floor.
6   We sit _____ each other in the same office.

2 Work in pairs. One person chooses an object in the classroom and describes where it is. The other person guesses what the object is.

Example:
It's on the left of the teacher's desk ...

3 Complete the questions with the present perfect or past simple form of the verbs.

A: How long [1] _____ you _____ (work) here ?
B: About three years. I [2] _____ (join) the newspaper when I left university.
A: So, [3] _____ you always _____ (want) to be a journalist?
B: Not particularly. But when I [4] _____ (be) young, I wrote stories.
A: What [5] _____ you _____ (study) at university?
B: Spanish.
A: [6] _____ you ever _____ (live) in Spain?
B: No, but I [7] _____ (spend) a summer in Argentina.
A: Really? [8] _____ you _____ (travel) around a lot?
B: Yes, I did. Especially in the region of Patagonia.

4 Prepare three questions for your partner starting with *How long have you ...?* Then ask and answer your questions using *since* or *for* in your answers.

> **I CAN**
> describe location and movement using prepositions
> talk and ask questions about events and experiences in the past

Vocabulary

5 Work in pairs. Look at the photo of the balloon seller. Do you think he enjoys this job? Why? / Why not?

6 Complete the text about the balloon seller with the correct form of *make* or *do*.

Nguyen [1] _____ two jobs. During the day he sells balloons and in the evening he [2] _____ money by working in a restaurant. He helps to [3] _____ food in the kitchen. He works long days but he is saving so he can complete his studies. If he [4] _____ well at college he can go to university.

> **I CAN**
> talk about different jobs and work

Real life

7 Match these questions at a job interview (1–5) with the responses (a–e).

1   Do you have any weaknesses?
2   What are you main strengths?
3   Would you say you're ambitious?
4   How well do you work with other people?
5   Do you have any questions for me?

a   Yes, fairly.
b   I get annoyed if other people aren't working hard.
c   Quite well.
d   Yes, just one ...
e   I'm careful and like to get things right.

8 Work in pairs. Take turns to ask and answer the questions in Exercise 7. Respond with your own answers.

> **I CAN**
> ask interview questions
> answer questions about myself and my job

Speaking

9 Imagine your dream job. Think about these questions.

- What would you like to do? Why?
- How many hours a week would you like to work?
- How much money would you want to earn?

Work in pairs. Tell your partner about your dream job.

Unit 8 Technology

Robots and humans working together
Photo by Robert Markowitz and Bill Stafford, NASA

FEATURES

1 Look at the photo and the caption. How do you think they are going to 'work together'? In what ways do robots already work with humans?

2 ✷ **2.7** Listen to someone talking about the importance of technology in our lives. Answer the questions.

1 What everyday jobs does technology do for humans?
2 Under what circumstances does technology ever make mistakes?
3 Where does the robot in the photo work? What does it do?

3 Which of these comments are true for a robot, a human or both?

> has new ideas   finds solutions and solves problems
> never gets hungry or tired   can make a mistake
> doesn't get bored   always follows instructions
> makes decisions   invents things

4 Work in groups. Compare humans and technology. Think of two more advantages or disadvantages for each.

8a Invention for the eyes

Speaking

1 Work in pairs. What problems did these famous inventions solve? Check your answers on page 153.

> Braille   electric light bulb
> microwave oven   post-it note   telescope

2 Think of one more invention that solved a problem and tell the class. Compare everyone's inventions and decide which was the most important in human history.

Listening

3 💿 **2.8** This Tibetan man is wearing a new type of glasses. Listen to a science programme about the glasses. Answer the questions.

1 What is a problem for many people in the world?
2 How can the glasses solve this problem?
3 In which parts of the world do people now wear the glasses?

4 💿 **2.9** Listen to the first half of the programme again. Number the instructions on the diagram in the correct order (1–4).

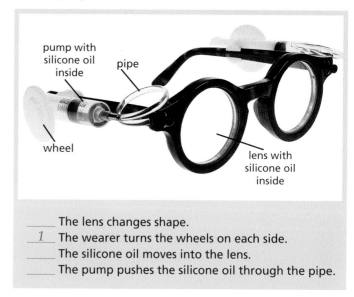

pump with silicone oil inside
pipe
wheel
lens with silicone oil inside

_____ The lens changes shape.
__1__ The wearer turns the wheels on each side.
_____ The silicone oil moves into the lens.
_____ The pump pushes the silicone oil through the pipe.

5 💿 **2.10** Listen to the second half of the programme again. Are the sentences true (T) or false (F)?

1 Joshua had to do experiments with the glasses before they worked properly.
2 The first man who used the glasses made clothes.
3 The glasses are expensive to produce.
4 Thirty thousand people will have the glasses by 2020.

6 How does Joshua's invention compare with your list of other inventions in Exercise 2? Does it solve a bigger problem?

Grammar **defining relative clauses**

7 Look at the sentences (a–c) from the science programme. Answer the questions.

a These people live in parts of the world where there aren't many opticians.
b There is a scientist who has found a solution to the problem.
c Joshua Silver has invented glasses which don't need an optician.

1 Which word (*where*, *who* or *which*) do we use to talk about a) a person, b) a place and c) a thing?
2 In sentence a, the highlighted part is called the defining relative clause. It gives essential information to help people identify which person, place or thing we are talking about. Underline the defining relative clause in sentences b and c.

> ▶ **DEFINING RELATIVE CLAUSES**
>
> *The first person **who** <u>used the new glasses</u> was a man in Ghana.*
>
> *Silver started an organisation **which** <u>is called the 'Centre for Vision in the Developing World'</u>.*
>
> *The organisation has worked in many places **where** <u>over thirty thousand people now wear the glasses</u>.*
>
> You can use *that* instead of *who* or *which* (but not *where*). It's less formal.
> *Tim Berners Lee is the man that invented the World Wide Web.*
> *It's the invention that's changed the world.*
> *This is the room ~~that~~ where he invented it.*
>
> For further information and practice, see page 163.

8 Look at the grammar box. Then complete the sentences with *who, which* or *where*. Underline the defining relative clause.

1 Einstein was a scientist _____ changed the way we think.
2 The Hubble Telescope in space can see places _____ no one has ever been.
3 Concorde was the first commercial aeroplane _____ flew at supersonic speed.
4 Silicon Valley is a place _____ many successful technology companies like Apple and Microsoft are based.
5 In 1800 Alessandro Volta built a machine _____ was the first battery.
6 Hedy Lamarr was a woman _____ was famous as an actress in the 1940s. She was also the co-inventor of a secret communication system.

9 In which sentences in Exercise 8 can you use *that* at the beginning of the relative clause?

10 Complete the text on the right about another invention, *Lifestraw*. Use these phrases and a relative pronoun (*who, which* or *where*).

> cleans the water   ~~need clean water~~
> there is a lake, river   can break
> there is no safe
> specialise in solving problems like this

11 Think of a famous person, a famous invention and a famous place or city. Write a sentence to define each one. Then swap sentences with your partner. Can he/she guess what they are?

Example:
It's a thing which you put in your computer.
It's small but it has a large memory. (a USB memory stick)

Lifestraw

There are still over one billion people in the world [1] *who need clean water*. They live in regions [2] _____ water supply. Now, some inventors [3] _____ have developed *Lifestraw*. It's an invention [4] _____ while you drink. It doesn't have any moving parts [5] _____ so it lasts a long time and it's cheap to produce ($2 each). It's also small and easy to carry to places [6] _____ or other sources of water.

Speaking

12 Work in groups. Invent a new kind of robot which helps people. Discuss these questions and draw a simple design of the robot with any important information on a large sheet of paper.

- What is the robot for (e.g. cleaning the house)?
- Who will use it (e.g. busy working people)?
- Where can you use it (e.g. around the office)?

13 Prepare and give a short presentation for the class about your new invention.

> *Our new invention is a robot which …*

> *It's for people who …*

> *You can use it in places where …*

TALK ABOUT ▶ **A NEW INVENTION** ▶ PLANNING AN EXPEDITION ▶ IMPROVING DESIGN ▶ HOW SOMETHING WORKS
WRITE ▶ **AN ARGUMENT FOR TECHNOLOGY**

95

8b Technology for explorers

Vocabulary the Internet

1 Complete the comments from different people about how they use the Internet with these verbs.

| do download log on search ~~set up~~ |
| subscribe upload write |

1 I _set up_ an account with a social networking site because it's a good way to keep in touch with old friends.
2 Does anyone buy CDs anymore? I don't. It's much easier to _____ music.
3 I _____ a weekly blog with all my family's news.
4 A lot of my friends _____ online gaming but I find it all a bit boring.
5 When I need to find information quickly, the first thing I do is to _____ the web.
6 I _____ to a daily podcast which gives me all the latest news.
7 My friends and family _____ and share their photos all the time.
8 Online banking is so easy. You just _____ with a password and your account details.

2 Which of the sentences in Exercise 1 are true for you? Change any sentences which are untrue or give more details.

> I write a blog but I don't write about my family. I describe what my friends and I like doing.

> ▶ **WORDBUILDING verb prefixes**
>
> Many prefixes can change or add new meaning to a verb. For example, the verb *load* can be **down**load, **up**load, **un**load, **over**load, **re**load.
>
> For further information and practice, see Workbook page 67.

Reading

3 Read the blog on the right. Answer the questions.

1 How does Jay Gifford use the internet?
2 Why does he think modern technology is important for explorers?

4 Read the blog again. Which of these things does Jay write about on his social networking sites?

- where he is
- what he is doing at the moment
- his plans for later
- his recent news
- his opinions

NGM BLOGWILD

Kamchatka Project
Posted by Jay Gifford | July 15, 2:55 PM

After travelling round the world for almost half a week and moving through three international airports and nineteen time zones, we finally step off the helicopter. We are at the beginning of the Karimskaya River in the region of Kamchatka. It's a bright sunny day and in the far distance I can see the Karimski volcano. This is probably the wildest place in Russia but if the weather is this good for the next few days, the expedition will go well.

In the past, when explorers arrived in a strange place, they put up their tents or cooked a meal. But nowadays, when explorers arrive in a new place, they log on to their social networking site using a satellite phone. I write, 'Just landed. Need to relax for a few hours.' Explorers in the past wrote about their adventures in books which were published months or years later. Nowadays, I post a message in seconds.

Sites like Facebook and Twitter also help if we have a problem. Someone in our group touched a strange plant and suddenly his skin was red and painful. I asked for advice on Twitter: 'Hand touched a strange plant. It's red and hot. Any advice?' Minutes later, someone who knew the region replied, 'Probably a Pushki plant. If it is, it'll hurt but it won't kill you!' In the age of the modern explorer, communication like this really helps to make decisions and sometimes it even saves lives.

Continue reading this entry »
Posted by Jay Gifford | Comments (21)
Filed Under: Kamchatka, Karimskaya, Wild, River

Grammar zero and first conditional

5 Look at the sentences (a–c) from the blog in Exercise 3. Answer the questions (1–2).

a If the weather is this good for the next few days, the expedition will go well.

b Sites like Facebook and Twitter also help if we have a problem.

c When explorers arrive in a new place, they log on to their social networking site.

1 Which sentences talks about things that are generally true?

2 Which sentence talks about a possible future situation?

► **ZERO and FIRST CONDITIONAL**

zero conditional
if/when + present simple, present simple
When we have news, we text all our friends.
We text all our friends if we have news.

first conditional
if + present simple, *will (won't)*
If I hear any news, I'll text you.
I'll text you if I hear any news.

For further information and practice, see page 163.

6 🔘 **2.11** Look at the grammar box. Complete the conversation between two explorers planning a canoeing expedition with the correct form of the verbs. Then listen and check your answers.

A: So, what are we going to take with us?

B: Well, I don't know what the weather's going to be like. If it rains, we ¹ _____ (need) all this waterproof clothing.

A: Yes, but if we take all that, there ² _____ (not / be) space for anything else. Anyway, when I go canoeing, I ³ _____ (always / get) wet. Why are you packing that?

B: If we don't have a map, we ⁴ _____ (probably / get) lost.

A: Don't worry. If I ⁵ _____ (bring) my GPS, we'll know exactly where we are at all times. What about food?

B: I normally take tins and packets of food when I ⁶ _____ (go) on a trip like this.

A: Good idea. If you carry the food in your canoe, I ⁷ _____ (pack) both the tents in mine.

B: Maybe that's not such a good idea. If something ⁸ _____ (happen) to one of us, then the other person either won't have any food or won't have a tent.

A: Well, hopefully that ⁹ _____ (not / happen) if we're careful.

7 Pronunciation intonation in conditional sentences

a 🔘 **2.12** In conditional sentences, when the *if/when* clause is first, the intonation rises and then falls. Listen and repeat.

If it rains, we'll need this.

b Work in pairs. Practise reading the conversation in Exercise 6. Pay attention to the rising and falling intonation where necessary.

Vocabulary and speaking

8 Work in groups. You are going to the mountains for two days. The weather forecast is for sun on the first day and rain on the second. Because you are walking and camping, you don't want to take too many items. You have tents, rucksacks and food. Discuss these other items and choose five others to take. Explain your reasons for taking them.

camera	gas cooker	GPS	hairdryer	hat	laptop
matches	mobile phone	sun cream	sunglasses		torch
towel	umbrella	video game player			

If we take ..., we won't need ...

We'll need ... if it rains ...

TALK ABOUT ► A NEW INVENTION ► **PLANNING AN EXPEDITION** ► IMPROVING DESIGN ► HOW SOMETHING WORKS
WRITE ► AN ARGUMENT FOR TECHNOLOGY

97

8c Designs from nature

Reading

1 Look at the photos at the top of page 99. How is the robot similar to the gecko?

2 Read the first two paragraphs of the article. Answer these questions.

  1 Why are geckos amazing?
  2 What are the scientists interested in?
  3 What is the problem with the robot?
  4 Why do people study plants and animals?

3 Look at the photos (1–4). Inventors and designers studied these plants and animals for the inventions (A–D) at the bottom of the article on page 99. Try to match the animal or plant to the invention. Then check your answers by reading the rest of the article.

Critical thinking supporting the main argument

4 The main argument of this article is that the design of animals can improve the design of our own world. Which of these sentences support or restate the argument?

  1 Scientists want to use the design of a gecko on their own robot.
  2 Animals and plants can teach humans a lot about design and engineering.
  3 Most humans have never seen a whale.
  4 Mercedes Benz is producing a new kind of car.
  5 Engineers in Canada are studying whales' flippers because they move so effectively through water.

Word focus *have*

5 Look at two uses of *have* (a–b) when it is the main verb (i.e. not an auxiliary verb). Then match *have* in the sentences from the article (1–5) with the two uses.

> **have** /hæv/
> **a** possessing or owning something (including physical appearance, ideas, illnesses, etc.)
> **b** actions or experiences

  1 It has four feet. *a*
  2 It still has a more difficult time when it tries to walk upside down.
  3 When they have a problem, nature often has the answer.
  4 Most people have some Velcro on an item of clothing.
  5 He had a closer look.

6 We can also use *have got* instead of *have* when talking about possessing or owning something (e.g. *It's got four feet*). Look at these nouns. We can use *have* with all of them, but which ones can't use *have got*?

> a bad cold   a chat   a new car   a rest   blonde hair
> fun   a good time

Speaking

7 Work in groups. Read the three pieces of information about different animals. Discuss how these animals could help humans. Which products in our life could they improve?

> • Spiders have got silk which is very light and very strong. It's stronger than many human-made materials, including steel.
> • The Abalone is a type of shellfish. It's got a shell that is much stronger than many types of stone.
> • Glow worms have a cold light which is more efficient than a light bulb.

boxfish

lotus leaf

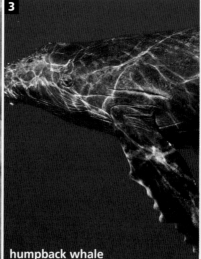
humpback whale

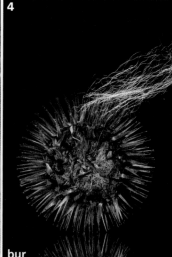
bur

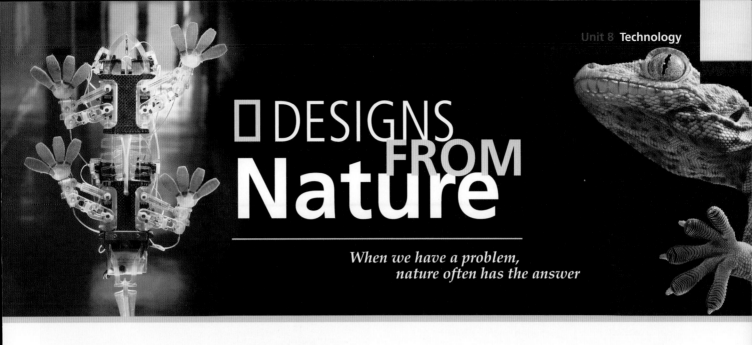

DESIGNS FROM Nature

*When we have a problem,
nature often has the answer*

In a room at Stanford University, scientists are studying a small animal called a gecko. It's an amazing animal because it can move very quickly up and down a tree and it can even walk upside down on ceilings. The scientists are particularly interested in the gecko's feet. They want to use the same design on their own robot. The metal robot looks very similar to the gecko. It has four feet which can also walk up walls made of glass or plastic. However, it still has a more difficult time when it tries to walk upside down.

Animals and plants can teach humans a lot about design and engineering. As a result, many engineers, scientists and designers spend time studying them. When they have a problem, nature often has the answer. This science is called biomimetics. *Bio-* means 'studying living things' and *mimetics* means 'copying the movement of things'. In other words, scientists – or biomimeticists – study animals and plants in order to copy the design.

Take, for example, a whale. Engineers in Canada are studying their flippers because they move so effectively through water. The engineers believe the shape can also improve the movement of wind turbines. Similarly, the boxfish is another animal from the sea which is helping car manufacturers in Germany. Mercedes Benz is using the shape of the fish for one of its new cars. The shape makes it faster and more fuel efficient.

Velcro is probably the most famous example of biomimetics. Most people have some Velcro on an item of clothing. It was invented by the Swiss engineer George de Mestral in 1948. He was walking in the countryside when he pulled a plant's bur from his trousers. He noticed how the bur stuck so well to his clothes. He worked on his idea and the result was Velcro, which became an affordable alternative to the traditional zip.

In 1982, Wilhelm Bartlott was another inventor who had a great idea when he was studying the leaves of a lotus plant. Bartlett noticed that water always ran off the leaf. When he had a closer look, he also noticed how the leaf cleaned itself. Bartlott copied the leaf's special surface and now you can find it in specialised paint products where water and dirt never stay on the paint.

In conclusion, biomimetics has helped to design our world and there are many more future possibilities. Unfortunately, it might take a long time to discover all the possibilities. This isn't really surprising because it's taken nature thousands of years to design its animals and plants.

> **flipper** (n) /ˈflɪpə(r)/ the flat arm or leg of a sea animal, used for swimming
> **bur** (n) /bɜː/ a seed from a plant
> **zip** (n) /zɪp/ two rows of metal teeth-like parts which come together (e.g. on a coat)

TALK ABOUT ▶ A NEW INVENTION ▶ PLANNING AN EXPEDITION ▷ IMPROVING DESIGN ▶ HOW SOMETHING WORKS
WRITE ▶ AN ARGUMENT FOR TECHNOLOGY

99

8d Gadgets

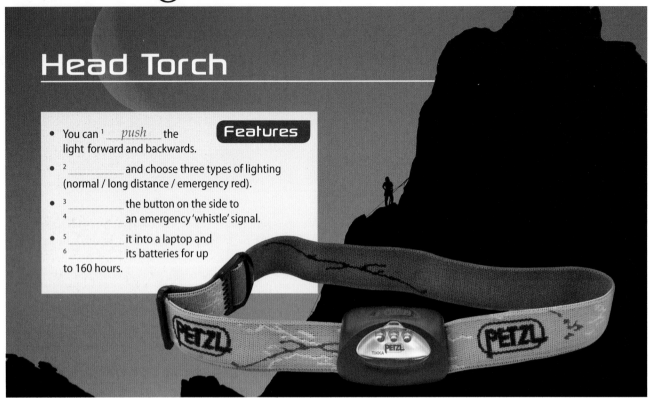

Vocabulary technology verbs

1 Look at the photo of the head torch in the advert above. What is it used for? Would it be useful for you? Would you buy one?

2 Complete the list of features (1–6) for the head torch with these verbs.

| plug | press | push | recharge | send | switch on |

3 Pronunciation linking

a 🎵 **2.13** A word ending with a consonant sound links to the next word if it starts with a vowel sound. Listen and practise saying these instructions.

1 Switch‿it‿on.
2 Plug‿it‿into a laptop.
3 Recharge‿it‿overnight.
4 Send‿an‿email.
5 Click‿on the link.

b Work in pairs. Think of more items you often use at home or at work and make sentences using the verbs in Exercises 2 and 3a. Pay attention to linking where necessary.

> *I switch‿on my mobile‿in the morning and recharge‿it‿overnight.*

Real life asking how something works

4 🎵 **2.14** Listen to two people who are going on a camping trip. They talk about the head torch. Tick the features in Exercise 2 that they discuss.

5 🎵 **2.14** Listen to the conversation again. Tick the questions in the box you hear.

> ▶ **ASKING HOW SOMETHING WORKS**
>
> Where do I switch it on?
> How did you do that?
> What happens if I press this button?
> What is this for?
> How long does the battery last?
> Why do you need to do that?
> How do you make it switch on / record?

6 Work in pairs. Take turns to ask and explain how something works. Use these objects or gadgets in your bag or in the school.

> a mobile phone   a CD player
> an MP3 player   a computer
> an interactive whiteboard   a DVD player
> a vending machine

8e An argument for technology

Writing a paragraph

1 Read the paragraph. Where do you think it comes from? Choose the correct option (1–3).

1 an instruction manual
2 a report on energy in the workplace
3 a message to a colleague at work about the lighting

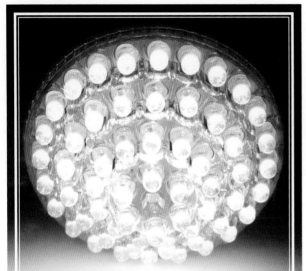

LED lighting is a more effective form of modern lighting technology. Firstly, LED lights last longer than normal lights. For example, a normal light bulb lasts for around 5,000 hours. LED light bulbs last 100,000 hours. Furthermore, LED light bulbs change 80% of electricity into light. Normal bulbs only change 20%. In other words, LED lights need less electricity to produce more light. On the other hand, one disadvantage is that LED lights are more expensive than normal lights. However, they don't have to be changed every year and they use less energy. As a result, they are cheaper.

2 Writing skill connecting words

Look back at the highlighted connecting words in the paragraph in Exercise 1. Match the words with their uses (1–6).

1 to sequence ideas and sentences: _firstly_
2 to introduce an example: _____
3 to add supporting information: _____
4 to say the same thing in a different way:
_____
5 to introduce contrasting information: _____,

6 to introduce a result: _____

3 Writing skill supporting sentences

The first sentence in the paragraph about LED lighting is the topic sentence. It gives a general introduction to the main idea of the paragraph. Afterwards, all the other sentences support this main idea. Which of these sentences (1–8) are topic sentences (T) and which are supporting sentences (S)?

1 The Internet has completely changed our access to information.
2 Take, for example, how many books and articles you can read online.
3 For example, closed circuit television (CCTV) is on our streets and in public places.
4 There are many different ways to use technology in security.
5 In other words, all your personal information can be put onto one identity card.
6 Firstly, Russia put the first satellite in space in 1957. Now there are thousands in space.
7 Over the last fifty years, there have been many great achievements in space travel and technology.
8 Furthermore, robots have now landed and travelled on Mars.

4 Read these notes for a paragraph about GPS technology. Write the paragraph using the notes and connecting words from Exercise 2.

> Main argument:
> GPS is a good idea for anyone who travels a lot
> Supporting ideas:
> 1 GPS maps are always up-to-date and accurate
> 2 more expensive than a normal map but safer to use when driving
> 3 saves time (and money on petrol)

5 Choose one of these types of technology and prepare to write a paragraph about why it is useful. Write your paragraph with three supporting ideas.

mobile phones   email   wireless technology
music downloads   your own idea

6 Use these questions to check your paragraph.

• Have you used a topic sentence?
• Have you used three supporting sentences?
• Have you used connecting words?

Wind power

The people of Spirit Lake are using the power of the wind to ensure a better future for everyone.

Before you watch

1 Work in groups. Look at the photo and discuss the questions.

1 Where are the children in the picture?
2 What technology can you see? What is it for?
3 How will the children benefit from this technology?

While you watch

2 Watch the video and check your answers from Exercise 1.

3 Watch the video again and answer the questions.

1 How much money could the wind turbines save the school district in energy costs?

2 How would the district spend the money?

3 Why is it very important that the turbines in Spirit Lake can withstand strong winds?

4 What does the school district do with the energy from the larger turbine?

5 Why are farmers happy when the wind blows?

6 What do teachers encourage students to do?

4 Watch the video again. Complete the phrases with the correct number.

| 6,000 | 71,000 | 81,530 | 130 | 257 | 180 | 2 |

1 The number of wind turbines in Spirit Lake:

2 The amount of money the smaller turbine has saved the district: $
3 The height of a wind turbine: _____ feet
4 The strength of winds the wind turbines can withstand: _____ mph
5 The amount of money Charles Goodman will make in a year from his wind turbines: $ _____
6 The number of wind turbines in this piece of the Iowa countryside: _____
7 The number of homes in the town of Des Moines: _____

After you watch

5 **Roleplay a conversation between a salesperson and a head teacher**

Work in pairs.

Student A: You are a wind turbine salesperson. You are going to visit a school to explain the benefits of wind turbines. Write notes about three or four benefits.

Student B: You are the head teacher of a school. Read the notes below and prepare questions to ask the salesperson.

- You are interested in wind turbines but are not sure whether to build one for your school. Some parents have complained that wind turbines are very ugly.
- Think of three or four disadvantages of wind turbines.
- Ask the salesperson about the benefits of wind turbines.

Act out the conversation. Then change roles and repeat the conversation.

6 Jan Bolluyt says: 'So, you know, it's not just a small thing.' What is he referring to? Do you agree with him?

7 Work in pairs. Discuss these questions.

1 What types of alternative energy are used in your country?
2 What are the advantages and disadvantages of alternative energy compared to fossil fuels?
3 Where do you think we will get our energy in the future?

---

blade (n) /bleɪd/ the long, narrow part that makes a propeller turn when the wind hits it
blow (v) /bləʊ/ the wind does this when it moves
crop (n) /krɒp/ plants that farmers grow and harvest
encourage (v) /ɪnˈkʌrɪdʒ/ get someone to do something
ensure (v) /ɪnˈʃɔː/ guarantee
flat (adj) /flæt/ without hills or mountains
fossil fuel (n) /fɒsɪl ˈfjuːəl/ gas, oil or coal
foundation (n) /faʊnˈdeɪʃən/ a solid base under the ground that a structure sits on
grid (n) /grɪd/ a system of cables for distributing electricity
impressive (adj) /ɪmˈpresɪv/ causing a feeling of admiration
pay off (v) /peɪ ˈɒf/ finish paying for something
power (n) /ˈpaʊə/ electricity, energy
power (v) /ˈpaʊə/ send electricity to
rod (n) /rɒd/ a long, thin piece of metal or wood
save (v) /seɪv/ use less money
silo (n) /ˈsaɪləʊ/ a place where farmers put their crops after they harvest them
steel (n) /stiːl/ a type of metal
turbine (n) /ˈtɜːbaɪn/ a type of machine that produces energy from a moving propeller
withstand (v) /wɪðˈstænd/ resist

Grammar

1 Make sentences with a relative clause using the words.

1 the invention / has changed the modern world / the internet

The invention which has changed the modern world is the internet.

2 camping / an activity / I enjoy doing
3 GPS / a gadget / tells you where you are
4 my parents / the people / always happy to see me!
5 the thing / I hate about TV / the adverts
6 the Space Shuttle / the first spacecraft / travel from and to Earth

2 Complete these sentences for you. Then tell your partner why.

1 Someone who changed my life was …
2 Something which improved my life was …

3 Complete the sentences with these verbs. Use *will* ('ll) or *won't* where necessary.

| not call | not go | love | press | work |

1 When you _____ this button, the TV comes on.
2 If you put new batteries in, it _____ again.
3 When it's sunny, we _____ to go to the beach.
4 If he _____, then he doesn't want to come with us.
5 I _____ hiking if you don't go.

I CAN

describe people, places and things with extra information ☐

talk about situations that are generally true and possible in the future ☐

Vocabulary

4 Match the verbs (1–5) with the nouns (a–e).

1 make   a a problem
2 find   b a decision
3 solve   c an idea
4 make   d a solution
5 have   e mistakes

5 Complete the questions with words from Exercise 4. Then discuss the questions with your partner.

1 What's the best _____ you've ever had in your life?
2 What decisions do you _____ in your daily life or at work? How important are they?
3 What's the most common mistake you _____ in English?
4 Do you like to solve a _____ on your own or _____ a solution with others? Why?

6 Match two words (one from each box) and complete the sentences.

| click | log | plug | forward | into |
| push | set | turn | on (x2) | round | up |

1 I want to _____ but I've forgotten my password.
2 How do you _____ an online account?
3 _____ it _____ the wall socket and it'll recharge.
4 For maximum volume, _____ the dial _____ to number 10.
5 You can pull it backwards for reverse or _____ it _____ to go faster.
6 _____ the icon in the top corner to open the program.

Real life

7 Put these words in the correct order to make questions for asking how something works.

1 switch / it / where / do / I / on?
2 you / did / that? / do / how
3 if / I / happens / button? / press / this / what
4 the / battery / long / how / does / last?
5 that? / why / do / do / you / to / need
6 record? / how / it / do / you / make

8 Match these responses (a–e) with the questions in Exercise 7. One response answers two questions.

a So you don't lose any data.
b Eight hours.
c There.
d By pressing this.
e You turn it off.

I CAN

talk about using technology ☐

explain and ask how something works ☐

Speaking

9 Work in pairs. Explain to your partner how to use the DVD in the back of this book.

Unit 9 Language and learning

Learning
Photo by Cary Wolinsky

FEATURES

1 Look at the photo. Answer the questions.

1 What country do you think this classroom is in?
2 What are the pupils learning?

2 🔊 **2.15** Listen to a teacher talking about the photo. Check your answers. Which of these statements (1–3) are true?

1 The language has many words with the same sound but different meanings (called homophones).
2 The language has 26 characters.
3 It has borrowed words and characters from other languages.

3 Read the facts about the English language. Answer the questions. Then compare with your partner.

1 How many of the facts are true for your first language?
2 Rewrite the other facts so that they are true.

The *English language:*

- has 26 letters.
- is an official language in 53 countries.
- borrowed words from other languages in the past including German, French and Latin.
- has different varieties including American English and Australian English.
- normally uses this word order in a sentence: subject + verb + object.

TALK ABOUT ▶ **ADULT EDUCATION** ▶ **A GENERAL KNOWLEDGE QUIZ** ▶ **THE AUTHOR'S OPINION** ▶ **ENROLLING ON A COURSE**

WRITE ▶ **A FORM**

105

9a Ways of learning

Vocabulary education

1 Look at the pairs of words. Match the words with the correct definitions (a–b).

1 **lesson / subject**
   a a period of time when people learn something with a teacher
   b a topic you learn about at school (e.g. art, mathematics, geography)
2 **discipline / rules**
   a instructions that say what you must or mustn't do
   b making people follow instructions
3 **enrol / apply**
   a to join and pay for a course
   b to fill in a form to ask to join a course or to get a new job
4 **schedule / timetable**
   a days and times for subjects in school each week
   b a plan of events or tasks with times and dates
5 **teach / instruct**
   a to tell someone to do something
   b to help people learn a new subject or skill by explaining or demonstrating it
6 **qualification / skill**
   a knowledge or ability you need to do something well
   b an examination you pass because you need it to get a job or place at university

2 Pronunciation stress in two-syllable words

🔊 **2.16** Listen to the stressed syllable in these two-syllable verbs and nouns. How is the stress different between the nouns and verbs? Listen again and repeat.

1 lesson (n)
2 enrol (v)
3 subject (n)
4 instruct (v)
5 apply (v)

3 Work in pairs. Discuss the questions.

1 What was your favourite subject at school? Why?
2 Was there a lot of discipline at your school? Were there many rules?
3 What qualifications did you get from your education?
4 What do you think is the best way to get new knowledge or skills?

Listening

4 🔊 **2.17** Listen to a radio documentary about learning Kung Fu in China. Match the parts of the documentary (1–3) with the topics (a–c).

a Life at a Kung Fu school
b The history of the Shaolin Temple and Kung Fu
c Shaolin and Kung Fu in modern China

temple (n) /'templ/ religious building
punch (v) /pʌntʃ/ hit with fist of hand
brand (n) /brænd/ symbol of a product
demonstration (n) /ˌdemən'streɪʃn/
   when you show someone how to do
   something
kickboxer (n) /kɪk'bɒksə(r)/ person who
   does physical sport where competitors
   hit and kick each other

5 🔊 **2.17** Listen to the documentary again. Choose the correct options.

1 Many people in China learn about Kung Fu for the first time *from watching films and TV / at the Shaolin Temple.*
2 Students have learned Kung Fu at the temple since the *fifth / fifteenth* century.
3 Shaolin *only teaches Kung Fu / has different businesses.*
4 In the city of Dengfend there are 50,000 *schools / students* of Kung Fu.
5 *All the students / Not all the students* are at the school because they want to be.
6 There is a lot of *discipline / free time* in the school.

6 What are your views about learning Kung Fu in China? Complete the speech bubbles. Then compare your views with the class.

> One thing that surprised me was …

> I would / wouldn't like to learn something this way because …

> This new interest in Kung Fu probably will / won't last a long time because …

Grammar present simple passive / *by* + agent

7 Look at the sentences (a–b) and answer the questions (1–3).

a Teachers teach Kung Fu in hundreds of schools in China.
b Kung Fu is taught in hundreds of schools in China.

1 In sentence a, what is the object of the sentence? Who does the action?
2 In sentence b, what is the subject of the sentence? Does it say who does the action?
3 Look at the grammar box. Then underline all the verbs in the passive form in the audioscript on page 173.

▶ **PRESENT SIMPLE PASSIVE / BY + AGENT**

              subject   verb   object
ACTIVE SENTENCE: Hundreds of tourists **visit** the temple.
              subject   verb
PASSIVE SENTENCE: The temple **is visited** by hundreds of tourists.

We form the passive with the verb *to be* + past participle:
Kung Fu is / isn't taught …
Students are / aren't enrolled on courses.

We often use the passive when who / what does the action is not important or unknown. If necessary, we say who does the action using *by: by hundreds of tourists.*

For further information and practice, see page 164.

---

8 Complete the article about adult education with the present simple passive form of the verbs.

More and more adults [1] _____ (enrol) on courses nowadays. Some of them [2] _____ (send) for further training by their employers to acquire new skills. Others want a change of career, so new qualifications [3] _____ (need). For many adults, learning [4] _____ (not / see) as something only for school children. Studying a subject can be fun and a good way to socialise. And these days, many courses [5] _____ (not / take) in a real school. Adults are studying more in later life by distance or online learning. Books [6] _____ (send) to their home. Course material [7] _____ (email) by their online tutor. On some courses, the lessons [8] _____ (teach) with videoconferencing. It all helps with the belief that education doesn't have to stop when you leave school.

Adult education

9 Look at the sentences. Delete *by* + agent where you don't need it.

1 Degrees are normally taught ~~by lecturers~~ for three years.
2 Many degrees are now taught by lecturers working from home.
3 The ancient language of Latin isn't studied much by students anymore.
4 Latin isn't known by many people under the age of seventy anymore.
5 Paris is visited by twenty seven million tourists per year.
6 In my country, English is spoken by nearly everyone under the age of thirty.

Speaking

10 Work in groups. Discuss these questions.

1 In your country, is adult education seen as normal or something new?
2 Are employees in your workplace sent on training courses? What kinds of courses do they take? Are the courses paid for by the employee or the employer?
3 Are you enrolled on any other courses at the moment?
4 In your country, are many courses taught online these days? Who are these courses offered by? Have you ever studied online? How did it compare to traditional learning in a classroom?

9b The history of writing

Reading

1 Work in pairs. Think of two or three differences between speaking and writing. Then compare your ideas with the class.

Example
Writing needs extra objects, speaking doesn't.

2 Read the article about the history of writing. Find words or phrases that describe:

1 different forms of writing (e.g. cuneiform)
2 types of materials people have used for writing in the past (e.g. on stone or clay)
3 the reasons for writing (e.g. for people's identity)

Grammar **past simple passive**

3 Look at the sentences from the article (a–b). Answer the questions (1–3).

a The symbols were made of clay.
b The typewriter's keyboard is still used on computer keyboards today.

1 Which form do the sentences use: the active form or the passive form?
2 Which sentence is about the present? Which sentence is about the past?
3 How do you form the past simple passive?

> **▶ PAST SIMPLE PASSIVE**
>
> We form the past simple passive using *was/were* + past participle:
> *The first computer **was invented** in the early twentieth century.*
> *Computers **weren't used** by many people until later in the century.*
> *When **was** the first computer **invented**? / **Were** computers **invented** in the twentieth century?*
>
> For further information and practice, see page 165.

The history of Writing

3000 BC | 2000 | 1000 |

Nowadays, 85% of the world's population communicate by writing, but 5,000 years ago people only communicated by speaking. When words were written on a piece of stone for the first time, the world changed forever.

Mesopotamian cuneiform
(3200 BC to AD 75)
Cuneiform was used by speakers of fifteen different languages for three thousand years. The symbols were made with clay.

Egyptian hieroglyphs
(3200 BC to AD 394)
The Egyptians made these signs on the walls of pyramids which you can still see today. They represented objects, ideas, emotions and sounds. Around 2500 BC, 'papyrus' was made from a plant and it was written on by the Egyptians. Later, the Romans also used papyrus.

Indus Valley
(2800 to 1900 BC)
Stone objects were found in the Indus Valley. They were possibly used for people's identity or symbols of a tribe.

MESOPOTAMIAN   INDUS VALLEY
MAYA
LEVANTINE   CHINESE
EGYPTIAN

Chinese logograms
(1200 BC to present)
The earliest Chinese writing was done on bone.

108

4 Look at the grammar box on page 108. Then complete the sentences with the past simple passive form of the verbs. (Note that some of the sentences contain false information.)

1 Papyrus _____ (make) from a type of tree.
2 Objects from the Indus Valley _____ (use) as identity cards.
3 Early Chinese writing _____ (do) on bone.
4 The first alphabet _____ (not / create) by the Phoenicians.
5 Pictures _____ (not / use) by the Maya to represent dates and times.
6 Lots of books _____ (publish) because of Gutenberg's invention.
7 The typewriter _____ (invent) in 1873.
8 eBooks _____ (not / sell) before 2010.

5 Work in pairs. Read the article again and decide which sentences in Exercise 4 are false.

6 Make quiz questions about the article. Use the past simple passive form.

1 How / Cuneiform symbols / make? (Answer: With clay)
How were Cuneiform symbols made?
2 How / papyrus / use / by the Egyptians and the Romans? (Answer: For writing on)
3 In the Indus Valley, why / stone objects / possibly / use? (Answer: For people's identity or symbols of a tribe)
4 Where / the earliest Chinese writing / do? (Answer: On bone)
5 How / dates and time / represent / by the Maya? (Answer: With pictures)
6 By the end of fifteenth century, what / books / publish / with? (Answer: Gutenberg's printing press)
7 When / more eBooks / sell / by Amazon than paperback books? (Answer: In 2010)

Writing and speaking

7 Work in groups. Prepare a history general knowledge quiz for another group. Write five questions about historic or famous people, inventions, places, objects and important dates. Use the past passive form.

8 Work as a class. Ask your questions and find out which group has the best general knowledge.

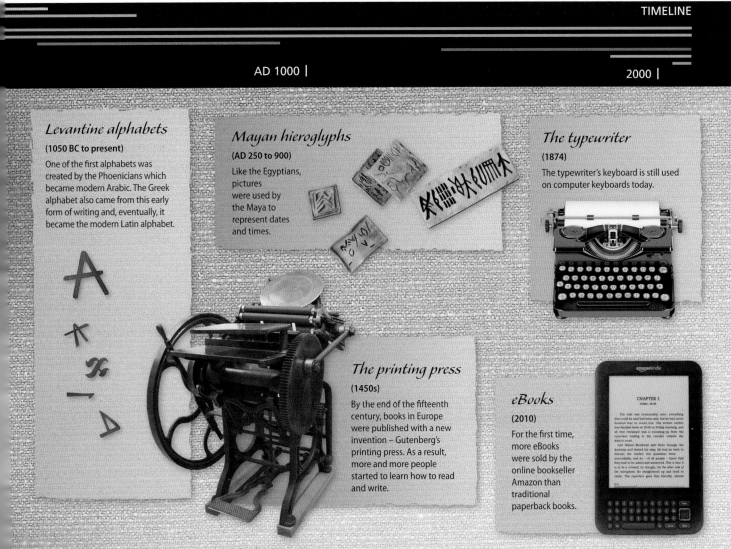

TIMELINE

AD 1000 |

2000 |

Levantine alphabets

(1050 BC to present)

One of the first alphabets was created by the Phoenicians which became modern Arabic. The Greek alphabet also came from this early form of writing and, eventually, it became the modern Latin alphabet.

Mayan hieroglyphs

(AD 250 to 900)

Like the Egyptians, pictures were used by the Maya to represent dates and times.

The typewriter

(1874)

The typewriter's keyboard is still used on computer keyboards today.

The printing press

(1450s)

By the end of the fifteenth century, books in Europe were published with a new invention – Gutenberg's printing press. As a result, more and more people started to learn how to read and write.

eBooks

(2010)

For the first time, more eBooks were sold by the online bookseller Amazon than traditional paperback books.

9c Saving languages

Reading

1 Does your country have different languages and cultures? What are they?

2 Read the article on page 111. Answer the questions.

1 What culture is it about?
2 What has happened to their languages? Why?
3 What is the purpose of the Enduring Voices Project and the Salish school?

3 Read the article again. Complete the summary with words from the article.

> Five hundred years ago, Europeans arrived on the continent of ¹_____. Eventually, the Europeans became more powerful than the native ²_____ and they moved these people to reservations. Their ³_____ and ⁴_____ began to disappear. Nowadays many native Americans speak ⁵_____ and live in ⁶_____. But on some of the reservations, the tribes are recording the language of the older generation. They are also setting up ⁷_____ for children to learn the languages so they might save it for the future.

Vocabulary phrasal verbs

4 Find the phrasal verbs (1–8) in the article. Match the phrasal verbs to their meanings (a–h).

1	take away	a	meet and discuss something
2	give up	b	learn informally
3	get together	c	remove from someone
4	die out	d	stop doing something
5	write down	e	become less common and disappear
6	pass on	f	start something new (e.g. a company or organisation)
7	pick up	g	write something with pen and paper
8	set up	h	give to someone (often your children)

> ▶ **WORDBUILDING phrasal verbs**
>
> A phrasal verb is a verb + particle: *pick + up = pick up, get + together = get together.*
> When you join these two words, it creates a new meaning.
>
> For further information and practice, see Workbook page 75.

5 Pronunciation stress in phrasal verbs

🔊 **2.18** Listen to the phrasal verbs in the sentences. Do we normally stress the verb or the particle in phrasal verbs? Listen again and repeat.

1 They **took away** the children.
2 They **gave up** smoking.

6 Complete the sentences about learning and studying with the correct form of the phrasal verbs in Exercise 4.

1 How much of your English do you _____ from listening to music or watching films in English?
2 How often do you and your friends _____ and practise speaking English?
3 Do you think traditional classrooms will _____ and everyone will learn online?
4 When you hear a new word, do you have to _____ it _____ or can you remember it?
5 Is it important for older people to _____ their knowledge to younger people or is it quicker to use the internet?

7 Work in pairs. Ask and answer the questions in Exercise 6 and give your opinion.

Critical thinking **fact or opinion**

8 An article can provide facts but also gives opinions. Look at these sentences from the article and decide which three include the author's opinion.

1 Five hundred years ago, Europeans arrived on a new continent.
2 And so a terrible part of history began.
3 But the good news is that some of these people are keeping their culture and language alive.
4 Many tribes also offer courses in the language.
5 The Salish tribe is an excellent example of how schools can help.
6 It has 30 students aged two to twelve during the day.

9 Look at the three opinion sentences in Exercise 8. Underline the words which show the sentence is an opinion. What kinds of words are they?

Speaking

10 Work in groups. Discuss these questions.

1 Overall, how much does the author support the Native Americans and their plans to save their language and culture?
2 How strong is his opinion in the article?
3 Do you agree with him?

SAVING LANGUAGES

Five hundred years ago, Europeans arrived on a new continent.

They brought new cultures and languages to this place which they called America. However, there were already people living there who had their own cultures and languages. And so a terrible part of history began.

As more Europeans arrived, there was a fight for the land with the native American Indians. By the end of the nineteenth century, the Indian tribes were moved to reservations. A lot of their children were taken away to boarding schools and these children were taught to speak English. By the end of the twentieth century more than half of the Native Americans in the US were living in cities. They gave up speaking their old tribal language and only used English. As a result, many Native American languages disappeared and with them their culture.

Some American Indian languages are still used today but they are usually spoken by the older members of the tribes who still live on the reservations. In North America there are 150–170 languages that have at least one speaker and many of these languages have under a hundred speakers.

One ancient language which is spoken by the Northern Paiute tribe has more than two hundred speakers. This means when the elders of the tribe get together, they still speak it. But for most of the younger members of the tribe, the everyday language is English.

But the good news is that some of these people are keeping their culture and language alive. They are also receiving help from the *National Geographic Society's* Enduring Voices Project. The aim of the project is to help languages around the world which are dying out. Linguists and experts meet these 'last speakers'. The team interview them and they are recorded with video, pictures and audio. They also tell old stories which are written down in English so people can learn more about the culture.

Recording the language and culture is only part of the project. The next stage is to pass on the language to the next generation. Some children pick up some of the language from their parents or grandparents but many tribes also offer courses in the language. The Salish tribe is an excellent example of how schools can help. The tribe lives in the Flathead Reservation in Montana. Their language is currently spoken by about 50 people who are aged over 75 years. No one under 50 speaks the language. So now, the local people have set up a school. It has 30 students aged two to twelve during the day and there are also courses for adults in the evening. It is schools and projects like these which – hopefully – might save languages for the future.

> **reservation** (n) /ˌrezə'veɪʃn/ an area of land where Native Americans live
> **boarding school** (n) /'bɔːdɪŋ skuːl/ a school where you live, study and sleep

TALK ABOUT ▶ ADULT EDUCATION ▶ A GENERAL KNOWLEDGE QUIZ ▶ THE AUTHOR'S OPINION ▶ ENROLLING ON A COURSE
WRITE ▶ A FORM

111

9d Enrolling on a course

Reading and speaking

1 Work in pairs. Read the web page about three evening classes and answer the questions.

1 What kind of people might be interested in each course?
2 Are the courses for people with no knowledge or experience of the subject?
3 Which course would you choose? Why?

http://corfieldcollege.com/courses/winter/evening

Contact Us | Sitemap | Accessibility

Enrol NOW!

New evening classes for the winter term

Calligraphy
A course for anyone interested in this beautiful and ancient art of writing. For beginners or those with experience.
Wednesday evenings 6.30–9.00 p.m. (10 weeks)

Preparing more effective PowerPoint presentations
Ideal for people who already give presentations for their work. The course is for people with some experience but introduces you to new techniques and helps you to create better, more professional-looking slides.
Mondays and Wednesdays 6.00–7.30 p.m. (5 weeks only)

Spanish for beginners
Learn Spanish for your next holiday or for business trips. Useful language for restaurants, shopping, hotels and general conversation.
Tuesdays and Thursdays 7.00–9.00 p.m. (10 weeks)

Real life describing a process

2 2.19 Listen to a telephone conversation about enrolling on one of the courses. Are the sentences true (T) or false (F)?

1 There are no more places on the course *Preparing more effective PowerPoint presentations.*
2 To enrol, you have to fill in an enrolment form.
3 There is an interview for the course.
4 You have to pay for the course immediately.
5 You have to pay a deposit immediately in order to reserve a place.
6 For this course, you have to buy a lot of books.

3 2.19 Look at these expressions for describing a process. Listen to the conversation again and tick the expressions the speakers use.

▶ DESCRIBING A PROCESS

Firstly, you need to …
The first thing you're asked to
  do is …
Next, the form is sent …
When you've completed the online
  enrolment form …
Then send us payment.
After we've received payment …
Once you've enrolled …
Having done that, you need to …
At the end, click 'enrol now'.

---

4 Work in pairs. Practise a similar telephone conversation.

Student A: You are the caller. Choose one of the other courses in Exercise 1. Ask about the course and how to enrol.

Student B: You are the administrator. Answer the call and describe the process for enrolling to the caller.

Then change roles and repeat the conversation.

5 Roleplay another conversation between someone in a job recruitment agency and someone looking for a job.

Student A: Turn to page 153 and follow the instructions.

Student B: Turn to page 154 and follow the instructions.

TALK ABOUT ▶ ADULT EDUCATION ▶ A GENERAL KNOWLEDGE QUIZ ▶ THE AUTHOR'S OPINION ▶ **ENROLLING ON A COURSE**
WRITE ▶ A FORM

9e Providing information

Writing **filling in a form**

1 Work in pairs. Answer the questions.

1   What kinds of forms do you have to fill in?
2   What kind of information do you have to provide?
3   Do you ever find them confusing or complicated?

2 Look at the forms. What is each one for?

A

Title	
First Name	
Middle initial	
Surname	
Address	
Postcode	
Gender	
DOB	
No. of dependents	
Country of origin	
First language	

Current occupation	
Do you smoke?	
Yes No	
Current medications	

Details of past surgery or operations

B

PLEASE USE CAPITAL LETTERS

PASSPORT NO.   PLACE OF ISSUE

NATIONALITY   MARITAL STATUS

QUALIFICATIONS (DEGREE, ETC.)

Have you visited this country before? (If yes, give details)

Have you ever been refused entry or a visa on a previous occasion? (If yes, give details)

Contact details of person in case of emergency (e.g. spouse, next of kin)

For office use only:
Issued/Refused on   by

3 Writing skill **providing the correct information**

a Match the questions (1–8) with the places on the forms in Exercise 2 where you write the information.

1   Are you married, single or divorced? *marital status*
2   Do you take any types of medicine?
3   How many children do you have?
4   Where did you receive your current passport?
5   Where were you born?
6   Why weren't you allowed into this country two years ago?
7   Who do we call if you need help (e.g. your husband, wife or someone related to you)?
8   What is the first letter of your middle name?

b Look at the forms again. Notice how forms use certain conventions and abbreviations. Answer the questions. Then check your answers on page 153.

1   How many abbreviations can you find in the forms? What do you think they mean?
2   What do you think these abbreviations mean?
    Titles: Mr, Mrs, Ms, Dr, Prof
    Qualifications: BA, BSc, MBA, PhD
3   Which form has a section you do not write in?
4   Which form does not want you to write in lower-case (small) letters?

4 Work in pairs. Design a one-page enrolment form for a language school. Make a list of all the information you need about the students. Then prepare the form.

5 Exchange your form with another pair. Use these questions to check their form. Afterwards, give your feedback on the form.

• Is the form easy to follow?
• Do you know what to write in each part?
• Is all the information they want useful and relevant?

9f Disappearing voices

When a language disappears, we lose information about the world.

Aka speakers watch playback of an Aka story told by Biga Nimasow. (left to right) Kumshi Parasow, Shigi Nimasow, Biga Nimasow. Palizi, East Kameng District, Arunachal Pradesh, India.
Photo: Jeremy Fahringer

Before you watch

1 Work in groups. Look at the photo and the caption. Discuss the questions.

1 What are the people in the photo doing?
2 What do you think the caption means? What kind of information do you think we lose?

2 Work in pairs. Tick the things you think you are going to see in this video.

> a camera   a classroom   a computer
> a digital recorder   headphones   a map
> a microphone   pen and paper

While you watch

3 Watch the video and check your answers from Exercise 2.

4 Watch the first part of the video (to 02.17). Are the sentences true (T) or false (F)?

1 Chris Rainier is a member of the Living Tongues Institute.
2 7,000 languages are expected to disappear in the next 50 years.
3 The three men helped to create the Enduring Voices project.
4 After Australia, the team went to northeast India.
5 The team never have any problems with their equipment.
6 There is no written record of many of the local languages.

5 Watch the second part of the video (02.17 to the end). Answer these questions.

1 What language do most of the older people in Hong speak; Apatani, English or Hindi?

2 Why do the team want to meet younger people in Hong?

3 What does a language technology kit contain?

4 What are the language technology kits for?

5 What do the researchers hope the language technology kits will do?

6 Complete what the people say with these words. Then watch the whole video to check.

> awareness   interesting   language   loss
> speakers   younger

'Every two weeks around the planet a ¹＿＿＿＿ disappears. Completely disappears forever and ever. So what we're doing with the Enduring Voices project is really, kind of, trying to bring ²＿＿＿＿ to this whole issue of language ³＿＿＿＿ around the planet.

'We definitely want to find ⁴＿＿＿＿ speakers because they're the ones that will be showing the shift. The older ⁵＿＿＿＿ of course will have the language. So it will be ⁶＿＿＿＿ to see if people who've been schooled in the modern times, if they've still kept it.'

After you watch

7 Roleplay **saying what you think and giving reasons**

Work in pairs.

Student A: You are a young person from Hong. Look at the information below and make notes.

• You speak a little Apatani with older people but you and your friends prefer to speak English and Hindi. You think Apatani is old-fashioned and you do not care if it disappears.

Student B: You are a researcher from the Enduring Voices project.

• Find out what languages the young person speaks, and why. Then try to persuade him/her that it is important to preserve Apatani. Give reasons.

Act out the conversation. Then change roles and repeat the conversation.

8 Work in pairs. Discuss these questions.

1 Has your native language changed in your lifetime? In what ways?
2 Do you think it is in danger from global languages? Why? / Why not?
3 Do you think the fact that English is the dominant global language is a good thing or not?

---

abandon (v) /ə'bændən/ stop using
awareness (n) /ə'weənəs/ knowledge or understanding of a subject or situation
disappear (v) /ˈdɪsə'pɪə/ stop existing
enduring (adj) /ɪn'djʊərɪŋ/ lasting for a long time
equipment (n) /ɪ'kwɪpmənt/ instruments or tools needed for a job
extinct (adj) /ek'stɪŋkt/ not existing any more

loss (n) /lɒs/ the state of no longer having something
neglect (v) /nɪ'glekt/ forget about
remote (adj) /rɪ'məʊt/ distant and difficult to get to
researcher (n) /rɪ'sɜːtʃə/ somebody who does research (makes a detailed study of something to find out information)
school (v) /skuːl/ educate a child
shift (n) /ʃɪft/ a change in something

Grammar

1 Choose the correct options to complete the article.

The language of 'Koro' [1] *speaks / is spoken* by about a thousand people in north eastern India. It [2] *discovered / was discovered* by accident when a team of linguists [3] *began / was begun* working in the Indian state of Arunachal Pradesh. They were studying two other languages when they realised a third language [4] *used / was used* in conversations between local people. The team quickly [5] *started / was started* studying it. The 'new' language [6] *doesn't write / isn't written down* anywhere so local people [7] *recorded / were recorded* so that the team could study their words. Not many people under the age of 20 know 'Koro' so it's important that the language [8] *saves / is saved* before it dies out.

2 Work in pairs. Make questions about the article in Exercise 1 using these prompts. Use the passive form.

1 How many people / Koro / speak / by?
2 who / Koro / discover / by
3 Koro / write down / or / speak?
4 Koro / know / by many people under twenty?

3 Change your partner and take turns to ask and answer your questions. Do you think your partner's questions are all correct?

> **I CAN**
>
> use the active or passive form of the present simple and past simple tense
>
> ask questions using the passive form of the present simple and past simple tense

Vocabulary

4 Choose the correct option (a–c) to complete the sentences.

1 What time is your history _____?
  a lesson   b subject   c timetable
2 I'm _____ for a place at university but I don't know if they'll accept me.
  a studying   b applying   c enrolling
3 What _____ do you get at the end of this course?
  a skill   b qualification   c education
4 Mr Smith is great at _____ us maths. He makes it really fun!
  a learning   b instructing   c teaching

5 Complete the sentences with these particles.

> away   down   on   out   up (x2)

1 I gave _____ studying French after I left school.
2 My friend finds it easy to pick _____ languages. She knows about six!
3 I never write letters anymore. I think writing like this is dying _____.
4 Where's my dictionary? Did someone take it _____ with them?
5 My mother was from Bulgaria and tried to pass _____ her language to me but I don't remember any words now.
6 I'm going to read this text aloud and I want you to write _____ every word you hear.

> **I CAN**
>
> talk about language and learning

Real life

6 Replace the words in bold with these phrases.

> After that   Having   The first thing you do is   When

1 **Firstly, you need to** type in the word you need.
2 **When you've** done that, press enter.
3 **Then** read the definition of the word.
4 **Once** you've finished, remember to switch the dictionary off.

7 Work in pairs. Think of a process in your life (e.g. at work). Write down the four or five stages. Then explain the process to your partner using phrases from Exercise 6.

> **I CAN**
>
> describe a process

Speaking

8 Work in pairs. Talk about when you were at school. Explain who or what was your favourite:
- teacher
- subject
- time of day
- classroom

Unit 10 Travel and holidays

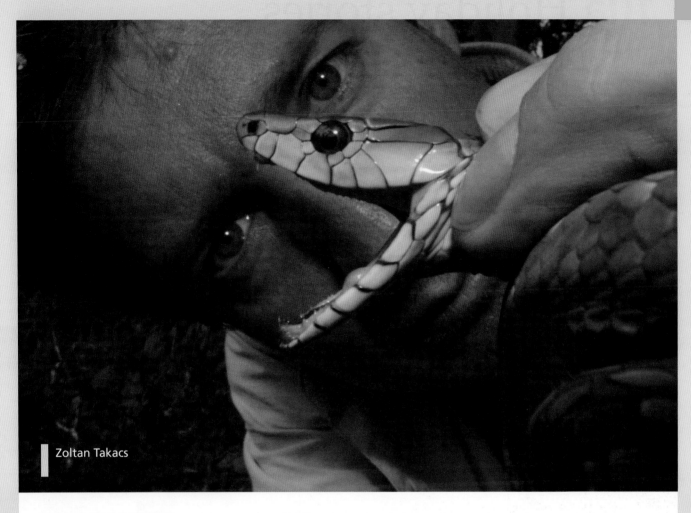

Zoltan Takacs

FEATURES

1 The photo shows the explorer Zoltan Takacs in another country. Do you think he is travelling for his work or is he on holiday? Explain your opinion.

2 2.20 Listen to an interview with Zoltan about travel and holidays. Which of these statements are true for him?

1 He travels and studies snakes for his job.
2 He often goes on holiday.
3 He always takes certain items when he travels.
4 He usually travels on his own.
5 He always plans where he is going to stay before he leaves home.
6 He thinks travel and holidays are about exploration and discovering new things.

3 Match these words to the categories (a–d). Then add one more word to each category. Compare your ideas with the class.

> camera   camping   cruise   five-star hotel
> package tour   self-catering   sightseeing   sunbathing
> sleeping bag   sun tan lotion   tent   water sports

a type of holiday   c travel items
b accommodation   d holiday activities

4 What kinds of holiday do you prefer? What kinds of holiday don't you take? Why not?

TALK ABOUT ▸ A HOLIDAY YOU REMEMBER ▸ THE HOLIDAY OF A LIFETIME ▸ A TOURIST WEBPAGE ▸ TOUR INFORMATION
WRITE ▸ A FORMAL LETTER

10a Holiday stories

Reading

1 Do you usually leave a tip in restaurants or hotels? How much do you tip? Do you know if there is a difference between tipping in your country and other countries?

2 Read the holiday story about tipping in another country. Answer the questions.

1 What was the description of the holiday in the brochure?
2 What was the problem?
3 How did she solve the problem?

3 Read the story again. Number the events (a–i) in the correct order 1–9.

a gave the manager a tip
b arrived at the hotel
c the engineer didn't fix the shower
d gave the engineer a tip
e read the holiday brochure

f turned on the shower
g called reception
h moved to room 405
i waited at reception

4 Discuss the questions.

1 What did the writer learn in this story?
2 Do you think it's important to do things differently in other countries?
3 Have you ever learned any cultural differences in other countries or meeting people from there?

I was so excited after I had found the holiday in the brochure. It said: 'Enjoy a week of sightseeing in one of Europe's most beautiful cities while staying at one of its most luxurious hotels.' Now I wasn't so sure. I had waited fifteen minutes at reception when I arrived and now the shower in my room wasn't working. I called hotel reception.
'Hello. This is room 308. There isn't any water in my bathroom.'
'Are you sure?'
'Of course I'm sure!'
'I'll send our hotel engineer immediately.'
An hour later, the engineer came to look at the shower. He hit the pipes a few times and looked worried. 'Sorry, but I cannot fix it today. Maybe, tomorrow.' Then he held out his hand. I couldn't believe it! He wanted a tip for doing nothing! I was furious. But suddenly, I had a better idea. Quickly, I gave the engineer a few coins. He hadn't fixed my shower but he had taught me something about staying in his country. Two minutes later I was at the reception desk. I explained the problem to the receptionist and he apologised: 'This is a terrible situation, but what can we do?' I knew exactly what to do. I gave the hotel manager a very large tip. Fifteen minutes later I moved into room 405. It was twice the size of room 308, it had a wonderful view of the city, a comfortable bed and, most importantly, there was water in the bathroom.

Holiday STORIES

118

Grammar past perfect simple

5 Look at the sentence from the story and answer the questions.

I was so excited after I had found the holiday in the brochure.

1 Which action happened first?
2 Which verb is in the past simple tense?
3 How do we form the past perfect simple?

> ▶ **PAST PERFECT SIMPLE**
>
> I **had waited** fifteen minutes at reception when I arrived.
> He **hadn't fixed** my shower but he had taught me something about staying in his country.
>
> Note: In spoken English we often use '*d (= had)*
>
> For further information and practice, see page 165.

6 Complete the sentences with the past simple or past perfect form of the verbs.

1 When we landed in London from Chicago, our connecting flight to Dubai _____ (leave) so we had to stay overnight at the airport.
2 When she reached Rome, her luggage _____ (not arrive) and she spent an hour at lost luggage.
3 The hotel hadn't expected them until the evening so they _____ (go) for lunch while room service prepared the rooms.
4 We _____ (not eat) for hours but we finally found a restaurant that was open.
5 I realised I _____ (lose) my passport as soon as I put my hand in my pocket.
6 By the end of the week they _____ (have) a wonderful time in Istanbul.

7 Pronunciation '*d*

🎧 **2.21** Listen to the last two sentences in Exercise 6. Notice the pronunciation of '*d*. Then listen again and repeat.

Listening

8 🎧 **2.22** Listen to two conversations about holidays. Answer the questions.

1 What problems were there with each holiday?
2 Were the problems solved?
3 What happened in the end?

Grammar subject and object questions

9 Look at the questions and answers (a–b) from the second conversation in Exercise 8. Answer the questions (1–3).

a **Who** took it?
  A man outside the hotel took my bag.
b **When** did it happen?
  It happened after we'd arrived.

1 Which question asks about the subject (subject question)?
2 Which question asks about the object (object question)?
3 Does the subject question or the object question need the auxiliary verb *did*?

> ▶ **SUBJECT and OBJECT QUESTIONS**
>
> **Subject questions**
>
> | subject | verb | object |
> |---|---|---|
> | **Who** | booked | the holiday? |
> | **My friend** | booked | the holiday. |
>
> **Object questions**
> **How much** did she pay?
> She paid **one hundred dollars**.
>
> For further information and practice, see page 165.

10 Look at the grammar box. Then underline all the questions in the audioscript of the two conversations from Exercise 8 on page 173. Which are subject and which are object questions?

11 Work in pairs. Write subject or object questions about the holiday story in Exercise 2.

1 Where / find the holiday? (In a brochure.)
  Where did she find the holiday?
2 Who / call? (The person at reception.)
3 Who / look at the shower? (The hotel engineer.)
4 What / the hotel engineer do? (Nothing.)
5 What / happen / next? (She went to reception.)
6 What / give the man at the front desk? (A large tip.)
7 Where / move to? (Room 405.)

Speaking

12 Think of a holiday or journey you went on. Make notes under these headings:

- the type of accommodation and/or transport
- other people who went with you and local people you met
- one day or thing you remember in particular (What happened? Did anything go wrong?)

13 Work in pairs. Take turns to ask questions about each other's holiday or journey.

Where did you ...?

Who ...?

What happened next?

TALK ABOUT ▶ A HOLIDAY YOU REMEMBER ▶ THE HOLIDAY OF A LIFETIME ▶ A TOURIST WEBPAGE ▶ TOUR INFORMATION
WRITE ▶ A FORMAL LETTER

119

10b Adventure holidays

NATIONAL GEOGRAPHIC
ADVENTURES

Unique trips
for the
Active Traveller

Get ready for the holiday of a lifetime with *National Geographic*! Walk through some of the world's most stunning mountain ranges. Kayak down legendary rivers like the Amazon. Let our expert guides take you to the birthplaces of ancient civilisations and introduce you to the fascinating people who live there now: from the Hadza tribesmen of Tanzania to Bhutanese villagers. This is your opportunity for a unique adventure with active itineraries that combine spectacular places, cultural interaction and physical challenge: the perfect mix for an unforgettable adventure.

Vocabulary holiday adjectives

1 Look at the website. What sort of person do you think would choose this kind of holiday?

2 Match the highlighted adjectives in the website with these synonyms and definitions.

1 to describe an important or memorable event or experience _____
2 very old _____
3 very interesting _____
4 impressive or dramatic _____ ,

5 very famous _____
6 only one of its kind _____

3 Work in pairs. Imagine your partner wants to go on an adventure holiday. Try to convince him/her to visit your country or a country you know. Talk about the country's:

• geographic regions and wildlife
• important cities and famous places
• history and culture

Listening

4 🔊 **2.23** Listen to part of a radio interview about travel with Madelaine from *National Geographic*. Answer the questions.

1 What kind of new job does Madelaine have?
2 What are some of her responsibilities?

5 🔊 **2.23** Listen again. Are the sentences true (T) or false (F)?

1 Madelaine's job is sometimes boring.
2 *National Geographic* holidays are quite traditional.
3 Madelaine is going to the Galápagos Archipelago for the first time.
4 Some people on the tour come on their own.
5 You have to do the same activities as other people in the group.
6 You have to be fairly fit to do this kind of holiday.

6 Does Madelaine's job sound exciting to you? Which parts of the world would you like to work in?

Grammar *-ed* / *-ing* adjectives

7 Look at the adjectives in the two sentences from the radio interview in Exercise 4. Answer the questions.

*You're also very **excited** about your new job.*

*This tour is very **exciting** because I've never been there before.*

1 Which adjective describes how a person feels?
2 Which adjective describes a place, person or thing?

> ▶ **–ED / -ING ADJECTIVES**
>
> We use **-ed** adjectives to describe feelings:
> *He feels bored / excited / worried / annoyed,* etc.
> We use **-ing** adjectives to describe …
> • places: *Venice is fascinating.*
> • people: *Her brother is so boring.*
> • things: *This film is exciting.*
>
> For further information and practice, see page 166.

8 Look at the grammar box. Then choose the correct adjectives to complete the conversation.

A: So, how was your holiday?
B: I had an ¹ *amazed / amazing* time. I'm so ² *bored / boring* to be back at work.
A: I'm sure. Where did you go exactly?
B: We went hiking in Patagonia! It's a ³ *fascinated / fascinating* place.
A: Yes, I watched an ⁴ *interested / interesting* TV programme about it once. The mountains there are enormous. They looked like a ⁵ *frightened / frightening* place to climb.
B: Well, we had a fantastic guide so I wasn't ⁶ *worried / worrying*.
A: What were the rest of the people in the group like?
B: Really nice. Except for one man who really ⁷ *annoyed / annoying* me. He kept complaining about all the walking. He said he was ⁸ *tired / tiring* all the time.
A: Sounds like he booked the wrong holiday!

9 Pronunciation number of syllables

🔊 **2.24** Listen to the sixteen adjectives in Exercise 8. Write the number of syllables you hear in each word. Then listen again and repeat.

Example:
1 amazed (2), amazing (3)

10 Work in pairs. Talk about these topics using the *-ing* or *-ed* form of these adjectives.

amaze	annoy	bore	excite	fascinate	interest
tire	worry				

1 a place you visited recently
2 a new project you have
3 the last book you read
4 a person you met recently for the first time
5 a TV programme you saw last week
6 a present you received recently

> *I recently visited London. I was excited because it was the first time I'd ever been but in fact it was a bit boring …*

> ▶ **WORDBUILDING dependent prepositions**
>
> We often use a preposition with **-ed** adjectives: *fascinated by, worried about.*
>
> For further information and practice, see Workbook page 83.

Speaking

11 Work in groups of three or four. Imagine you have each won $1,000 from a travel magazine to spend on 'the holiday of a lifetime'. You can choose any holiday lasting seven days but you must all travel as a group. Follow these steps:

1 Think about the kind of holiday you are interested in and make notes about it.
2 Take turns to tell the group about the kind of holiday you want.
3 As a group, try to agree and plan a holiday which everyone will enjoy. You will need to discuss:
   • the destination
   • the type of accommodation
   • the type of activities (daytime and evening)
   • the type of itinerary (flexible or fixed?)
4 Present your holiday to the rest of the class.

TALK ABOUT ▶ A HOLIDAY YOU REMEMBER ▶ THE HOLIDAY OF A LIFETIME ▶ A TOURIST WEBPAGE ▶ TOUR INFORMATION
WRITE ▶ A FORMAL LETTER

121

10c A tour under Paris

Reading

1 What is Paris famous for? Why do millions of tourists visit it every year?

2 Look at the man in the photo and the title of the article on page 123. Predict the answers to these questions.

1 Where is this man?
2 What do you think he might find there?
3 Why do you think he is there?

3 Read the article. Check your predictions in Exercise 2 and underline any words or sentences which explain:

1 what is under Paris.
2 why people go there.

4 Read the article again and choose the correct answers (a–c). There is more than one answer for some questions.

1 What does the author describe about different parts of Paris?
  a what he sees
  b what he hears
  c what he smells

2 In paragraph 1, what time of the day does he describe?
  a early in the morning
  b midday
  c late at night

3 Why were the tunnels built?
  a no one knows
  b for many different reasons
  c He doesn't say.

4 Are tourists allowed to go underground?
  a Yes, nowadays they can go everywhere.
  b It depends where they want to go.
  c No, never.

5 Why does the writer say it's dangerous in the tunnels?
  a There are criminals down there.
  b The tunnels might fall down on you.
  c You might get lost.

6 Why is Dominique and Yopie's room difficult to find?
  a It isn't on a map.
  b It's at the end of a two-hour walk through many tunnels.
  c They never show people where it is.

Critical thinking **reading between the lines**

5 Which of the statements (1–5) do you think are probably true? Underline the parts of the article which make you think this.

1 The author travels a lot and often visits Paris.
2 The tunnels below Paris have a long history.
3 Many young people go under Paris because they don't enjoy life above ground.
4 The author broke the law in order to write this article.
5 Dominique and Yopie are employed by a tour company.

Vocabulary **places in a city**

6 Find these places in the article. Do you think the places are above ground, underground, or both?

avenue   canal   catacombs   cellar   district
cemetery   tunnel

7 Match the places in Exercise 6 with the definitions (1–7).

1 long underground passage
2 official area of a town
3 wide straight road through a city, often with trees on both sides
4 man-made river
5 tunnels and rooms underground where dead people are buried
6 an area of land where dead people are buried
7 underground room for storing food or wine

8 Think of a famous city in your country. Which parts are popular with tourists? Has it got many of the places in Exercise 6?

Speaking and writing

9 Work in pairs. Imagine Paris decides to open more of the tunnels to tourists. You are a tour company and want to offer a new tour called 'Paris Underground'. Use the information from the article and discuss the type of tourist you will attract and which parts of the tunnels they will be interested in.

10 Write a short paragraph for the webpage about the tour on your company's website.

A TOUR
under Paris

The great avenues are quiet, the shops are closed. There's the smell of fresh bread from a bakery somewhere. It would be hard to say which time of the day in Paris I prefer but this is probably it. Soon the streets will be full of people and traffic. As with most other cities, you see the real Paris when the city wakes up.

There is, however, another part of Paris which is silent and free from people 24 hours a day. Under the city are hundreds of kilometres of tunnels. There are sewers and old subways but there are also spaces of all kinds: canals and catacombs, wine cellars which have been made into nightclubs and galleries. During the 19th century, the Parisians needed more stone for buildings above the ground so they dug tunnels beneath the city. After that, many farmers grew mushrooms in them. During World War II, the French Resistance fighters also used them. Since the 1970s, many groups of young people spend days and nights below the city in these tunnels. It's a place for parties, theatre performances, art galleries – anything goes here!

Everywhere you go under Paris, there is history and legend. Historians and novelists often refer to them in their books. For example, Victor Hugo mentions the tunnels in his famous novel *Les Miserables* and in the story and musical *The Phantom of the Opera* there is a pond beneath the old opera house. Most people think this is myth but in fact there is an underground pond here with fish. A 'normal' tourist can visit parts of Paris beneath the ground. For example, there are the catacombs beneath the Montparnasse district. Here you can see the bones and skeletons of about six millions Parisians. The bodies came from cemeteries above the ground two centuries ago when the city needed more space.

However, it's illegal to enter other parts of the tunnels and police often search the area. It's also very dangerous because some of the tunnels might collapse. Nevertheless, there are people who will take you to visit them. I have found two 'unofficial' tour guides – Dominique and Yopie (not their real names). They take me through many tunnels and after a couple of hours we arrive at a room which isn't on any map. Yopie and some of his friends built it. The room is comfortable and clean with a table and chairs and a bed. Yopie tells me there are many other places like this. 'Many people come down here to party, some people to paint … We do what we want here.'

> **myth** (n) /mɪθ/ a fictional story
> **illegal** (adj) /ɪˈliːgl̩/ against the law
> **collapse** (v) /kəˈlæps/ fall down

TALK ABOUT ▶ A HOLIDAY YOU REMEMBER ▶ THE HOLIDAY OF A LIFETIME ▶ A TOURIST WEBPAGE ▶ TOUR INFORMATION
WRITE ▶ A FORMAL LETTER

10d At tourist information

Reading and listening

1 Work in pairs. Look at the advert on the right and answer the questions.

1 Would you go on this tour? Why? / Why not?
2 What kind of information is missing?
3 What questions would you ask at a tourist information office to find out the information?

Example:
What days is it open? / Is it open today?

Real life **direct and indirect questions**

2 🎧 **2.25** Listen to a conversation at a tourist information office about visiting the Catacombs of Paris. Complete the advert in Exercise 1 with the missing information.

3 🎧 **2.25** The man asks five questions using direct and indirect questions. Listen again and complete the questions (1–5).

▶ DIRECT and INDIRECT QUESTIONS	
Direct questions	**Indirect questions**
Is it open today?	Can you tell me if ¹ _____ ?
² _____ open?	Do you know what time it opens?
How long does it last?	I'd like to know ³ _____ .
⁴ _____ much walking?	I was wondering if there's much walking.
How many steps are there?	Do you have any idea ⁵ _____ ?

4 Look at the direct and indirect questions in Exercise 3. Answer the questions (1–3).

1 Which questions are more polite?
2 Which questions use the same word order as an affirmative sentence?
3 Do you use *if* in indirect questions with *wh-/how* questions or with *yes/no* questions?

5 Pronunciation /dʒə/

🎧 **2.26** Listen to these two indirect questions. How does the speaker pronounce the first two words? Listen again and repeat.

1 Do you know if there's a taxi rank near here?
2 Do you have any idea how much it costs?

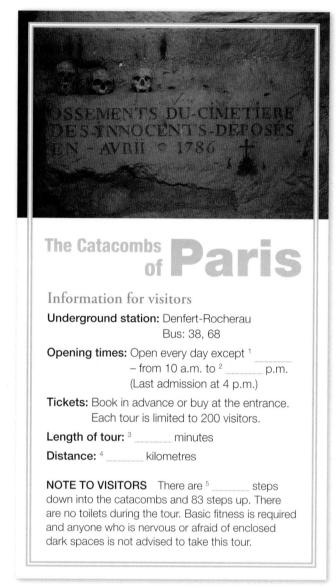

The Catacombs of Paris

Information for visitors

Underground station: Denfert-Rocherau
Bus: 38, 68

Opening times: Open every day except ¹ _____ – from 10 a.m. to ² _____ p.m.
(Last admission at 4 p.m.)

Tickets: Book in advance or buy at the entrance. Each tour is limited to 200 visitors.

Length of tour: ³ _____ minutes

Distance: ⁴ _____ kilometres

NOTE TO VISITORS There are ⁵ _____ steps down into the catacombs and 83 steps up. There are no toilets during the tour. Basic fitness is required and anyone who is nervous or afraid of enclosed dark spaces is not advised to take this tour.

6 Make these direct questions into indirect questions using the words in italics.

1 Which bus do I take?
  Can you tell me …?
2 Is there a post office near here?
  Do you know if …?
3 What time does the gallery open?
  I'd like to know …
4 Are there any good restaurants nearby?
  I was wondering if …
5 How much does it cost?
  Do you have any idea …?

7 Work in pairs. Practice two conversations between a tourist and a person at tourist information. Use the box in Exercise 3 to help you.

Student A: Turn to page 154.
Student B: Turn to page 155.

10e Requesting information

Writing a formal letter

1 When you want to go on holiday, how do you find out information about the holiday (e.g. online, from a high-street travel agent, by letter or phone)?

2 Read the letter and answer the questions.

1 What is the writer's purpose?
2 What information does the writer want from the travel company?

3 Writing skill formal expressions

The phrases (1–10) are less formal. Find similar, but more formal, phrases in the letter in Exercise 1.

Starting
1 Hi …
2 It's about …

Asking for more information
3 Can you send me more information about …?
4 What level of fitness do I need?
5 Can you tell me what 'average' means?
6 Please tell me when you will know the tour dates.
7 Will this also happen when we stay in hostels …?

Ending
8 Thanks for any help or information.
9 Hope to hear from you soon.
10 All the best

4 Look at the holiday advertisement for a cruise. Write to the tour company and request further details including:

- details about the exact length of the cruise (in weeks)
- exact starting location in South America
- are all meals included in the cost?
- the exact prices of cabins with a view of the sea

5 Work in pairs. Exchange letters. Use these questions to check your partner's letter.

- Has he/she used a formal style of writing?
- Has he/she used indirect phrases and expressions?

Dear Sir or Madam,

I am writing with regard to the 'Explorer's Holidays' on your website. I would like to request further details of your next expedition to Alaska.

First of all, I was wondering what level of fitness is required for this kind of trip. The website says participants should have an average level of fitness. I'd be grateful if you could define 'average' for me.

Secondly, the website says that you will confirm the exact dates for next year in the near future. I'd like to know when the tour dates will be available.

My last question is about accommodation. I understand that for the parts of the journey with camping, we will share a tent with someone else in the group. Can you tell me if this is also the case for staying in the hostels and cabins or whether we will have our own private rooms?

Thank you in advance for providing any further details of the tour. I look forward to hearing from you.

Best regards,

Dr Walter P Faversham

Cruise of a lifetime to the Antarctic

BOOK NOW!

Summer cruise starting in South America to the Antarctic coast

FIVE-STAR meals. Evening meal with the Captain available.

Price ranges from £2,000 to £3,500. Price depends on size and choice of cabins (with or without view of sea).

TALK ABOUT ▶ A HOLIDAY YOU REMEMBER ▶ THE HOLIDAY OF A LIFETIME ▶ A TOURIST WEBPAGE ▶ TOUR INFORMATION
WRITE ▶ A FORMAL LETTER

125

10f Living in Venice

This is the part of Venice that most visitors never see.

Before you watch

1 The photo shows people living and working in Venice. Read the sentences and choose the option you think is correct.

1 *Late afternoon / Early morning* is the best time for shopping in the outdoor markets.
2 Residents say it's a very *clean / dirty* city to live in.
3 The population of Venice is getting *younger / older*.
4 Property *is / isn't* very expensive.
5 Getting home from work is often very *easy / difficult*.
6 Venice is *less expensive than / as expensive as* many other cities.

While you watch

2 Watch the video and check your answers from Exercise 1.

3 Watch the video again and number the things in the order you first see them.

a a trader peeling vegetables
b early morning in the Piazza San Marco
c sunset in Venice
d musicians playing violins
e a gondolier
f a fish market
g a man jogging

4 Make notes about the advantages and disadvantages of living in Venice. Then compare your notes with a partner.

Advantages	
Disadvantages	

5 Match the people (1–3) with what they say (a–g).

1 Giovanni dal Missier
2 the narrator
3 Gino Penzo

a In a few hours, thousands of people will come to this square.
b We have many, many kinds of fish.
c My son, he doesn't … live in Venice. I am very sorry.
d The tourists come to experience a city that feels like it's still in the fifteenth century.
e Anyone who comes to Venice will fall in love.
f I know that it's a … gift to live in a city (like) Venice.
g For those who stay, it can be a wonderful experience.

After you watch

6 Roleplay a conversation between a tourist and a tour guide

Work in pairs.

Student A: You are a tour guide showing a visitor your town or city. Use the information below to make notes.

Student B: You are a tourist visiting a town or city. Find out what it's like to live there. Use the information below to prepare questions to ask the tour guide.

- the best places to see
- the advantages of living in the town or city
- the disadvantages of living in the town or city

Act out the conversation. When you have finished, change roles and act out the conversation again.

7 Giovanni dal Missier says: 'I get bored with the people, with the tourists.' Do you sympathise with him? Why? / Why not?

8 Work in pairs. Discuss these questions.

1 Which is the most visited tourist city in your country? Why do visitors go there?
2 Would you like to live in a city with lots of tourists? Why? / Why not?
3 What benefits does tourism bring? What are the disadvantages?

---

advantages (n) /əd'vɑːntɪdʒɪz/ good things
challenge (n) /'tʃælɪndʒ/ something difficult
crowd (n) /kraʊd/ many people in the same place
disadvantages (n) /'dɪsədvɑːntɪdʒɪz/ bad things
earn a living (v) /ɜːn ə 'lɪvɪŋ/ make enough money to live
gift (n) /gɪft/ a present

huge (adj) /hjuːdʒ/ very big
increase (v) /ɪn'kriːs/ get bigger
population (n) /pɒpjuː'leɪʃən/ the people who live in a place
property (n) /'prɒpəti/ houses
trader (n) /'treɪdə/ a person who buys and sells things

UNIT 10 REVIEW

Grammar

1 Complete the conversation with the past simple or past perfect simple form of the verbs.

A: How was your holiday?
B: It was fine, in the end.
A: Why? What ¹ _____ (happen)?
B: Well, we arrived at the hotel but they ² _____ (not / receive) our reservation. So we ³ _____ (not / have) a room and they were full.
A: Oh no! ⁴ _____ you _____ (book) the hotel?
B: Yes, I had. Anyway, they ⁵ _____ (phone) another hotel and fortunately they ⁶ _____ (have) rooms.
A: That was lucky.
B: Yes, but it was in another town.
A: So what ⁷ _____ you _____ (do)?
B: Well, I was really angry after everything that ⁸ _____ (happen), but the manager ⁹ _____ (paid) for a taxi to the other hotel.
A: That was nice.
B: Yes, and it was funny because we ¹⁰ _____ (see) our new hotel in the brochure months ago but it ¹¹ _____ (be) more expensive so we ¹² _____ (book) the other one!
A: Brilliant!

> **I CAN**
> tell stories and describe what happened to me
> ask questions about the past

2 Complete the adjectives with -ing or -ed.

1 Do you feel bor_____?
2 This book is very interest_____.
3 We had an amaz_____ time in Peru.
4 Stop being annoy_____ and leave me alone!
5 This is so excit_____!
6 I'm really frighten_____!

3 Work in pairs. Look at the photo. How do they feel? How would you describe the activity they are doing?

> **I CAN**
> describe how people feel
> describe places, people and things

Vocabulary

4 Delete the incorrect word in each group and say why.

1 old, historical, ~~unforgettable~~, ancient
   the others are synonyms of 'old'
2 sun tan lotion, camping, package tour, cruise
3 stunning, huge, beautiful, spectacular
4 sleeping bag, tent, camera, water sports
5 five-star, sunbathing, self-catering, hostel
6 cellars, tunnels, bridges, catacombs

5 What's your dream holiday? Make notes about the location, accommodation and activities.

6 Work in pairs. Tell your partner about your dream holiday.

> **I CAN**
> talk about tourist locations and holidays

Real life

7 Imagine you are a tourist in your town or city. Complete these indirect questions to ask for information.

1 Can you tell me _____?
2 I'd like to know _____.
3 Do you know _____?
4 I was wondering _____.

8 Rewrite your questions in Exercise 7 as direct questions.

> **I CAN**
> ask for tourist information using direct and indirect questions

Speaking

9 Work in pairs. Comment on these different aspects of holidays and travel using the phrases and your own words.

> adventure holidays   waiting at airports
> hot beaches   visiting new countries
> looking at other people's holiday photos
> queuing to visit tourist sites
> new exotic food   flying

We both like / dislike … are interested in …
get bored of … get excited / worried about …
get angry with …

Unit 11 History

Captain Scott's hut
Photo by Antarctic Heritage Trust/Barcroft India

FEATURES

1 The hut in the photo is about one hundred years old. Which part of the world do you think it is in? Who do you think Captain Scott was? What do you think he did?

2 **2.27** Listen to a historian talking about the hut and check your ideas in Exercise 1. Then answer the questions.

1 What objects can you see inside the hut?
2 Why is it important to look after the hut?
3 The historian says, 'the hut has become a time capsule'. What do you think he means by a *time capsule*?

3 Work in groups. Some people and organisations put objects in a 'time capsule' and bury it under the ground so that future historians will learn more about our present day society. Imagine you are going to make a time capsule. It only has space for five items. Discuss which five objects will be most useful for future historians. Use these examples or your own ideas.

a copy of today's newspaper   a tin of food
a DVD showing a film of daily life
a CD with some popular music   a menu from a restaurant
drawings and diaries   money (coins and notes)   a clock
a popular novel

4 Present your final list for the time capsule to the class and explain the reasons for your choices.

TALK ABOUT ▶ HOW WE USED TO LIVE ▶ REPORTING AN INTERVIEW ▶ RESEARCHING A BIOGRAPHY ▶ A PRESENTATION

WRITE ▶ A BIOGRAPHY

11a An ancient civilisation

Speaking

1 Do you live in or near a town or city with lots of historical places? Which of these does it have? What do you know about the history of each place?

> ancient roads and bridges   castles
> city walls   museums   pyramids
> old religious buildings   a palace
> statues of historical people

2 Which of these are the reasons why your town or city looks after some of the places you described in Exercise 1?

1 The place is unique and you cannot see it anywhere else.
2 Someone famous lived or worked in the building.
3 The architecture is important.
4 There are important objects inside.

Vocabulary archaeology

3 Read the text about an ancient pyramid in Mexico City. Match the highlighted words with the definitions (1–6).

1 to dig in an area of land to find buildings and objects from the past
2 the action of finding something you didn't know was there
3 people who study societies from the past by looking at their buildings, tools and other objects
4 the act of killing an animal (or human) for your god(s)
5 a human society from the past
6 metal or stone images of someone or something

> ▶ **WORDBUILDING word roots**
>
> Parts of many English words come from the ancient languages of Greek and Latin. For example, the first part of the word *archaeology* comes from a Greek word meaning *ancient, old, from the beginning*. The *ex-* in the word *excavation* is a Latin prefix meaning *out of*. Sometimes you can guess the historical meaning of a new word if you know some of these word roots.
>
> For further information and practice, see Workbook page 91.

In 1978 archaeologists made an important discovery right in the middle of modern Mexico City. It was a fourteenth-century pyramid from the ancient civilisation of the Aztecs. They started to excavate different rooms inside. In some rooms they found objects such as plates and cooking pots. In others, there were small religious statues or knives which the people used to make a sacrifice to their gods.

Listening

4 🔊 **2.28** Listen to an interview with an archaeologist who is still working at the excavation site in Exercise 3. What has she found in the pyramid? Why is it important?

5 🔊 **2.28** Listen again. Match the objects (1–5) from the excavation to their purpose (a–e).

1	pots and plates	a	for doing business
2	gold and jade	b	for cooking
3	statues	c	for sacrificing
4	knives	d	for hunting
5	(the skeleton of) a dog	e	for religious importance

Grammar *used to*

6 Look at the sentences (a–d) from the interview in Exercise 4. Answer the questions (1–4).

a   Archaeologists discovered this pyramid in 1978.
b   The Aztecs used to sacrifice animals.
c   Did the Aztecs use to keep dogs as pets?
d   No, they didn't use to have pets.

1   Which sentence, a or b, describes a single action at a specific time in the past?
2   Which sentence, a or b, describes a past situation or habit which doesn't happen now?
3   What form of the verb follows *used to*?
4   How does the negative and question form of *used to* change?

▶ USED TO

I/you/he/she/it/we/they **used to live** in this house.
I/you/he/she/it/we/they **didn't use to live** in this house.
Did I/you/he/she/it/we/they **use to live** in this house?
Yes, I did. / No, I didn't.

We don't use *used to* with a particular time in the past.
Use the past simple:
I ~~used to live~~ in this house in 1989. ✗
I lived in this house in 1989. ✓

For further information and practice, see page 166.

---

7 Look at the grammar box. Then complete the text about another ancient civilisation with the correct form of *used to*. Use the past simple where *used to* is not possible.

In 1928, some miners in Nigeria ¹ *discovered* (discover) a small clay statue in the ground. It was from an ancient civilisation called 'The Nok' who ² *used to live* (live) in Central Nigeria. Archaeologists ³ _____ (not know) anything about The Nok but nowadays there is much more information about them.

The Nok ⁴ _____ (live) in the fourth century B.C.E. They were different from other civilisations in this period because they ⁵ _____ (not / work) with stone. Instead, they ⁶ _____ (produce) iron and other metals. As a result they ⁷ _____ (make) strong tools. They could dig the land and they ⁸ _____ (grow) their own food. This is one of the earliest examples of farming in history.

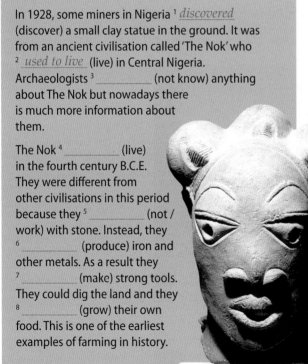

8 Pronunciation /s/ or /z/

a 🔊 2.29 Listen to the change in pronunciation of the words *use or used*. What is the rule for the /s/ or the /z/?

*The Nok **used** to live in Africa but they didn't **use** to live in Europe. They **used** iron but they didn't **use** any stone.*

b Practise saying the sentences in part a.

9 Work in pairs. Test each other's knowledge of other ancient civilisations. Use the prompts to ask questions with *used to*. In some cases, both answers are correct, only one is correct or neither are correct.

1   Ancient Egyptians: build pyramids / castles
2   Ancient Greeks: watch theatre / sport
3   The Celts: live in South America / in Asia
4   North American Indians: grow corn / potatoes

> *Did the ancient Egyptians use to build pyramids and castles?*

> *They used to build pyramids but they didn't use to build castles.*

10 🔊 2.30 Listen and check your questions and answers in Exercise 9.

Speaking

11 Work in pairs. Look at the list of topics of more recent history. Discuss what people used to do and what they do now for each one.

- fashion
- information (e.g. news)
- communication
- music and entertainment
- transport

> *How did people use to listen to music?*

> *What kind of clothes did people use to wear?*

> *Did people use to travel by …?*

> *Do people still … today?*

11b Modern history

Speaking

1 What do you think is the most important moment of world history in your lifetime? Why?

2 Work in groups. Think of one important historical moment for each of these topics.

> world politics
> famous individuals
> space exploration
> culture and the arts
> countries and cities
> technology

3 Compare your ideas from Exercise 2 with the rest of the class. Then choose the three most important moments in history.

Reading

4 Read the article. Number the paragraphs (A–E) in the correct order.

5 Answer the questions with information from the article about times and dates.

1 What date did the space age begin?
2 How many years later did an American walk on the moon?
3 When did the US lead the space race?
4 How many years later did they agree on plans for the ISS?
5 When did the ISS start orbiting the Earth?
6 When did 'space tourism' begin?
7 What period of history does the speaker talk about at the end?

6 Work in pairs. Discuss the questions.

1 What is an important date and year in your country's history?
2 Which is your favourite decade in history?
3 Which century in your country's history is the most interesting?
4 Do you remember what you were doing at the turn of the last century?
5 How do you think life will change in the next half century?

MOMENTS IN

SPACE
history

A

Eight years later, an American finally walked on the moon and during the early seventies the US led the Soviet Union in the space race. However, space travel was expensive and they needed to co-operate more. As a result, in 1975 astronauts from both countries flew two spacecraft and met in space. Afterwards, one astronaut said that the mission showed that the Soviet Union and America could work together.

B

At the beginning of the twenty-first century, businessman Dennis Tito paid twenty million dollars and told the world he loved space as he spent eight days on the ISS. Since then, space tourism has developed with plans for regular tours and floating hotels.

C *1*

On October 4, 1957, the Soviet Union sent Sputnik 1 into space and a new age in history began – The Space Age. The Soviets launched more Sputnik satellites in the fifties and by 1961 they had put the first man into space.

D

And what about the next half a century? In 2009, a Russian Space Chief said Russia was planning a nuclear spaceship for Mars. In 2010, the US president Barack Obama told an audience that by the mid-2030s the US would send humans to Mars. The race for Mars has already started.

E

Nearly two decades later, leaders from both countries said they had agreed on plans for a new international space station (ISS) and by the turn of the century the ISS had started orbiting the Earth. Nowadays, the ISS is used by scientists from all over the world.

Grammar reported speech

7 Look at the example of reported speech from the article in Exercise 4 and the direct speech equivalent. Which words change in reported speech?

Reported speech: One astronaut said that the mission showed that the Soviet Union and America could work together.

Direct speech: One astronaut said, 'The mission shows that the Soviet Union and America can work together.'

8 Look at the examples of direct speech. Then look back at the article in Exercise 4 and find their equivalents in reported speech. How do the pronouns and tenses change?

1 Tito said, 'I love space.'
2 The two leaders of both countries said, 'We agreed on plans for a new international space station.'
3 A Russian Space Chief said, 'Russia is planning a nuclear spaceship for Mars.'
4 Barack Obama told an audience that, 'By the mid-2030s the US will send humans to Mars.'

▶ REPORTED SPEECH	
Direct speech →	**Reported speech**
Present simple	Past simple
Present continuous	Past continuous
Past simple	Past perfect
Present perfect	Past perfect
will	*would*

For further information and practice, see page 167.

9 Look at the grammar box. Then complete the direct and reported speech sentences.

1 The boy said, 'One day I want to be an astronaut.'
The boy said that one day _____ to be an astronaut.
2 Last year the president said he had plans for a new mission to the moon.
Last year the president said, '_____ for a new mission to the moon.'
3 In 2010, Astronomers said, 'The Hubble Telescope has found a new planet.'
In 2010, Astronomers said that the Hubble Telescope _____ a new planet.
4 Scientists said the robot had discovered water on the planet.
Scientists said, 'The robot _____ water on the planet.'
5 The radio announcer said, 'The rocket is landing.'
The radio announcer said the rocket _____.
6 The Government said they were discussing the problem.
The Government said, 'We _____ the problem.'
7 China said, 'We will visit the moon in the next few years.'
China said it _____ the moon in the next few years.
8 They said they couldn't afford the ticket into space.
They said, 'We _____ the ticket into space.'

Vocabulary *say* or *tell*

10 Look back at the article in Exercise 4 and underline examples of *say (said)* or *tell (told)*. Then complete this rule with *say* or *tell*.

[1] _____ always needs an object such as *me, him, her, you, us, them, everyone*. Do not follow [2] _____ with an object.

11 Choose the correct options to complete the conversation.

A: Did I [1] *say / tell* you there was a great TV programme on last night?
B: No, what was it about?
A: Space travel in the next century. They [2] *said / told* humans would soon land on Mars.
B: Really? When did they [3] *say / tell* it would happen?
A: The presenter didn't [4] *say / tell* us exactly but I think before the year 2050.
B: I read another article and it [5] *said / told* there would be a hotel on the moon soon.
A: Yes, but someone [6] *said / told* me a few years ago that there were going to be space hotels orbiting the Earth soon but nothing's happened yet.

Speaking

12 Work in pairs. Interview each other with these questions and write down your partner's answers.

1 What's one thing you want to do in your lifetime (e.g. jump out of an aeroplane, travel into space)?
2 Which was your favourite subject at school (e.g. history, geography)?
3 What famous historical places have you visited (e.g. Stonehenge, The Great Wall of China)?
4 Do you think you will travel to space in your lifetime? Where will you go (e.g. Mars, the moon)?

13 Work with a new partner and report your original partner's answers. Use *say* or *tell* and reported speech.

He said he wanted …

She told me it had been …

TALK ABOUT ▶ HOW WE USED TO LIVE ▶ REPORTING AN INTERVIEW ▶ RESEARCHING A BIOGRAPHY ▶ A PRESENTATION
WRITE ▶ A BIOGRAPHY

133

11c The life of Jane Goodall

Reading

1 Do you ever read biographies? What kind of people do you like to read about (e.g. people from history, celebrities)?

2 Read the biography about the life of Jane Goodall on page 135. Which paragraphs are about her life during these different times?

1 the sixties
2 the seventies
3 the eighties
4 the nineties up to the present day

3 Read the biography again and answer the questions. Underline the information in the article which gives you the answer. Then compare your answers and the information you underlined with your partner.

1 Who was Jane travelling with when she first arrived in Gombe?
2 How soon after she arrived did she try to find her first chimpanzee?
3 How qualified was she for this kind of work?
4 What did she discover about chimpanzees?
5 When did scientists and academics start reading about her work?
6 Why did Gombe become a dangerous place?
7 Did all the foreigners, including Jane, leave the region?
8 Why were there only about a hundred chimpanzees living in Gombe by the end of the eighties?
9 Has Jane retired?
10 What does she do in her spare time?

Critical thinking **relevance**

4 The statements (a–d) could be included as useful background information at the end of four of the paragraphs in the article. Match them with the correct paragraph.

a This was new and surprising scientific information at that time.
b Even ordinary people around the world were starting to recognise her name.
c This was the start of a lifetime of studying the behaviour of the chimps in Africa.
d This work continues to the present day.

Word focus *set*

5 Find four phrasal verbs with *set* in the biography. Then complete the definitions (1–4) with the correct particle.

1 set _____: start a journey
2 set _____: start something new such as a new business
3 set _____: start doing something with energy and enthusiasm
4 set _____: start something with a particular aim

6 Complete the questions with a phrasal verb with *set*. Then ask and answer the questions with your partner.

1 What time did you _____ to work/college this morning?
2 What time did you _____ starting work?
3 Did you always _____ to do the job you have now?
4 Have you ever wanted to _____ your own business?

Writing and speaking

7 Work in pairs. Imagine you are biographers and you are going to write a biography of Jane Goodall. Prepare seven or eight interview questions for her based on the information in the article.

Example:
Do you remember your first day in Gombe?
What did you have with you?
Why did you set off into the forest?

8 Work with a new partner and roleplay an interview between the biographer and Jane Goodall. Take turns to be the interviewer and Jane.

On the morning of July 14, 1960,

Jane Goodall arrived on the east shore of Lake Tanganyika and the Gombe National Park. She had brought a tent, a cup without a handle, a pair of binoculars and her mother. A group of local men met the strange pair of women and helped carry their camping gear. Then, around 5 p.m., somebody reported that they had seen a chimpanzee. Straight away, Jane set off into the forest to find her first chimpanzee.

As a young woman, Jane Goodall had no scientific qualifications but this didn't stop her from following her childhood dream of studying chimpanzees in Africa. She had set out to study the animals and find out how they really lived. After many months of difficult work she made three important discoveries: chimpanzees ate meat, they used tools to get food and they also made tools.

Every evening, Jane wrote her findings in a diary and she began to publish articles in journals such as *National Geographic* magazine. After a while, scientists and academics started reading her studies and Jane was offered a place at a university. After more years of research she became Doctor Jane Goodall in 1966. Her work was also making her famous. There was a film documentary *Miss Goodall and the Wild Chimpanzees* (1963) and then the first of many books called *My Friends the Wild Chimpanzees* (1969).

> **rebel** (n) /ˈrebl/ soldier who fights against government soldiers
> **fled** (to flee) (v) /fled/ left quickly because of a dangerous situation
> **deforestation** (n) /ˌdiːˌfɒrɪˈsteɪʃn/ when trees and forests disappear
> **sanctuary** (n) /ˈsæŋktʃuərɪ/ a safe place
> **trade** (n) /treɪd/ buying and selling

During the seventies, Gombe became a dangerous place to work. It is on the border of four different countries and there was fighting between soldiers and rebels. Many foreigners fled the region but Jane stayed. In the end, she needed a military escort in order to continue her work. In one of her diaries from this period she notices that chimpanzees can also be violent: 'I thought the chimps were nicer than we are. But time has revealed that they are not. They can be just as awful.'

A different problem developed in Gombe in the 1980s. The human population in the region was increasing which caused deforestation. As a result of this there were only about a hundred chimpanzees living in Gombe by the end of the decade. Jane realised that something had to be done so chimpanzees and humans could live together so she set about helping the local community to grow more trees in the region.

After 1989, Jane left her career in Gombe in order to do other work. Firstly, she started travelling and giving lectures. She protested about the cruelty to chimpanzees used in medical research laboratories. She also set up sanctuaries for chimps which had been captured or were orphans because of the trade in chimpanzee meat. Nowadays, she spends about 300 days a year giving interviews, talks and lectures, meeting with government officials and raising money for the Jane Goodall Institute which continues her research. She has very little spare time left but she still spends part of every year in the forest in Gombe, watching her chimpanzees.

The life of Jane Goodall

11d A journey to Machu Picchu

Real life **giving a short presentation**

1 Do you ever give talks or presentations in your own language (or in English)? What are they about? Why would people give talks or presentations in these situations?

- at work
- at school or university
- at the meeting of a local club or town council
- at a special occasion (e.g. a wedding)

2 🎵 **2.31** Listen to parts of a presentation about Peru and Machu Picchu. Which of the topics (1–6) does the presenter talk about?

1 the people in Peru and their customs
2 the history of Machu Picchu
3 the history of the Incas
4 the capital city of Peru
5 his own journey
6 the food in Peru

3 🎵 **2.31** Listen again and complete these expressions for giving a short presentation.

> ▶ **GIVING A SHORT PRESENTATION**
>
> Good morning and ¹ _____ _____ all for coming.
> Today I would like to ² _____ about …
> Let me ³ _____ by telling you about …
> So, that's everything I wanted to ⁴ _____ about …
> Now, let's ⁵ _____ onto …
> The ⁶ _____ part of my presentation is about …
> I'd like to ⁷ _____ you some of my photos.
> That's the ⁸ _____ of my talk. To sum up …
> Are there any ⁹ _____?

4 Pronunciation pausing

a 🎵 **2.32** Presenters often pause at the end of a sentence, the end of a phrase, or before and after important words they want to emphasise. Listen and read the first part of the presentation. Notice the first five pauses (/) and write in the other pauses.

Good morning / and thank you all for coming. / Today / I'd like to talk about / my holiday in Peru / and in particular, about my journey to Machu Picchu. It's also called 'The Lost City of the Incas'. Let me begin by telling you about the history of Machu Picchu.

b Work in pairs. Try reading the same part of the presentation with similar pauses.

5 Prepare a short presentation for your partner. Think about a historical place you have visited and make notes for these questions:

- Where is it?
- Why is it important?
- Who lived there in the past?

11e The greatest mountaineer

Writing a biography

1 Think of three pieces of information you would expect to find in a biography. Compare your ideas with your partner.

2 Read the biography about Reinhold Messner. Does it include your ideas from Exercise 1? Which paragraph (1–4) has information about the topics (a–f)? Two paragraphs each contain two topics.

  a When and where the person was born
  b Childhood and early life
  c Why the person became well-known, famous or important
  d Something the person said or a famous quotation
  e What other people think or have said about the person
  f When the person died or what the person is doing now

3 Writing skill punctuation in direct speech

a The first sentence in the biography of Messner includes direct speech. Underline three more examples of sentences with direct speech in the text.

b Answer these questions about punctuation rules for direct speech.

  1 Where do you put the two quotation marks?
  2 Do you always put a full stop at the end of the quotation or only if it ends the sentence?
  3 Where do you put the comma? What does it separate?

c Write in the missing punctuation.

  1 My grandfather always told me you should follow your dreams
  2 Yes we can said Barack Obama when he campaigned to become the US President
  3 Film critics say she's the greatest actress of her generation
  4 Education is the most powerful weapon said Nelson Mandela

4 Write a short biography (100–120 words) about someone famous or someone you admire. Try to include all the topics in Exercise 2 and remember to use the correct punctuation with quotations or direct speech.

The world's greatest mountaineer

1 Reinhold Messner has been described as 'the greatest mountaineer in history'. He's famous for being the first man to climb Mount Everest without oxygen in 1980. But he was also the first man to climb all fourteen of the world's mountains over eight thousand feet.

2 Messner was born in 1944 in a small village in the mountains of northern Italy. When he talks about the area he still says, 'it's the most beautiful place in the world.' His father was a climber and took his son up a mountain when he was only five. As a teenager Messner climbed with his younger brother Günther.

3 In their twenties, the two brothers started climbing in the Himalayas but Günther died in an accident and Reinhold lost six toes. Nevertheless, Messner continued climbing and he became a legend among other mountaineers. The climber Hans Kammerlander believes Reinhold changed climbing. 'Reinhold had so many new ideas,' says Kammerlander. 'He found new ways, new techniques.'

4 Nowadays Messner spends more time at home with his family and he has written over sixty books. In 2006 he opened the Messner Mountain Museum where people can find out more about the world he loves.

1 foot = 0.3048 metres

5 Exchange your biography with a partner. Use these questions to check your partner's biography.

  • Which topics in Exercise 2 has he/she included?
  • Is the punctuation correct?

11f The lost city of Machu Picchu

The lost city is no longer lost.

Before you watch

1 Work in groups. Look at the photo and discuss the questions.

1 Who are the people in the photo?
2 Where are they?
3 What are they doing?
4 What do you think the caption means?

2 Tick the things you think you are going to see in the video.

bicycles	buses	cameras	children	dogs
mountains	a river	ruins	a train	umbrellas

While you watch

3 Watch the video and check your answers from Exercise 2.

4 Choose the correct option to complete the summary.

Machu Picchu is an ancient city ¹ *8,000 / 18,000* feet up in the ² *Andes / Pyrenees*. It is over ³ *1,000 / 500* years old. It is sometimes called the lost city of the ⁴ *Incas / Aztecs*. When their civilisation ended, few people knew Machu Picchu existed but in ⁵ *1911 / 2001* an explorer, Hiram ⁶ *Bingham / Birmingham*, found it again.

5 Are these sentences true (T) or false (F)? Watch the video again to check your answers.

1 It is always sunny at Machu Picchu.
2 The lost city is not very popular with tourists.
3 You can't walk around the ruins.
4 Machu Picchu is now a very noisy place.
5 Local people would like more tourists to visit Machu Picchu.
6 Conservationists say that tourism is good for the environment.
7 Many parts of Peru are very poor.
8 Aguas Calientes is a very large city.

6 Match the people (1–3) with what they say (a–f).

1 Julio (tour guide)
2 José (hotel owner)
3 The narrator

a It is a magic attraction.
b Why not be like the rest of the world?
c Why keep it to the few?
d Machu Picchu is one of the magnetic centres of the ancient world.
e This beautiful quiet place is covered in sunshine
f Even in the rain and fog, it's wonderful to walk through the ruins.

After you watch

7 Roleplay discussing the future of Machu Picchu

Work in pairs.

Student A: You are a conservationist. Read the information below and make notes. Argue your point of view with your partner.

• You want to limit the number of tourists who visit the ancient city.
• Give reasons (for example, too many people are destroying the ruins, people leave a lot of rubbish).

Student B: You work in the tourist industry. Read the information below and make notes. Argue your point of view with your partner.

• You want to increase access to Machu Picchu.
• Give your reasons (for example, more tourists means more money for the local economy, hotel owners will benefit).

Act out the discussion. Then change roles and repeat the discussion.

8 According to the narrator, time may be running out for the 'Lost City of the Inca'. What do you think she means by this?

9 Work in pairs. Discuss these questions.

1 Are there any ancient sites or ruins in your country? Who built them? Are they tourist attractions?
2 Does tourism have a positive or negative impact on these places? Why? / Why not?
3 How can ancient monuments best be preserved for future generations?

---

ancient (adj) /ˈeɪnʃənt/ very old
conservationist (n) /kɒnsɜːˈveɪʃənɪst/ a person who works to preserve a natural or ancient place
explorer (n) /ɪksˈplɔːrə/ a person who goes to places where people do not normally go
fog (n) /fɒg/ low cloud that makes it difficult to see
ruins (n) /ˈruːɪnz/ destroyed buildings
run out (v) /rʌn ˈaʊt/ come to the end, finish
stall (n) /stɔːl/ a temporary shop without walls
step (n) /stɛp/ the place where you put your foot when you go up stairs
summit (n) /ˈsʌmɪt/ the top of a mountain
tourist (n) /ˈtʊərɪst/ a person who visits a place on holiday

Grammar

1 Complete the sentences with the correct form of *used to*.

1 We _____ live in England but now we live in Scotland.
2 I _____ have short hair but now it's much longer.
3 They _____ like vegetables, but now they love them!
4 There _____ be trees all around my house but now there are other houses.
5 The town _____ have cafés and restaurants, but now there are lots of places to eat and drink.

2 Work in pairs. Comment on these aspects of your appearance in the past and now.

- length and/or colour of hair
- height
- wearing glasses
- colours and style of clothes

> *I used to have long hair and now I don't.*

3 Rewrite the direct speech into reported speech.

1 'I want to fly in space.'
He said he _____ .
2 'I'm driving home.'
She said she _____ .
3 'We visited the pyramid in Giza.'
They said they _____ .
4 'He's gone to the museum.'
You said he _____ .
5 'One day I'll go on holiday to Rome.'
Matt said one day he _____ .

4 Complete the sentences with *say* or *tell*.

1 _____ him to hurry up!
2 Did she _____ what time she was coming?
3 Don't _____ me the answer. I'll work it out.
4 Did the archaeologist _____ who built this house?

5 Work in pairs. Tell your partner something:

- the news reader on the TV or radio said this morning.
- your English teacher told you in the lesson today.

> **I CAN**
> talk about past situations and habits ☐
> report what people said or told me ☐

Vocabulary

6 Look at the photo. What does it show? What do you think they were for?

7 Complete the text with these words and check your ideas in Exercise 6.

> archaeologists civilisation excavations
> pyramids sacrifices statue

> The Inca [1] _____ was the largest in South America in the thirteenth and fourteenth century. Today, you can visit the huge [2] _____ that they built and [3] _____ are still finding objects from their past. For example, the [4] _____ on the left of the photo is a llama. It was found in [5] _____ at a site which they used for animal and human [6] _____ .

> **I CAN**
> talk about history and archaeology ☐

Real life

8 Put these sentences from different parts of the presentation in the order the speaker said them (1–7).

Today I'd like to talk about my visit to Italy.
1 Good morning everyone and thank you for coming.
So that's everything about Pisa and its leaning tower.
But before I finish, are there any questions?
Let me begin by telling you a bit about the city of Pisa.
That's the end of my talk.
Now let's move onto my next stop which was the city of Florence.

> **I CAN**
> give a short presentation ☐

Speaking

9 Discuss as a class. What's your favourite historical period? Why? What do you like about it (e.g. the clothes, the architecture, the art)?

Unit 12 Nature

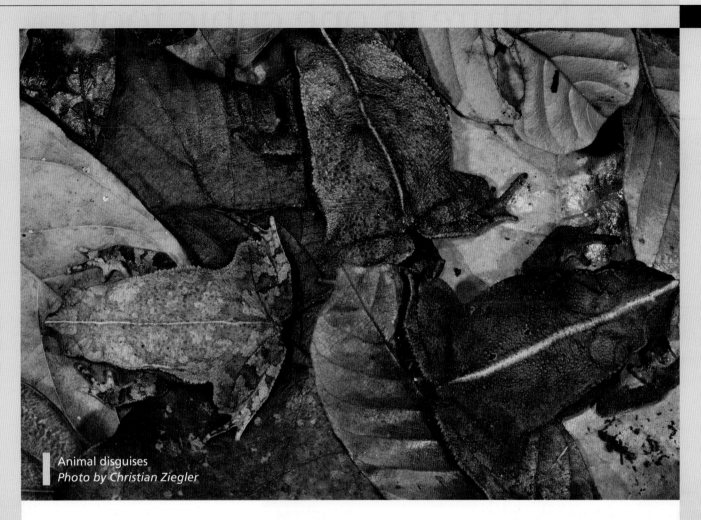

Animal disguises
Photo by Christian Ziegler

FEATURES

1 Look at the photo. Describe what you can see.

2 🔊 **2.33** Listen to a nature expert talking about the photo. Answer the questions.

1 Which animals does she talk about?
2 Where is each animal hiding or hunting?

3 Match these words to the correct category (1–7) in the diagram. Then think of one more word for each category.

> butterfly   eagle   horse   shark   snake   toad   tree

NATURE
1 PLANT   ANIMAL
2 INSECT   3 AMPHIBIAN   4 MAMMAL   5 REPTILE   6 BIRD   7 FISH

4 Work in pairs. Complete these sentences with the name of an animal (or animals) and give reasons.

I've never seen ...

I'd love to have a ... as a pet.

I'm really scared of ...

12a Nature in one cubic foot

Listening

1 Work in pairs. Discuss the questions.

  1 Do you like taking photos?
  2 Do you ever take photos of nature? Why? / Why not?

2 Match the photos (A–D) with the locations (1–4).

  1 forest   3 ocean
  2 mountain   4 river

3 🔊 **2.34** Listen to a documentary about David Liittschwager, the photographer. Why does he take photos of the green metal frame?

> **cube** (n) /kjuːb/ a shape that has six equal square sides (cubic = adj)
> **ecosystem** (n) /iːkəʊsɪstəm/ all the plants and animals that live in a particular area

4 🔊 **2.34** Listen to the documentary again. Are the sentences true (T) or false (F)?

  1 The narrator thinks most people look at the natural world and see everything.
  2 David Liittschwager thinks there is natural beauty everywhere.
  3 He took his green cubic foot to many different parts of the world.
  4 He spent three weeks taking photos around the world.
  5 He photographed living things that were smaller than one millimetre in size.
  6 In total, he photographed over a thousand organisms in each cubic foot.

5 Work in pairs. Describe the view from a window in your house. Use these questions to help you.

  • Can you see any natural locations such as mountains or rivers?
  • Do you look at buildings and roads?
  • How important is it for you to look at nature?

Grammar *any-*, *every-*, *no-*, *some-* and *-thing*, *-where*, *-one*, *-body*

6 Look at the highlighted words in these sentences from the documentary in Exercise 3. Does the yellow part of the word talk about a place, a person or an object?

1 **Everyone** looks at nature differently.
2 Maybe you're **somebody** who has no interest in nature.
3 If you go **anywhere** green, you don't notice **anything**.
4 **Nowhere** in the world is without natural beauty.

7 Look at the green part of the highlighted words in Exercise 6. Complete the sentences with *any-*, *every-*, *some-* or *no-*.

1 _____ one loves taking photos. It's very popular.
2 _____ one likes that photo. We all look terrible in it.
3 _____ one can take a photo. It's easy.
4 _____ one took my photo. It's in today's newspaper.

> ► **ANY-, EVERY-, NO-, SOME-** and **-THING, -WHERE, -ONE, -BODY**
>
> **Affirmative (*every-*, *any-*, *some-*)**
> *Everyone likes nature.*
> *Anybody can take a photo.*
> *Let's go somewhere.*
>
> **Negative (*no-*, *any-*)**
> *No one uses the park in my city.*
> *People don't notice anything there.*
>
> For further information and practice, see page 168.

8 Look at the grammar box. Then read the information about four different ecosystems on the right. Complete the words. Sometimes more than one answer is possible.

Speaking

9 Look at these slogans from different advertisements. What are they advertising?

10 Work in groups. Imagine you work for a local tourist company which wants to attract more visitors to the region. Write four slogans to use on your advertisements.

11 When you are ready, choose your best idea and tell the class. Which is the best slogan?

FOUR DIFFERENT ECOSYSTEMS

FOREST
Central Park   New York

[1] Any_____ who visits New York visits Central Park but it isn't [2] some_____ that's famous for its natural life. However, the forest is full of plants and animals.

CORAL REEF
Moorea   French Polynesia

[3] _____where is as beautiful as a coral reef and there's always [4] _____thing to look at: from the multi-coloured coral to the orange, green and yellow sea life.

MOUNTAINS
Table Mountain   South Africa

Possibly, there isn't [5] _____ where else in the world with an ecosystem as rich as this one. [6] Every_____ you look, there are different types of plants.

FRESH WATER
Duck River   Tennessee

[7] _____body in Tennessee who likes fishing knows about the Duck River. It's one of the most biodiverse rivers in the USA.

Everywhere you look, you'll find nature's beauty.

Enjoy the peace and quiet but sshh! Don't tell anyone!

Everybody is looking for natural paradise
... We know where it is.

12b The power of nature

Vocabulary and reading extreme weather

1 Match these weather words with the pictures (A–F).

> flood   hurricane   lightning   snow storm
> thunderstorm   tornado

2 Discuss the questions.

1 Which parts of the world often have the extreme weather in Exercise 1?
2 Which types of extreme weather do you have in your country?
3 What time of year is typical for this kind of weather?

3 Read the article below. What type of extreme weather is it about?

4 Read the article again. Complete the diagram with the phrases (1–5).

1 sees a tornado
2 drives away from the tornado
3 drives towards the tornado
4 is lucky
5 is very unlucky

Rex Geyer   Both   Tim Samaras

1

The POWER of nature

It's early evening and Rex Geyer and his family are eating dinner. On the TV, the weather man is telling everyone to look out for tornadoes. If a tornado hit Rex's house, it would destroy it. [1] _____ Suddenly, Rex's brother rushes through the front door. 'Tornado! We have to go now!' he shouts. The whole family run to the car. [2] _____ As they drive away to safety, two cars go past in the opposite direction – straight towards the tornado.

If anyone else drove in that direction, they'd be mad. But the people in the cars are Tim Samaras and Pat Porter who follow and study tornadoes. This year they are trying to put a 'probe' into the middle of a tornado. So far they haven't been successful. If the tornado passed over the probe, it would record a lot of useful scientific data so they are keen to try. [3] _____

As Tim and Pat drive closer, the tornado gets bigger. They put a probe on the ground and, at the last moment, they drive away. [4] _____ The tornado passes right over the probe and gives Tim and Pat new and exciting scientific data. Unfortunately, for Rex and his family, the news is not so good. The following day they return to their house but it's gone. Rex says, 'There was nothing left, no trees, no house, nothing.'

5 Complete the gaps in the article (1–4) with the sentences (a–d).

   a Maybe they'll be lucky this time.
   b Tornadoes travel at over two hundred miles an hour and the biggest are a kilometre wide.
   c This time it works!
   d They leave everything except for a mobile phone.

6 Work in pairs. Complete the comments about the people in the article with your own words.

   1 I feel sorry for Rex because …
   2 I think people like Tim and Pat have to be a bit crazy because …
   3 Rex and his family were unlucky but they were also lucky because …

Grammar second conditional

7 Look at the sentences (a–b) from the article. Answer the questions (1–2).

   a Tornadoes travel at over two hundred miles an hour and the biggest are a kilometre wide.
   b If a tornado hit Rex's house, it would destroy it.

   1 Which sentence describes something real or a fact?
   2 Which describes something unreal or imagined?

8 Match the two parts of this grammar explanation.

In second conditional sentences:
1 we use *if + past simple* in the *if-clause* to
2 we use *would/wouldn't* + infinitive in the main clause to

a describe the situation.
b describe the imagined result of the situation.

> ▶ **SECOND CONDITIONAL**
>
> *If a tornado **came**, **I'd leave** immediately!*
> *I **wouldn't wait** to look at a tornado **if** it **came** towards me.*
> *What **would you do if** a tornado **came** towards your house?*
>
> For further information and practice, see page 168.

---

9 Complete the text about the Gulf Stream in the Atlantic Ocean with the correct form of the verbs. Add *would/wouldn't* where necessary.

If the climate changed …

The Gulf Stream is a current of warm water which begins in Florida and travels across the Atlantic Ocean. As a result, countries on the west coast of Europe have warmer climates.
If there ¹ _____ (be) no gulf stream, life in Europe ² _____ (change) forever and countries like Great Britain ³ _____ (become) much colder, especially in the winter. If the sea was colder, spring and summer ⁴ _____ (not / last) as long. Farmers ⁵ _____ (not / produce) certain types of food and heating costs ⁶ _____ (go up). If the Gulf Stream never ⁷ _____ (return), eventually Europe ⁸ _____ (have) another ice age. As the world's climate changes, some scientists believe this might actually happen.

10 Pronunciation *would / 'd*

  a 🔊 **2.35** Listen to a short conversation. How many times do you hear the words *would, wouldn't* or *'d*?

  b Look at the audioscript on page 174 and check your answers. Then practise reading the conversation aloud with your partner.

11 Work in pairs. Practise similar conversations to the one in Exercise 10. Use these questions to help you.

   1 Would you live in another country if you could? Where would you move to?
   2 Would you like to meet someone famous? Who? What would you ask them?
   3 Would you go into space if you had the opportunity? Which planet would you like to visit?

Speaking

12 Work in groups. Imagine you work for a special department in the government and you must plan for any future possibility. Discuss what action you would take for each of the following situations. Afterwards present your ideas to the class.

What would happen if:

- the weather became much colder?
- the level of the sea and rivers rose?
- there wasn't enough oil?

> *If the weather became much colder, we'd need more heating.*

12c Changing Greenland

Reading

1 Work in groups of four. What do you know about Greenland? Brainstorm as much information as possible.

2 Work in your groups again. The article on page 147 has four paragraphs. Each student reads one paragraph and answers the questions (1–4).

1 What recent changes are there in Greenland?
2 What are the problems and dilemmas for Greenlanders?

3 Take turns to report your answers back to the rest of the group. Write notes about the other paragraphs.

4 Read the whole article and check all your information.

Critical thinking close reading

5 Read sentences 1–7. Write answers A, B or C.

A = The sentence is true. The information is in the text.
B = The sentence is false. The information is in the text.
C = We don't know if it's true or false. The information isn't in the text.

1 Greenland has the smallest population in the world.
2 25% of the population live in the cities.
3 Sea levels around Greenland are rising.
4 There are plans to drill for oil around the coast.
5 The country has a difficult choice about the oil.
6 Farmers have longer periods to grow their crops.
7 The author thinks they might not sing the song because the winters won't be long in a hundred years' time.

Vocabulary society and economics

6 Find these adjectives and nouns in the article and match them with the nouns.

Adjective	Noun
1 economic	resources
2 social	season
3 traditional	economy
4 modern	difficulties
5 strong	development
6 natural	problems
7 growing	industry

> ▶ **WORDBUILDING adjective + noun collocations**
>
> Pairs of words with this combination are common in English.
> *The country has had* **economic difficulties**.
> *Its* **traditional industry** *is fishing.*

For further information and practice, see Workbook page 99.

7 Pronunciation word stress

🔊 **2.36** Listen to the answers in Exercise 6 and underline the stressed syllable in each word. Then listen again and repeat.

eco<u>no</u>mic <u>diff</u>iculties

Grammar *will / might*

8 Look at the highlighted verbs in these sentences from the article. Both make predictions about the future. Which verb is more certain? Which verb is less certain?

1 Oil production will begin in the next few years.
2 Drier summers might create new problems.

> ▶ **WILL and *MIGHT***
>
> | | modal | + main verb |
> |---|---|---|
> | I/you/he/she/ it/we/they | will might | change in the future. |

Speaking

9 What do you think will or might change in your country in the next ten years? Make predictions for these areas about your country.

- population and cities
- the economic situation and taxes
- social problems and difficulties
- technological developments and traditional industries
- any other issues affecting your country

10 Work in groups. Compare your predictions. How similar or different are your predictions?

There might be less countryside because ...

More people will move to the cities because ...

If more people have modern technology, there will / might ...

Changing Greenland

Greenland is the largest island in the world but has a small population of 56,000. Many of these 'Greenlanders' live close to the coastline because a large part of the country is covered with ice and glaciers. More than a quarter of all the people live in the capital, Nuuk. Since the 1960s, the country has had economic difficulties and social problems. Its traditional industry – and its biggest – is fishing but the country still imports much more than it exports. Now, however, life is about to change dramatically for many Greenlanders – and all because of the weather.

Most scientists agree that the world's climate is getting warmer and you can already see the difference in Greenland. For example, small icebergs – about the size of city buses – are floating near to the coast. They have broken off from much larger areas of ice further out in the ocean because of the change in temperature. Furthermore, the huge sheet of ice which covers Greenland is shrinking by about 75 cubic kilometres each year. If all of Greenland's ice melted, sea levels across the world would rise by 7.5 metres.

One industry that is benefiting from the melting ice is the oil industry. Nowadays, the sea around the west coast of Greenland has no ice for six months of the year. This means oil companies can explore this area. They plan to drill for oil in the next few years. Greenlanders have mixed feelings about this modern development. The country's prime minister, Kuupik Kleist, explains the dilemma: 'The Arctic people are the ones most exposed to climate change but we need a strong economy and we have to utilise the opportunities that oil could bring us … we don't have any other natural resources for the time being that hold as much potential as oil.'

Farming will also change. The growing season is longer with spring arriving earlier and longer summers. On the one hand, if the country produced more of its own food, it wouldn't need to import so much. On the other hand, some farmers are worried. They think the drier summers might create new problems. For example, last year, it was so dry, farmers produced half the normal amount of food. I spent my last night in the town of Qaqortoq with farming families at their annual celebration before the summer begins. After dinner, everyone started singing this traditional song. The song is about the importance of summer in a place where, in the past, the winters were long and the summers were short. As nature and the weather changes in Greenland, I wondered if they would still sing this song in a hundred years' time. They might not.

> **Summer, summer, how wonderful**
> **How incredibly good.**
> **The frost is gone,**
> **The frost is gone …**

dilemma (n) /dɪˈlemə/ problem or difficult choice
iceberg (n) /ˈaɪsbɜːɡ/ large piece of ice in the sea with a small part of it above the water

12d Saving the zoo

Speaking and reading

1 Do you ever visit zoos? Why? / Why not?

2 Look at the photo and read the newspaper extract below. Answer the questions.

1 Is it certain that the zoo will close?
2 What problem does the council need to solve?
3 What would happen to the animals if it closed?

'Animals will have nowhere to go if zoo closes,' says City Council

The city's zoo might close in six months' time if the city council cannot solve the problem of low visitor numbers and lack of money. The zoo's manager is also worried about the animals at the zoo. 'If the zoo closed, they couldn't go back into the wild. We'd have to find them a new home.'

Real life finding a solution

3 🎵 **2.37** Listen to a conversation between the leader of the city council and the zoo's manager. Are the sentences true (T) or false (F)?

1 If the zoo doesn't receive more money, it will close.
2 Lots of people visit the zoo.
3 The zoo manager thinks the zoo helps to save animals from extinction.
4 The zoo manager likes the suggestion about advertising.
5 The zoo manager likes the suggestion about sponsorship.

4 🎵 **2.37** Complete the sentences with these phrases. Then listen again and check.

But if we don't	I'm sorry but	that isn't	we can't
What about	What if you	why don't you	You might

1 _____ giving us more money?
2 _____ the council doesn't have any more money for the zoo.
3 _____ find a solution soon, then we'll have to close it.
4 _____ advertised the zoo more?
5 But if we don't have any money, _____ advertise.
6 Well, _____ try sponsorship. You know, ask a company to support the zoo.
7 Actually, _____ a bad idea.
8 _____ be right!

5 Match the sentences in Exercise 4 with the correct section in the box.

▶ FINDING A SOLUTION

Stating and explaining the problem The problem is that …	**Responding positively** That's a good idea.
Making suggestions We could also …	**Responding negatively** Yes, but … No, that won't work.

6 Work in groups of four. Imagine you all work for the zoo and want to save it. Roleplay a conversation and discuss your suggestions.

Student A: You are the zoo manager and will lead the meeting. At the end of the discussion, choose the three best suggestions. Turn to page 154.
Student B: Turn to page 155.
Student C: Turn to page 154.
Student D: Turn to page 155.

TALK ABOUT ▶ PROMOTING YOUR REGION ▶ PLANNING FOR EVERY POSSIBILITY ▶ PREDICTING YOUR COUNTRY'S FUTURE
▶ FINDING A SOLUTION WRITE ▶ A PRESS RELEASE

12e Good news

Writing a press release

1 The manager of a zoo has sent this press release to the local and national newspapers. Read the press release and answer the questions.

1　Why is the new tiger important?
2　How will the zoo use the new sponsorship money from the local company?
3　What special events are they planning?

Your local zoo is delighted to announce the arrival of 'Tibor', a beautiful three-year-old Sumatran tiger. Sumatran tigers are the smallest species of tiger and there are only about 400 of them left in the world. Tibor's mother was killed in the wild so the zoo is proud to offer the young tiger a home as part of its excellent animal conservation programme.

This wonderful news also comes as the zoo is pleased to inform you of a new sponsorship deal with a local food manufacturing company. The sponsorship agreement means the zoo can:

• advertise nationally.
• give a home to more animals like Tibor.
• have longer opening hours in the summer.

During the summer, the zoo is also excited about its special events:

• live music every Thursday evening;
• 'animal adventure days' for children.

More events are also planned. We look forward to seeing everyone this summer!

2 Work in pairs. Discuss the questions.

1　What is the purpose of a press release?
2　Does it include general news, a special event or both?

3 Read the press release again. Notice how press releases usually contain a lot of positive words or phrases for giving good news. Underline examples of these kinds of words or phrases.

Example:
... *is delighted to announce* ...
... *beautiful* ...

4 Writing skill using bullet points

a Notice how the writer uses bullet points in the press release. Read the information below and tick (✓) the correct information about bullets.

We use bullet points with:
• the main information you want the reader to know about.　☐
• short, simple phrases or sentences.　☐
• paragraphs.　☐
• any extra or unnecessary information.　☐

b Read part of a press release. Then rewrite the press release using bullet points.

The council is delighted to announce a new sponsorship deal with a sports manufacturer to build a stadium which can be used by the football club and local schools. It also plans to use the area for a series of free outdoor summer concerts and other cultural events. The stadium will also include restaurant facilities for use at sporting and cultural events and for private and corporate events.

5 Work in pairs. Write another press release for the zoo using this information. Include one more item of news about the zoo.

The zoo has raised $5,000 from visitors and local companies to open a new area for two baby elephants. It is also opening a new café with a shop selling zoo souvenirs (for example, T-shirts, hats).

6 Exchange your press release with another pair. Read their press release and use these questions to check their press release.

• Does the press release include words and expressions for giving good news?
• Does it use bullet points effectively?

12f Cambodia Animal Rescue

Unfortunately, there is one
thing many of these animals
have in common ...

Before you watch

1 You are going to watch a video about an animal rescue centre in Cambodia. Work in pairs. Look at the photos and discuss the questions.

1 What kinds of animals can you see in the photo?
2 What do they 'have in common'?
3 How do you think the rescue centre helps them?

While you watch

2 Watch the video and check your answers from Exercise 1.

3 Watch the video again. Put the animals in the order you first see them on the video.

a scorpions
b a tiger
c an elephant
d crested eagles
e a bear
f crocodiles
g monkeys
h a gibbon

4 Watch the first part of the video (to 02.09) and answer the questions.

1 What do the letters MU stand for?

2 What does the MU do?

3 Does the government of Cambodia support the work of the MU?

4 What does the American group Wild Aid do?

5 Where did the little gibbon live before the rescue centre?

6 Which organisation sponsors Mimi?

7 Why did the family take Mimi to the rescue centre?

5 Complete the extract about poaching. Use words from the below to help you. Then watch the second part of the video (02.09 to the end) and check your answers.

^{1}_____ can make a lot of money by selling a tiger's body parts ^{2}_____ . In some Asian countries, certain parts of the tiger are ground into ^{3}_____ . This is processed and sold as an expensive traditional ^{4}_____ . People think that taking the product will ^{5}_____ their health.

After you watch

6 Roleplay talking about a plan

Work in pairs.

Student A: You want to go and work at the Animal Rescue Centre in Cambodia. Look at the information below and make notes.

- You plan to go for a year.
- You want to find out more about poaching in Cambodia.
- You want to help the animals at the rescue centre because you love animals.
- You have a particular interest in tigers and know they help a lot of these animals.

Student B: A friend of yours wants to go and work at the Animal Rescue Centre in Cambodia. Ask questions to find out why he/she wants to go and what he/she plans to do there.

Act out the conversation. Then change roles and repeat the conversation. For the second conversation, Student B should choose a different animal and reasons.

7 According to the narrator, what is 'the bigger problem'? Why is it still a problem?

8 Work in pairs. Discuss these questions.

1 How do you feel when you see the animals in the video?
2 Does animal poaching exist in your country? What animals do poachers catch? Why?
3 What can we do to protect animals from poaching?

---

grind (past tense: ground) (v) /graɪnd/ break something into small pieces of powder, usually in a machine
handle (v) /'hændl/ look after or control something or somebody
illegally (adv) /ɪ'liːgəli/ in a way not allowed by the law
improve (v) /ɪm'pruːv/ make better
medicine (n) /'medsɪn/ what you take to get better when you are ill
poacher (n) /'pəʊtʃə/ a person who catches or kills animals illegally
poaching (n) /'pəʊtʃɪŋ/ the activity of catching or killing animals illegally
powder (n) /'paʊdə/ a very fine, dry substance

release (v) /rɪ'liːs/ set free
rescue (v) /'reskjuː/ take someone or something out of a dangerous situation
sponsor (v) /'spɒnsə/ support an organisation by giving them money and help such as training, etc., often in return for publicity
support (v) /sʊ'pɔːt/ help
survive (v) /sə'vaɪv/ continue to live after an accident or dangerous event
victim (n) /'vɪktɪm/ a person or thing that has been affected by a dangerous event
the wild (n) /waɪld/ the natural environment

UNIT 12 REVIEW

Grammar

1 Complete the sentences with these pairs of words.

> anyone + anywhere   everyone + anything
> nobody + everybody   nowhere + everywhere
> someone + somewhere   something + nothing

1 _____ is as beautiful as this part of the country. _____ you look there are trees and plants.
2 _____ told me there's a snake _____ in the grass so be careful.
3 Has _____ seen Michelle? I can't find her _____.
4 _____ is hungry. Is there _____ in the fridge?
5 I left a message but _____ called me back. Is _____ on holiday?
6 I'd like _____ special to eat but _____ on the menu looks very interesting.

2 Complete the second conditional sentences with the correct form of the verbs.

1 If it was hotter, we _____ (go) to the beach.
2 The grass would be much greener if it _____ (rain).
3 Hurricanes would be more common if you _____ (live) in the southern USA.
4 We _____ (not / need) air conditioning if we moved north to a colder climate.
5 They wouldn't eat my cooking if they _____ (not / like) it!

3 Complete these sentences for you. Then compare your sentences with a partner.

1 If I had a million dollars, I'd …
2 If I could visit anywhere in the world, I'd go to …
3 If I lived in another country, I'd live in …

> **I CAN**
> talk about unreal and imagined situations ☐

Vocabulary

4 Match these words with the correct groups.

> in the sky   mammals   plants   reptiles
> types of storms

1 _____ : tree, grass, flower
2 _____ : cow, horse, human
3 _____ : dust, ice, snow
4 _____ : snake, turtle, crocodile
5 _____ : lightning, rain, sun

5 Work in pairs. Look at the photo. What does it show? How do you think the photographer took it?

> **I CAN**
> talk about animals and nature ☐

Real life

6 Match the two halves of the sentences.

1 What about
2 Why don't we
3 We won't get any visitors if we
4 The problem is that
5 If we don't advertise, we

a we don't advertise.
b advertising the zoo?
c advertise the zoo?
d don't advertise.
e won't get any visitors.

7 Work in pairs. Discuss these problems and make suggestions to solve the problems.

- unemployment in your country
- too much traffic on the roads
- cities are growing so there is less countryside for animals and nature

> **I CAN**
> discuss problems and make suggestions for solving them ☐

Speaking

8 Imagine you are the leader of your country. Write down three changes you would make.

If I was the leader of my country, I'd …

9 Make a short speech to your class about your plans for change. Can you convince the class that you would make a great leader?

UNIT 5a Exercise 10, page 59

Student A

Ask the caller about his/her views on recycling and what we need to do about the problem. It's your job to ask extra questions and argue with the caller about his/her views. Before you begin, prepare some of your questions for the caller. You can use some of the questions and ideas from the audioscript on page 171.

UNIT 5d Exercise 6, page 64

Student A

Conversation 1

You ordered some clothes online. You received an email from the company. The clothes are not in stock. Telephone the customer service helpline.

- Say why you are calling.
- Your order number is EI3304A.
- Spell your surname.
- Find out how long you have to wait for the clothes.
- Ask for a refund. The price was $149.50.

Conversation 2

You are a customer service assistant for a book supplier. Answer the telephone.

- Ask for the customer's order number and the title of the book.
- The book isn't in stock. You don't know when the book will arrive.
- Offer the caller a second-hand copy of the same book. It's £3.50.

UNIT 8a Exercise 1, page 94

UNIT 9d Exercise 5, page 112

Student A

You work for a job recruitment agency which helps people find a new job. Describe the process to someone who is looking for a new job.

- fill in an application form
- attend an interview with the recruitment agency
- match your skills to different jobs
- choose possible jobs
- contact employers
- start new job!

UNIT 9e Exercise 3b, page 113

1   DOB = date of birth
    No. = number
    e.g. = for example
    etc. = et cetera
2   Mr = used before the name of any man
    Mrs = used before the name of a married woman
    Ms = used before the name of a woman and we don't know if she is married or single
    Dr = Doctor
    Prof = Professor
    BA = Bachelor of Arts
    BSc = Bachelor of Science
    MBA = Master of Business Administration
    PhD = Doctor of philosophy (a qualification given when you become a doctor on your subject, not necessarily philosophy)
3   Form B: It says 'For office use only' at the bottom.
4   Form B: It says 'Please use capital letters' at the top.

Braille
A way for blind people to read by touching a series of dots on paper (invented in 1825 by Louis Braille).

Electric light bulb
Invented by Thomas Edison in the nineteenth century to provide brighter light for long periods of time using electricity.

Microwave oven
An oven which cooks food much faster than traditional ovens by using microwave radiation.

Post-it note
A piece of paper which can be stuck anywhere and reused. It solved the problem of losing your notes!

Telescope
It solved the problem of looking at objects a long distance away, for example, at objects in space.

UNIT 5a Exercise 10, page 59

Student B

Speak to the radio presenter. Explain your views about recycling and what we need to do about the problem in the future. Before you begin, prepare some of your comments and opinions. You can use some of the expressions and ideas from the audioscript on page 171.

UNIT 9d Exercise 5, page 112

Student B

You are looking for a job with a recruitment agency. Ask about the process of finding a job.

Examples:
How do I start looking for a job?
Do I need to fill in a form / attend an interview?
Then what happens?

UNIT 10d Exercise 7, page 124

Student A

1 You are the tourist. You want to ask about the missing information (1–3) and check some information (4) in this tour. Prepare indirect questions using these words.

1 I'd like to know how old …
2 I was wondering how often …
3 Do you know when …
4 Can you tell me if …

History
The Caves of Lascaux are in the Dordogne region of France. The paintings on the cave walls are over (1) _____ years old.

Tour information
Bus: The tour bus leaves your hotel (2) _____ .
Departure time: (3) _____ a.m. to 5 p.m.
Tour price: 100 euros (includes all entrance fees and lunch). Each tour is limited to 30 visitors only.

On some tours, there is also a visit to a beautiful local town. Check with your tour guide for details (4).

2 Now ask your questions about the tour of the Caves of Lascaux and complete the missing information.

3 You are the person at tourist information. Answer the tourist's questions about this tour.

Information for visitors
Underground: Metro A line
Bus: 714, 118
Parking is available 1 kilometre from the entrance.
Opening times: 9 a.m. to 1 p.m. and 2 to 5 p.m. every day except Wednesday
Tickets: Adults: 8 euros   Children: 5 euros
Time: 40 minutes

Note to visitors
This tour involves a lot of walking. Basic fitness is required.

UNIT 12d Exercise 6, page 148

Student A

You are the zoo manager and will lead the meeting. Here are two possible suggestions. You can also make more suggestions.

• Ask companies to sponsor different animals and they put their name near the animal.
• Hold an open day where everyone in the city can visit the zoo for free to learn more about their zoo.

When you are ready to begin the meeting, state and explain the problem and then discuss each suggestion. Start your meeting by saying: *Hello, everyone and thank you for coming. Today we are going to discuss the zoo. The problem is that …*

UNIT 12d Exercise 6, page 148

Student C

Here are two possible suggestions. You can also make more suggestions.

• Start a zoo shop which sells T-shirts, posters, hats, etc.
• Invite newspaper and TV journalists to a special day where you explain the importance of the zoo and its conservation work.

UNIT 5d Exercise 6, page 64

Student B

Conversation 1

You are a customer service assistant for a clothing company supplier. Answer the telephone.

- Ask for the customer's order number and his/her surname.
- The clothes aren't in stock but they will be in two weeks.
- Offer some different clothes at the same price.

Conversation 2

You ordered a book online called *Learn Spanish in One Week*. You received an email from the company. The book is not in stock. Telephone the customer service helpline.

- Say why you are calling.
- Your order number is AZE880.
- Find out how long you have to wait for the book.
- Ask for the price of the second-hand copy.
- Buy the second-hand book.

UNIT 10d Exercise 7, page 124

Student B

1 You are the tourist. You want to ask about the missing information (1–3) and check some information (4) in this tour. Prepare indirect questions using these words.

1 I'd like to know which …
2 I was wondering which day …
3 Do you know how much …
4 Can you tell me if …

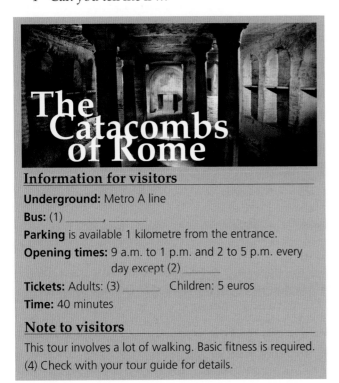

The Catacombs of Rome

Information for visitors

Underground: Metro A line
Bus: (1) _____, _____
Parking is available 1 kilometre from the entrance.
Opening times: 9 a.m. to 1 p.m. and 2 to 5 p.m. every day except (2) _____
Tickets: Adults: (3) _____   Children: 5 euros
Time: 40 minutes

Note to visitors

This tour involves a lot of walking. Basic fitness is required. (4) Check with your tour guide for details.

2 You are the person at tourist information. Answer your partner's questions about this tour.

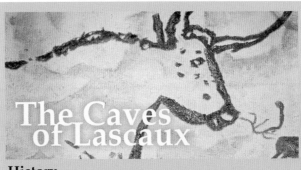

The Caves of Lascaux

History

The Caves of Lascaux are in the Dordogne region of France. The paintings on the cave walls are over 17,000 years old.

Tour information

Bus: The tour bus leaves your hotel every day.
Departure time: 9 a.m. to 5 p.m.
Tour price: 100 euros (includes all entrance fees and lunch). Each tour is limited to 30 visitors only.

On some tours, there is also a visit to a beautiful local town.

3 Now you are the tourist. Ask your questions about the Catacombs of Rome in Exercise 1 and complete the missing information.

UNIT 12d Exercise 6, page 148

Student B

Here are two possible suggestions. You can also make more suggestions.

- Offer special tickets with discounts such as a 'family ticket' or cheaper prices for children.
- Ask people to buy an animal but it lives at the zoo.

UNIT 12d Exercise 6, page 148

Student D

Here are two possible suggestions. You can also make more suggestions.

- Contact other zoos and exchange animals so people will come back to look at different animals.
- Have a parade with costumes and food through the city centre with some of the animals.

UNIT 1
Present simple and adverbs of frequency
Form

Affirmative	Negative	Interrogative
I/you/we/they work	I/you/we/they **don't** work	**do** I/you/we/they work?
he/she/it **works**	he/she/it **doesn't** work	**does** he/she/it work?

Use
We use the present simple to talk about:
- habits and routines. *I **eat** an apple every day.*
- things that are always true. *Lions **eat** meat.*

We often use adverbs of frequency (*always, usually, often, sometimes, rarely, never*) and expressions of frequency (*once a week, on Fridays, at the weekend, in the summer, every Saturday*) with the present simple to talk about how often we do something.

Adverbs of frequency usually go before the main verb or after the verb *to be*.
*I **sometimes** watch football on TV.*
*I am **always** very happy.*

Expressions of frequency usually go at the beginning or end of a sentence.
***At the weekend** they visit their grandparents.*
*They visit their grandparents **at the weekend**.*

Practice
1 Complete the sentences with the present simple form of the verbs and the adverbs / expressions of frequency.

1 I ___*walk*___ (walk) into town every Saturday.
2 Emily _____ (ride / often) her bike to work in summer.
3 When _____ he _____ (be / usually) at home?
4 I _____ (not be / often) in the office on Mondays.
5 He _____ (do / never) exercise at the weekend.
6 _____ the doctor _____ (work / every weekend)?

Present continuous
Form
We form the present continuous with the present simple of the verb *to be* plus the *-ing* form of the verb.

Affirmative	Negative	Interrogative
I am / you are / he is / she is / it is / we are / they **are washing**	I am not / you are not / he is not / she is not / it is not / we are not / they **are not washing**	Am I / are you / is he / is she / is it / are we / are they **washing**?

Use
We use the present continuous to talk about:
- things happening now. *He's **watching** the news on TV at the moment.*
- things happening around now, but not necessarily at the moment. *Vicky's **travelling** to several African countries this year.*
- current trends and changing situations. *Fewer people **are buying** cars this year.*

We don't usually use stative verbs (*be, have, like, love, hate, want*) in the present continuous.

Notes
Notice the spelling rules for the *-ing* form:
- for most verbs, add *-ing* (*walk → walk**ing**, play → play**ing**, read → read**ing***).
- for verbs ending in a consonant + vowel + consonant, double the last letter of the verb and add *-ing* (*sit → si**tt**ing, run → ru**nn**ing*).
- for verbs ending in *-e*, delete the final *e* and add *-ing* (*make → making, write → writing*).

Practice
2 Complete the sentences. Use the present continuous and present simple form of the verbs.

~~cook~~	not cycle	do	go	play	prepare

1 Carl usually ___*cooks*___ on Wednesday.
2 The boys often _____ hiking in the holidays.
3 _____ David _____ tennis at the moment?
4 She _____ to work today – it's raining.
5 Please wait. The pharmacist _____ the medicine.
6 We always _____ gardening at the weekend.

UNIT 2
Verb + *-ing* forms
Form
We add *-ing* to the main verb. The spelling rules are the same as for the present continuous.

verb	*-ing* form
walk	walking
swim	swimming
give	giving

Use
We use the verb + *-ing* form:
- as the subject of the sentence. The *-ing* form is often a noun. ***Eating** a lot of fruit is important.*
- after verbs such as *like, love, enjoy, prefer, don't like, hate, can't stand, (not) mind* as an object. *I love **walking** in the mountains.*
- after a preposition. *I'm very good at **playing** tennis.*

Practice

1 Complete the sentences with the *-ing* form of these verbs.

> ~~cycle~~   eat   go   shop   sit   visit   watch   write

1 I'm listening to a radio programme about _cycling_.
2 Do you enjoy _____ sport on TV?
3 _____ at home all day is boring!
4 We don't like _____ this football stadium.
5 Jenny is very good at _____ sports reports.
6 _____ for new football boots is always difficult.
7 He hates _____ to matches when his team loses.
8 _____ a lot before a game is bad for you.

like + -ing / 'd like to

Form
like + -ing

Affirmative	Negative	Interrogative
I/you/we/they **like watching** old films.	I/you/we/they **don't like watching** old films.	**Do** I/you/we/they **like watching** old films?
He/she/it **likes playing** in the park.	He/she/it **doesn't like playing** in the park.	**Does** he/she/it **like playing** in the park?

'd like to (= would like to)

Affirmative	Negative	Interrogative
I**'d**/you**'d**/he**'d**/she**'d**/it**'d**/we**'d**/they**'d like to** go there tomorrow.	I/you/he/she/it/we**'d**/they **wouldn't like to** go there tomorrow.	**Would** I/you/he/she/it/we/they **like to** go there tomorrow?

Use
like + -ing
We use *like + -ing* to talk about a general feeling which is true now.
*Richard **likes skiing** a lot.*
*Ella **doesn't like listening** to rap music.*

'd like to (= would like to)
We use *'d like to* to talk about a future ambition.
*I**'d like to visit** Kenya next year.*
*She **wouldn't like to work** in an office when she leaves school.*

Practice

2 Complete the sentences with *like + -ing* or *'d like to* and the verbs.

1 Andy _likes playing_ (like / play) football every Saturday.
2 The boys _____ (like / learn) how to swim next year.
3 _____ Mike _____ (like / drive) his new car?

4 I _____ (not like / compete) in this competition every week!
5 _____ you _____ (like / sit) here, sir?
6 Jo _____ (not like / travel) round the world next year.
7 My father _____ (like / cook) lunch for all the family every Sunday.
8 She _____ (like / watch) the match with us next week.

Modal verbs for rules
Form

I/you/he/she/it/we/they **must** wear goggles.	I/you/he/she/it/we/they **can** play here.	I/you/he/she/it/we/they **have to** hit the ball.
I/you/he/she/it/we/they **mustn't** (= must not) wear goggles.	I/you/he/she/it/we/they **can't** (= cannot) play here.	I/you/he/she/it/we/they **don't have to** hit the ball.

Notes
There are two important differences between *must* and *can* and regular verbs in the present simple:
* There is no third person *-s* with modal verbs.
  *She **must** go. I **can** stay.*
* There is no auxiliary *do* with modal verbs.
  *I **mustn't** lose. He **can't** play.*

Have to is a regular verb. *I **have to** go. He **has to** help. I **don't have to** play. She **doesn't have to** compete.*

Use
We use different modal verbs to talk about rules.
* When something is necessary and an obligation, we use *must, have to* and *mustn't*. *You **must** be home at eleven o'clock. You **have to** finish your homework tonight. He **mustn't** leave the house.*
* When something is allowed according to the rules, we use *can. Yes, you **can** go to the cinema on Friday.*
* When something is not necessary (but allowed), we use *don't have to. You **don't have to** wear a suit at the meeting.*
* When something is not allowed, we use *mustn't* and *can't. She **mustn't** tell anybody. He **can't** play football tomorrow.*

Practice

3 Put the words in the correct order.

1 get up he must tomorrow early
  He must get up early tomorrow.
2 competition finish at must ten o'clock the
  _____
3 send my have today application I to
  _____
4 tomorrow to don't they have to go work
  _____
5 argue referee team with the the can't
  _____

6 five o'clock to game have doesn't finish at the

7 for wear Tim can clothes casual the game

8 sports kit they forget their mustn't

UNIT 3
Comparatives and superlatives
Form

Adjective	Comparative	Superlative
▶ REGULAR		
new	newer	newest
hot	hotter	hottest
nice	nicer	nicest
easy	easier	easiest
interesting	more interesting	most interesting
▶ IRREGULAR		
good	better	best
bad	worse	worst

We add -er to regular short adjectives to form the comparative and we add -est to regular short adjectives to form the superlative:
new → newer → newest

We add *more* and *most* to form the comparative and superlative forms with longer adjectives:
interesting → more interesting → most interesting

Notice the spelling rules for comparative and superlative adjectives:
- for regular short adjectives, add -er / -est:
  long → longer → longest
- for adjectives ending in -e, add -r / -st:
  large → larger → largest
- for adjectives ending in -y (after a consonant), change the -y to -i: *happy → happier → happiest*
- for adjectives ending in consonant–vowel–consonant, double the final consonant:
  big → bigger → biggest; hot → hotter → hottest

We use *than* after a comparative adjective.
My bicycle is newer than yours.

We usually use *the* before a superlative adjective.
It's the quickest way to get to the station.

We use *much* to add emphasis to a comparative adjective.
Petrol cars are much more expensive than electric cars.

Use
We use comparative adjectives to compare two things.
Cars are faster than buses.

We use superlative adjectives to compare three or more things.
Blues whales are the biggest animals in the world.

Practice
1 Write sentences. Use the comparative (C) and superlative (S) forms.

1 India / Norway / hot (C)
  India is hotter than Norway.
2 cars / bikes / dangerous (C)
3 James / friendly / person / in our class (S)
4 Helena / good athlete / in the country (S)
5 cheetahs / tigers / fast (C)
6 Naomi / happy / person / in the office (S)
7 skiing / exciting sport / in the world (S)
8 sports cars / family cars / difficult to drive (C)

as ... as
Form

Affirmative	Negative	Interrogative
An elephant is **as heavy as** a car.	A bus **isn't** (is not) **as comfortable as** a car.	Is a horse **as strong as** an elephant?

Use
We use *as* + adjective + *as* to compare two things and say they are the same or equal.
*Robbie is **as** tall **as** his brother.*

We use *not as* + adjective + *as* to compare two things and say they are different or not equal.
*Paul is **not as** clever **as** Anna.*

Practice
2 Write comparative sentences and questions using *as ... as* (+) and *(not) as ... as* (–).

1 Rosa / old / Maria (+)
  Rosa is as old as Maria.
2 Alaska / cold / Canada (+)
3 cars / cheap / bicycles (–)
4 horse riding / healthy / running (?)
5 buses / quiet / trams (–)
6 books / exciting / films (?)
7 our car / clean / an electric car (+)
8 Russia / hot / Brazil (?)

UNIT 4
Past simple
Form

Affirmative	Negative	Interrogative
▶ **REGULAR**		
I/you/he/she/it/we/they **walked** all day.	I/you/he/she/it/we/they **didn't walk** all day.	**Did** I/you/he/she/it/we/they **walk** all day?
▶ **IRREGULAR**		
I/you/he/she/it/we/they **said**	I/you/he/she/it/we/they **didn't say**	**Did** I/you/he/she/it/we/they **say**?
		Short answers
		Yes, I/you/he/she/it/we/they **did**.
		No, I/you/he/she/it/we/they **didn't**.

We add -ed to regular verbs to form the past simple:
*work → work**ed**, walk → walk**ed**, play → play**ed***.

Notice the spelling rules for other regular verbs:
- for verbs ending in -e, we add -d: *die → die**d***
- for verbs ending in -y, we change the -y to i and add -ed: *try → tr**ied**, cry → cr**ied**, study → stud**ied***
- for verbs ending in vowel + consonant (not -w, -x or -y), we double the consonant: *stop → sto**pp**ed*

Some verbs have an irregular affirmative form in the past simple:
be → was / were, do → did, go → went, drive → drove, know → knew, take → took

We use the auxiliary verb *did / didn't* to form negatives and questions.
*Kirsten **didn't** go on the adventure.*
***Did** you live in Peru?*

We also use *did / didn't* to form short answers.
*Did you live in Peru? Yes, I **did**.*
*Did Kirsten go on the adventure? No, she **didn't**.*

Use

We use the past simple to talk about completed actions and events in the past. We often use a time phrase (*yesterday, last week, ten years ago*) with the past simple.
*I visited Paris **in January**.*
*They didn't see his new film **last night**.*

Practice

1 Write questions and answers using the past simple.

1 Where / he / go? go / Spain
Where did he go? He went to Spain.

2 Where / she / live? live / Rome

3 What / they / do? drive / Norway

4 When / Kerry / travel / the USA? travel / the USA / last year

5 Where / you / find / it? find / it / in South Africa

6 When / they / live / Canada? live / Canada / in 2010

Past continuous
Form

We form the past continuous with the past simple of the verb *to be* plus the *-ing* form of the verb.

Affirmative	Negative	Interrogative
I/he/she/it/ **was working** last week.	I/he/she/it/**wasn't working** last week.	**Was** I/he/she/it/**working** last week?
You/we/they **were working** last week.	You/we/they **weren't working** last week.	**Were** you/we/they **working** last week?

Use

We use the past continuous to:
- describe actions and situations in progress at a particular time in the past. *Paul **was watching** TV. Katy **was reading** a book.*
- talk about the background to a story. *The sun **was shining** and the birds **were singing**.*

We often use the past continuous with the past simple to talk about two actions that happened at the same time in the past. We can join the tenses with the words *when* or *while*.
*Tania was waiting at the station **when** the rest of the climbing team arrived. **While** the team were walking to the train, she ran to meet them.*
Remember, we don't usually use stative verbs (e.g. *be, like, believe, understand*) in the continuous form.

Practice

2 Complete the sentences with the past simple or the past continuous form of the verbs.

1 Jo ___*was driving*___ (drive) and Katya ___*was reading*___ (read) the map.
2 She _____ (sleep) when a noise _____ (wake) her up.
3 The team leader _____ (shout) and the wind _____ (blow).
4 While the boys _____ (make) a fire, it _____ (start) to rain.
5 Liz _____ (cook) supper and the others _____ (talk) about the expedition.
6 As they _____ (walk) in the mountains, the weather _____ (get) worse.
7 The rescue team _____ (arrive) while we _____ (decide) where to go.
8 While I _____ (swim), I _____ (see) a group of dolphins.

UNIT 5
Countable and uncountable nouns
Form and use
Some nouns are **countable**. These are nouns you can count and they have both a singular and a plural form. We use them with an indefinite article (*a/an*) and numbers.
*There is **a bag** on the table.*
*There are **two bags** on the table.*

Some nouns are **uncountable**. These are nouns you cannot count. They are singular and have no plural form. We use them with the definite article or no article. You cannot use them with *a/an* or numbers: *water (two waters), rubbish (two rubbishes).*
*We drink **water** eat every day.*
*The **water** is in the jug.*

Quantifiers
Form

Affirmative	Negative	Interrogative
▶ COUNTABLE NOUNS		
I've got **some** books.	I haven't got **any** books.	Are there **any** books?
There are **a lot of** books.	There aren't **many** books.	How **many** books have you got?
She's got **a few** books.		
▶ UNCOUNTABLE NOUNS		
I've got **some** water.	I haven't got **any** water.	Have you got **any** water?
There is **a lot of** water.	There isn't **much** water.	How **much** water have you got?
They've got **a little** water.		

Use
We use quantifiers with countable and uncountable nouns to talk about quantity.

Countable nouns
We use *some*, *a lot of* and *a few* in affirmative sentences.
*I've got **some** newspapers.*
*We've got **a lot of** bottles.*
*There are **a few** cans.*

We use *any* or *many* in negative sentences or questions.
*I haven't got **any** books.*
*There aren't **many** boxes.*
*Have you got **any** bags?*
*How **many** photos did you take?*

Uncountable nouns
We use *some*, *a lot of* and *a little* in affirmative sentences.
*I've got **some** water.*
*They've got **a lot of** food.*
*There is **a little** milk.*

We use *any* or *much* in negative sentences or questions.
*I haven't got **any** information.*
*There isn't **much** bread.*
*Have you got **any** rubbish?*
*How **much** water is there?*

Note: *a lot of = lots of* (there is no difference in meaning or use)

Practice
1 Choose the correct option.

1 There's *any* / *some* pollution in the river.
2 There isn't *much* / *many* food on the table.
3 Are there *much* / *any* plastic bags in the park?
4 I've got *a lot of* / *a few* drinking water.
5 How *any* / *many* recycling bins are there here?
6 Do you throw away *many* / *much* plastic?
7 He recycles *much* / *a little* rubbish.
8 How *much* / *many* air pollution is there?

Definite article (*the*) or no article
Form and use
We use the definite article (*the*):
- with something or someone you mentioned before. *Have they done a survey? Yes, They finished **the** survey last week.*
- when it is part of the name of something. ***The** USA introduced 'car pool' lanes.*
- with superlative phrases. *Consumers spend **the** most money on electronic equipment.*

We use no article:
- with most countries. *He lives in Canada and I live in Spain.*
- to talk about people and things in a general way. *People are trying to recycle more rubbish.*
- with certain expressions. *I don't work **at night**.*

Practice
2 Choose the correct option. Choose Ø for no article.

1 There's a black dog in my garden. It's *the* / Ø dog from next door!
2 Have you visited any recycling plants in *the* / Ø Germany?
3 He's *the* / Ø greenest person I know.
4 There were *the* / Ø children everywhere at the festival.
5 What time do you go to *the* / Ø work?
6 I'm going to a meeting about the environment in *the* / Ø Netherlands.
7 He is staying in London on *the* / Ø business.
8 How much did *the* / Ø computer cost?

UNIT 6
Verb patterns with *to* + infinitive
Form

We use *to* + infinitive after several structures. The form of the verb is always the same.

They intend/plan	**to go** to South America.
It's difficult	**to learn** Chinese.
She worked hard	**to buy** a new car.

Use

1 verb + *to* + infinitive

After certain verbs we use the *to* + infinitive form of another verb. This is often to talk about hopes, intentions and decisions.
*He decided **to stop** work.*
*She agreed **to travel** round the world.*
Common verbs which are followed by the *to* + infinitive form are: *intend, plan, want, hope, 'd like, decide, agree, refuse, promise.*
We don't use *to* + infinitive after modal verbs.
*She can't **play** tennis. We will **stay** here.*

2 adjective + *to* + infinitive

We use *to* + infinitive after certain adjectives, often to express a feeling about something.
*It's **fun to play** a musical instrument.*
*It's **difficult to live** on $50 a day.*

3 infinitive of purpose

We can use *to* + infinitive to explain the purpose of the main verb or an action (= in order to do something).
*Marco moved to New York **to go** to college.*
*They visited Greece **to learn** about Ancient Greece.*

Practice

1 Put the words in the correct order.

1 planning summer go diving to this we're
  We're planning to go diving this summer.

2 would like Australia Emma and Pip visit to

3 medicine get job she to studied good a

4 have pension to it's important a

5 wants his my brother leave job to

6 isn't to your save it easy money

7 promised email Brenda every to week

8 fun holiday a it's plan to

Future forms: *going to, will* and present continuous
Form
1 *going to*

Affirmative	Negative	Interrogative
I'm/you're/he's/she's/it's/we're/they're going to come to the party.	I'm not / you aren't / he isn't / she isn't / it isn't / we aren't / they aren't going to come to the party.	Am I / are you / is he / Is she / is it / are we / are they going to come to the party?

2 *will*

Affirmative	Negative	Interrogative
I/you/he/she/it/we/they 'll (will) go home later.	I/you/he/she/it/we/they won't (will not) go home later.	Will I/you/he/she/it/we/they go home later?

3 Present continuous

For the present continuous form see page 156.

Use
1 *going to*

We use *going to* + infinitive to talk about a plan or a future intention.
I'm going to make a costume.
She isn't going to take part in the celebrations.

2 *will* ('*ll*)

We use *will* to talk about a decision which is made during the conversation.
Tim: Oh no! There isn't any sugar left.
Sue: Don't worry. I'll buy some when I go into town.

3 Present continuous for future

We use the present continuous to talk about an arrangement with other people at a certain time in the future.
I'm leaving for the party at five o'clock.
We're moving house next month.
We usually use the present continuous, not *going to*, with the verbs *go* and *come*.
I'm going to the parade later.
He's coming to the festival with us.

Practice

2 Choose the correct option (a–c).

1 We ____ to Costa Rica on holiday next year.
   ⓐ are going   b are going to go   c will go
2 I've decided to do an evening class. I ____ Italian.
   a am studying   b am going to study
   c will study
3 Alex: I've left my money at home.
   Thomas: Never mind. I ____ the tickets.
   a am buying   b am going to buy   c 'll buy
4 What ____ next weekend?
   a are you doing   b are you going to do
   c will you do
5 I'm so excited! We ____ for Athens in a week!
   a are leaving   b are going to leave
   c will leave

6 Sam _____ in London next year.
  a 's working b 's going to work
  c 'll work
7 I don't know when it starts. I _____ out now.
  a am finding b am going to find
  c will find
8 _____ to stay with you?
  a Is he coming b Is he going to come
  c Will he come

UNIT 7
Prepositions of place and movement
Form
Prepositions of place
*The printer is **on** the desk.*
*The meeting room is **on** the first floor.*
*The office is **next to** the bank.*
*The meeting is **at** the conference centre.*

Common prepositions of place are:

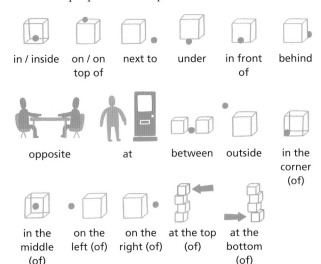

in / inside   on / on top of   next to   under   in front of   behind

opposite   at   between   outside   in the corner (of)

in the middle (of)   on the left (of)   on the right (of)   at the top (of)   at the bottom (of)

Prepositions of movement
*He walked **up** the stairs.*
*Claire went **through** the door.*
*The man got **into** the taxi.*

Common prepositions of movement are: *up, down, to, in, into, on, onto, over, under, across, along, round, around, through.*

Use
We use prepositions of place to describe where people and things are.
*Where's the coffee? It's **in** the cupboard.*
*Adrian is standing **in front of** the photocopier.*

We use prepositions of movement to talk about the direction someone or something moves. Prepositions of movement follow a verb of movement.
*Jack drove **along** the road.*
*The visitors are going **around** the factory.*
Common verbs of movement are: *go, climb, come, run* and *walk.*

Practice
1 Complete the text with these prepositions.

> along   ~~at~~   in   front   next   on   opposite
> through   up

Instructions for arrival
When you arrive [1] _____at_____ the office, go
[2] _____ the front door. Reception will be in
[3] _____ of you. All the meeting rooms are
[4] _____ the second floor. There isn't a lift, so go
[5] _____ the stairs. Your meeting is [6] _____
room 306. Coffee will be on the table, [7] _____
to the window. If you need the bathroom, walk
[8] _____ the corridor – it's [9] _____ the
photocopier.

Present perfect simple
Form
We form the present perfect simple with the present simple of the verb *to have* plus the past participle.

Affirmative	Negative	Interrogative
I/you/we/they **have found** the report.	I/you/we/they **haven't found** the report.	**Have** I/you/we/they **found** the report?
He/she/it **has found** the report.	He/she/it **hasn't found** the report.	**Has** he/she/it **found** the report?
		Short answers
		Yes, I/you/we/they **have.** **Yes,** he/she/it **has.** **No,** I/you/we/they **haven't.** **No,** he/she/it **hasn't.**

We add *-ed* to regular verbs to form the past participle: *work → work**ed**, walk → walk**ed**, play → play**ed**.*

The spelling rules for other regular verbs are the same as for the past simple tense (see page 159).

Many verbs have irregular past participles:
buy → bought, do → done, find → found, see → seen, take → taken, teach → taught

The verb *go* has two past participle forms: *been* and *gone*
*I've **been** to work today. (And now I'm back.)*
*He's **gone** to work today. (He isn't back yet.)*

We use the auxiliary verb *have/has* and *haven't/hasn't* to form negatives and questions.
*I **haven't** bought a farm.*
***Has** she seen her colleague this week?*

We also use *have/has* and *haven't/hasn't* to form short answers.
*Have you lived in Canada? Yes, I **have**.*

Use

We use the present perfect simple to talk about:
- an action that happened sometime in the past but we don't know the exact time. *I've worked in several banks in London.*
- an action that started in the past and is still true today. *Amy has lived in Paris since Christmas.* (She still lives in Paris.) *Mark hasn't found the watch he lost.* (The watch is still lost.)

When we use the present perfect simple we often do not say when the action happened.
I've been to Rome. (We do not say when.)

We use the past simple to describe a finished action at a definite time in the past. When we use the past simple, we often say when something happened.
I went to Rome last year.
We often use the present perfect simple with *for* and *since*. We use *for* to talk about the duration of a present situation, for example, *for 30 minutes, for two months.*
My sister has lived in London for six months.
We use *since* to show the starting point of a present situation, for example, *since 2.00 p.m., since Friday, since 2011.*
My sister has lived in London since September.

Practice

2 Complete the sentences with the present perfect simple form of the verbs.

1 John ___*has known*___ (know) his boss for about four months.
2 My sister _____ (work) for lots of different businesses.
3 We _____ (see) this training film three times before.
4 _____ your father _____ (visit) the factory in Madrid yet?
5 She _____ (not eat) Indian food before.
6 They _____ (not be) in the office since eight o'clock.
7 _____ you _____ (copy) the report?
8 Bob and Louise _____ (buy) a new car.

3 Complete the text with the present perfect simple or the past simple form of the verbs.

I [1] ___*have been*___ (be) a photographer for over 20 years, so I know what I'm doing. I [2] _____ (change) jobs ten times and I [3] _____ (work) in about fifteen different countries so I [4] _____ (often / live) abroad. My first job [5] _____ (be) as an assistant photographer for a magazine. I [6] _____ (take) photos for other people and I [7] _____ (develop) the pictures. Then I [8] _____ (start) working on a project about polar bears. The team [9] _____ (spend) many months on the sea ice of the Arctic and we [10] _____ (search) for the bears' homes. Eventually we [11] _____ (find) where the bears lived. Some bears [12] _____

(approach) me without fear. I [13] _____ (take) hundreds of photos of mothers, cubs and males. It was incredible and exciting, but I [14] _____ (never / be) so scared!

UNIT 8
Defining relative clauses
Form

He is the man *who (that)* invented the World Wide Web.
This is the system *which (that)* I told you about.
That is the place *where* we buy our computers.

Use

We use *who* (for people), *which* (for things) and *where* (for places) to introduce defining relative clauses. These clauses give us essential information about the person, place or thing we are talking about.
The person who discovered the solution was from China.
The factory which makes the machine employs 200 people.
The organisation where he works is called Novotech.

We can use *that* for people or things instead of *who* or *which*. This is less formal.
The person that discovered the solution was from China.
The factory that makes the machine employs 200 people.

Practice

1 Join the two sentences with the correct relative pronoun (*who, which, where*).

1 He's the man. He invented a new kind of bicycle.
He's the man who invented a new kind of bicycle.
2 That's the farm. They are experimenting with new crops at the farm.

3 There is the woman. She works in my father's laboratory.

4 These are the machines. They use less energy.

5 That is the nuclear power station. They had problems at the power station last year.

6 This is the documentary. I was watching it last week.

7 She's the doctor. She saved my father's life.

8 That's the factory. They developed the new lamps at the factory.

Zero and first conditional
Form
Zero conditional

If-clause (*If / When* + present simple), main clause (present simple)
If / When you drive very fast, it is more difficult to stop the car.

First conditional

If-clause (*If / When* + present simple), main clause (*will*)
If you **drive** very fast, it **will** be more difficult to stop.

We can use *if* in two positions:
- *If*-clause first: *If you travel abroad, you need a passport.*
- Main clause first: *You need a passport if you travel abroad.*

When the *if*-clause is at the beginning of the sentence, we use a comma to separate it from the main clause.

Use

Zero conditional

We use the zero conditional to talk about facts or things that are generally true.
If you want to travel in the USA, you need a visa.
When you cool water to zero degrees, it freezes.

When you talk about things that are generally true, you can use *if* or *when*. There's no difference in meaning.

First conditional

We use the first conditional to talk about a possible future situation.
If it rains tomorrow, we won't go to the mountains.

When you talk about situations in the future, there is a difference between *if* and *when*. We use *when* + present simple to talk about a certain future action.
When Jack **arrives**, I'll ask him to help us.

Practice

2 Complete the sentences with the correct form of the verbs.

1 When a mosquito lands on your skin, it ___tries___ (try) to suck your blood.
2 If a dog wags its tail, it _____ (mean) that it is happy.
3 If the weather is good, we _____ (explore) the forest on Saturday.
4 If they find a cure for cancer, many people _____ (live) much longer.
5 When he comes home from an expedition, he _____ (be) usually very tired.
6 When Oliver gets here tomorrow, I _____ (not tell) him about my problems.
7 Those fish _____ (die) if you don't clean the fish tank!
8 People _____ (become) dehydrated when they don't drink enough water.

UNIT 9

Present simple passive / *by* + agent
Form

We form the present simple passive with the present simple of the verb *to be* (*am / is / are*) + past participle.

Affirmative and negative		
Uniform	**is/isn't**	**worn** at the school.
Students	**are/aren't**	**taught** in big classes.

Interrogative		
Is	uniform	**worn** at the school?
Are	students	**taught** in big classes?

Use

We use the present simple passive when we want to focus on an action or the object of the action, rather than the person who is doing the action. The object of the active sentence becomes the subject of the passive sentence.

Active: Students take the exam in the summer.
(subject) (object)

Passive: The exam is taken by students in the summer.
(subject) (object)

by + agent

In an active sentence, you know who did the action.
Teachers teach Kung Fu in many countries.

In a passive sentence, we can say who did the action (the agent) using *by*.
Kung Fu is taught **by teachers** *in many countries.*

We use *by* + agent when it is important to know who did the action.
Kung Fu is taught in many countries **by specially trained teachers.**

It isn't always necessary to use *by* + agent. We don't usually use the agent when it is obvious who has done the action, when we don't know the name of the agent or when it isn't important or relevant.
Uniform is worn at the school ~~by students~~.
Lunch is served ~~by someone~~ *every day at 1.00.*

Practice

1 Rewrite the sentences in the present simple passive form. Use *by* + agent where appropriate.

1 They teach French at that school.
   French is taught at that school.
2 She does her homework on a computer.

3 Tutors usually provide lecture notes via the Internet.

4 They keep old books in that part of the library.

5 Do you use laptops at your school?

6 The students print out course material during the course.

7 Their employers don't pay for the English classes.

8 Students often complete course work online.

Past simple passive

Form

We form the past simple passive with the past simple of the verb *to be* (*was / were*) + past participle.

Affirmative and negative		
Black ink	**was/wasn't**	**invented** by the Egyptians.
Spices	**were/weren't**	**discovered** in Asia.

Interrogative		
Was	black ink	**invented** by the Egyptians?
Were	spices	**discovered** in Asia?

Use

We use the past simple passive when we want to focus on a past action or the object of the past action, rather than the person who did the action. The object of the active sentence becomes the subject of the passive sentence.

Active: subject   object
Scribes wrote letters for the Pharoahs.
Passive: subject   object
Letters were written by scribes for the Pharoahs.

Practice

2 Complete the text with the past simple passive form of the verbs.

carve	discover	~~find~~	leave	make	paint
record	use	worship			

There are cave paintings and cave art all over Europe. Famous examples [1] *were found* in Lascaux, France and Altimera, in Spain many years ago. In 2003, new paintings [2] _____ by researchers in Nottinghamshire, northern England. The question is, why [3] _____ they _____? There are many theories but many experts agree that early hunters and priests or 'shamen' gathered before a hunt to pray for good luck. Animal gods or spirits [4] _____ in the hope that the hunt would be successful. After the hunt, the events [5] _____ in drawings or paintings. Natural dyes and colours [6] _____ and paints [7] _____ from substances such as blood, plants and earth. Often, animals [8] _____ from wood or stone and sometimes these objects [9] _____ next to the paintings. Whatever the origins of the cave paintings, people are still amazed by their beauty and mystery.

UNIT 10

Past perfect simple

Form

We form the past perfect simple with the past simple of the verb *have* (*had*) + past participle.

Affirmative	Negative	Interrogative
I/you/he/she/it/we/they **had worked** hard.	I/you/he/she/it/we/they **hadn't** (had not) **worked** hard.	**Had** I/you/he/she/it/we/they **worked** hard?

Short answers
Yes, I/you/he/she/it/we/they **had**.
No, I/you/he/she/it/we/they **hadn't**.

Note: In spoken English we often use *'d* (= *had*). Don't confuse the contracted forms of *had* and *would*.
I'd worked in the hotel for five years. (= I had worked)
I'd like to work in that hotel. (= I would like to work)

Use

We use the past perfect simple to talk about an action in the past that happened before another action or before a certain time in the past.
I had visited Rome twice before I went to Venice.
We often use the past perfect simple and the past simple together.
I had bought my ticket online before I arrived at the station.

We often use the following time expressions with the past perfect simple: *already, just, before, previously, recently* and *earlier*.
I had just bought my ticket when the train arrived at the station.

Practice

1 Complete the sentences with the past simple or past perfect simple form of the verbs.

1 James _____*went*_____ (go) to Spain after he _____*had visited*_____ (visit) Portugal.
2 We _____ (be) in Brighton for two weeks before Mark _____ (arrive).
3 They _____ (cancel) their flights two days after they _____ (book) them!
4 I _____ (not meet) any other travellers until I _____ (get) to the mountains.
5 _____ they _____ (travel) abroad before they _____ (visit) Italy?
6 When I _____ (arrive) at the hostel I realised I _____ (forget) my sleeping bag.
7 I _____ (not explore) the jungle before I _____ (get) to Costa Rica.
8 They _____ (check) into the same hotel that they _____ (stay) in previously.

Subject and object questions

Form

▶ SUBJECT QUESTIONS		
subject	verb	object
Who	cancelled	the flight?
What	happened	to Tim

We do not use an auxiliary verb (*do, does, did*) with subject questions.

▶ OBJECT QUESTIONS

question word	auxiliary	subject	main verb
What	does	he	like?
Who	did	she	visit?

We use an auxiliary verb (*do, does, did*) with object questions.

Use

In **subject questions** the question word (*who, what, which, whose, how much / many*) is the subject of the verb. The word order is the same as in the affirmative sentence.
Who cancelled the flight? Paul cancelled the flight.

In **object questions** the question word is not the subject of the verb and the word order is not the same as in the affirmative sentence.
Who did she visit? She visited her parents.

Note that we cannot form subject questions with the following question words: *where, when, why, how.*
Where did they go on holiday? (not ~~Where they went on holiday?~~)
How does she travel? (not ~~How she travels?~~)

Practice

2 Write subject questions (S) and object questions (O).

1   Who / work / here (S)
    Who works here?

2   What / be / that (S)

3   Where / you / live (O)

4   How much / the holiday / cost (O)

5   Which / resort / be / this (S)

6   Where / they / go / last year (O)

7   When / you / want / to catch / the train (O)

8   What / country / be / this (S)

-ing / -ed adjectives and dependent prepositions

Form

-ed adjectives
*I'm **bored**.*
*He is **interested** in rock climbing.*

-ing adjectives
*This book is very **boring**.*
*He is an **interesting** person.*

Use

We use *-ed* adjectives to describe how a person feels about something or someone.
*They were **amazed** by the quality of the photos.*
*He was **excited** to see his friends.*

We use *-ing* adjectives to describe a place, person or thing.
*London is an **exciting** city.*
*Digital cameras are **amazing** inventions.*

-ed adjectives are often followed by dependent prepositions: *amazed **by**, annoyed **with**, bored **with**, excited **about**, fascinated **by**, interested **in**, tired **of**, worried **about**.*

Dependent prepositions are followed by nouns or gerunds.
*They were worried about **the flight**.*
*They were worried about **flying**.*

Practice

3 Complete the sentences with the *-ed* or *-ing* form of the adjectives.

annoy	~~bore~~	excite	fascinate	interest
please	tire	worry		

1   The new adventure film was really *boring* .
2   The plane journey was very _____ . We went to bed when we arrived.
3   India is a _____ country to travel in. There are so many things to see.
4   We weren't very _____ with the hotel. It was dirty and rundown.
5   They weren't very _____ in going to the museum – the queues were too long.
6   Emily was very _____ with the tour guide. He didn't know anything!
7   There's an _____ trip to the coast at the weekend. I've never been diving before!
8   We were _____ about the storms in the USA. They are often very damaging.

UNIT 11

used to

Form

Affirmative	Negative	Interrogative
I/you/he/she/it/we/they **used to** play hockey at university.	I/you/he/she/it/we/they **didn't use to** play hockey at university.	**Did** I/you/he/she/it/we/they **use to** play hockey at university?
		Short answers
		Yes, I/you/he/she/it/we/they **did**.
		No, I/you/he/she/it/we/they **didn't**.

We use an infinitive without *to* after *used to*.
*The gallery **used to open** at 9.00 a.m.*
*It **didn't use to have** a restaurant.*

Note that the negative and interrogative forms do not have a final -d in *use to*.
*Sophie **didn't use to** like sightseeing.*
***Did** Sophie **use to** like sightseeing?*

Use

We use *used to* to talk about a situation, a state or a habit in the past which doesn't happen now.
- State: *I **used to have** long hair when I was young.*
- Habit: *I **used to play** tennis three times a week.*

We don't use *used to* with a particular time in the past. We use the past simple instead.
I used to go to university ~~in 2005~~.
I went to university in 2005.

The past situation, state or habit may or may not still be true in the present.
I used to live in Oxford, but now I live in Paris.
They didn't use to eat meat, and they still don't now.

We can only use *used to* to talk about the past. We cannot use it to talk about the present.
*I **used to** visit museums every week. (past)*
*I **usually visit** museums every week. (present)*

Practice

1 Complete the sentences with *used to* and the verbs.

1 Victorian children ___used to play___ (play) with lots of dolls.
2 In ancient Rome, captured warriors _____ (work) as slaves.
3 _____ the Vikings _____ (wear) make-up?
4 Before the electric light, people _____ (go) to bed early.
5 The Celts _____ (not sleep) in beds.
6 In 1914, 48% of people _____ (drive) a Ford car.

Reported speech

Form

When we report what someone said, we often move the tense 'backwards'.

▶ DIRECT SPEECH	▶ REPORTED SPEECH
Present simple	**Past simple**
Alfie: I **live** in London.	Alfie said that he **lived** in London.
Present continuous	**Past continuous**
Mary: I **am working** very hard.	Mary said that she **was working** very hard.
Past simple	**Past perfect simple**
Mick: I **wanted** to be an astronaut.	Mick said that he **had wanted** to be an astronaut.
Present perfect simple	**Past perfect simple**
Sue: I **have read** the travel guide.	Sue said that she **had read** the travel guide.
will	*would*
Jack: I **will meet** you at the café.	Jack said that he **would meet** me at the café.

We often need to make other changes when we report what someone said:
- Pronouns: *I → he / she; we → they; my → his / her; our → their; you (object) → me*
- Time expressions: *now → then; today → that day; tomorrow → the next day; yesterday → the previous day; last night → the night before*

Use

We use reported speech to say what another person said to us or when we report someone's words from the past.
Direct speech: *'I **am getting** married **tomorrow**.'*
Reported speech: *She said that she **was getting** married **the next day**.*

We can use the conjunction *that* in reported speech. There is no difference.
Direct speech: *'I think Manchester United will win.'*
Reported speech: *Paul said **that** he thought Manchester United would win. = Paul said he thought Manchester United would win.*

We often use the verb *say* to report someone's words. We don't follow *say* with an object.
*'I think Manchester United will win.' → Paul **said** (that) he thought Manchester United would win.*

We can use *tell* to report someone's words and to say who someone is talking to. *Tell* always needs an object such as *me, him, her, you, us them, everyone.*
*'I think Manchester United will win.' → Paul **told me** (that) he thought Manchester United would win.*

Practice

2 Change the direct speech into reported speech.

1 The famous model: I like diamonds.
   The famous model said that she liked diamonds.
2 The politician: I don't want to talk to them.

3 The writer: I haven't got any new ideas.

4 The businessman: I'm going to Russia on Friday.

5 The organiser: We won't be able to build the Olympic stadium on time.

6 The government: We've cut taxes for the poor.

7 The scientist: Did you understand the experiment?

8 The famous actor: I didn't see the first James Bond film.

UNIT 12

any-, *every-*, *no-*, *some-* and *-thing*, *-where*, *-one*, *-body*

Form

	-thing (object / action)	*-where* (place)	*-one* (person)	*-body* (person)
any-	anything	anywhere	anyone	anybody
every-	everything	everywhere	everyone	everybody
no-	nothing	nowhere	no one	nobody
some-	something	somewhere	someone	somebody

When we use these pronouns as subjects, the verb is in the singular form.
*Everyone **likes** taking photos.*
*There **isn't** anyone here.*

Use

We use indefinite pronouns to talk in general about things, people or places. We use *every-*, *any-* and *some-* in the affirmative.
***Everything** is fascinating on this trip.*
*I'm looking for **something** to eat.*

We use *no-* and *not any* in negative sentences.
*I haven't got **anywhere** to go.*
*There wasn't **anything** to do.*

Note that *not any-* = *no-*. There is no difference between them.
*There **isn't anywhere** to sit. = There is **nowhere** to sit.*

We use *any-* in questions.
*Have you visited **anywhere** interesting today?*

There is no difference between the two 'person' words.
*There is **no one** on the island. = There is **nobody** on the island.*

We can use these pronouns before adjectives to give more detail.
*Lucy discovered **somewhere beautiful** on holiday.*

Practice

1 Complete the sentences with the words.

> ~~something~~   anyone   everything   anything
> somewhere   anywhere   somebody
> everybody

1 I'm going to see ___*something*___ exciting at the park.
2 We are driving to _____ beautiful tomorrow.
3 Are you meeting _____ you know there?
4 He didn't buy me _____ for my birthday!
5 I just saw _____ running into our garden.
6 Did you go _____ interesting when you were in Spain?
7 _____ wanted to hear the latest news.
8 Please leave _____ where it is and don't move.

Second conditional

Form

If-clause (*If / When* + past simple), main clause (*would / wouldn't* + infinitive)
***If** there **was** a hurricane, it **would destroy** the village.*

Main clause (*would / wouldn't* + infinitive) *if*-clause (*if* + past simple)
*People **would move** out if the sea levels **rose**.*

Use

We use the second conditional to talk about unreal or imagined situations. We use *if* + past simple in the *if*-clause to describe the situation. We use *would / wouldn't* + infinitive in the main clause to describe the imagined result of, or reaction to, the situation.
*If I **had** a lot of money, I **would donate** it to charity.*
*What **would** you **say if** you **met** a famous explorer?*

When we give advice, we often use *If I were you* rather than *If I was you*:
*If I **were** you, I would go on holiday.*

Practice

2 Choose the correct options.

1 If I (*was*)/ *would be* rich, I *went* /(*would go*) on a safari in Africa.
2 If it *rained / would rain* more, the crops *were / would grow* better.
3 If Ben *moved / would move* to London, he *found / would find* a good job.
4 What *did you do / would you do* if there *was / would be* a snow storm?
5 If there *was / would be* a tsunami, it *destroyed / would destroy* the town.
6 I *didn't tell / wouldn't tell* her if she *asked / would ask* me.
7 He *drove / wouldn't drive* to work if there *was / would be* ice on the road.
8 *Did you take / Would you take* me to the mountains if the weather *was / would be* nice?

Unit 1

1.1

People sometimes think Mary and Gerald are married but in fact they're just good friends. They have known each other for forty years because they regularly go ballroom dancing. Every week they meet and practise dancing. Mary Hall is eighty-five years old and Gerald Kavanagh is eighty. So, after all these years, why do they dance? Probably because it's good for their health for two reasons. It's good physical exercise, but dancing is also about learning new movements so it's good for your mental health as well. Dancing is one good reason for their long and happy life.

1.2

This quiz is a good way for people to find out how they sleep. It shows them what kind of person they are. People with mostly A answers usually sleep very well. They have regular routines and they are hardly ever tired. People with B answers sleep fairly well. Most adults wake up once or twice a night and that's normal. But these people probably have busy working lives or families so they always want extra hours in bed. Try to go to bed earlier and sleep for an extra hour at weekends. People with mostly C answers have the biggest problems. These people don't relax before bedtime. They regularly work in the evening or do exercise. Don't misunderstand me. Sport is good for your health but not late at night.

1.4

P = Presenter, D = David McLain

P: No one knows exactly the reason why some people live longer than others. Why are they so healthy? Is it their diet? Do they go to the gym more than others? Well, one man is trying to answer these questions and that man is explorer and journalist David McLain. He's currently travelling to places and regions with large numbers of people aged a hundred and over and asking the questions: Why are they so healthy? What are they doing that the rest of us aren't? At the moment he's working on the Island of Sardinia in Italy but he's speaking to us right now on the phone. David, thank you for joining us today.

D: Hello.

P: So, first of all. Tell us why you decided to visit Sardinia.

D: Well, Sardinia is an interesting place because men live the same amount of time as women. That isn't normal for most countries. Men normally die younger.

P: And does anyone know the reason why people live longer in Sardinia?

D: There are different ideas about this but possibly one explanation is that the family is so important here. Every Sunday the whole family meets and they eat a huge meal together. Research shows that in countries where people live longer, the family is important. But also on Sardinia, the older mother or grandmother often has authority in the family. As men get older, they have less responsibility in Sardinian culture. So, perhaps the older men have less stress, which means they're living longer.

P: I see. So, do you think people live longer in traditional societies?

D: That's an interesting question. It's true that even on Sardinia the younger generation are eating more food like chips and burgers. Also young people are moving to the city, so they are doing less exercise because of their lifestyle. So, it will be interesting to come back to Sardinia in twenty years and see if people are still living longer …

1.6

Conversation 1

C = Customer, P = Pharmacist

C: Hello. I've got a sore throat and a runny nose. I feel terrible.

P: Have you got a temperature as well?

C: No, it's normal.

P: Well, you should take this medicine twice a day. It's good for a sore throat.

C: Thanks.

P: And try drinking hot water with honey and lemon. That helps.

C: OK. I will.

P: Oh, and you need a box of tissues. If you still feel ill in a few days, see a doctor.

Conversation 2

P = Patient, D = Doctor

P: I've got an earache in this ear. I couldn't sleep last night because it was so painful.

D: Let me have a look. … ah … yes, it's very red in there. What about the other one?

P: It feels fine.

D: Hmm. It's a bit red as well. Do you feel sick at all?

P: No, not really.

D: Let me check your temperature. … Yes, it's higher than normal. I'll give you something for it. You need to take one of these pills twice a day for seven days. Drink lots of water and come back if you don't feel better.

Unit 2

1.7

The swimming race in the photo is one part of three races in total. The competitors swim for 3.86 kilometres (that's two point four miles), cycle for 180 kilometres and run a marathon at the end. It's called the Ironman triathlon and the men swimming in the photo are all competing at the annual Ironman world championship in Hawaii. Hundreds of people compete but thousands of spectators also watch the famous contest. They all want to see someone win the ultimate test of fitness.

1.9

M = Meg, P = Paul, K = Kirsty

M: I love getting up early every morning and going to the pool. It's really quiet at this time and there are only one or two other people. I'm not very good at swimming but I've got problems with my back so it helps with that.

P: I prefer watching sports to doing them. Especially running. We have to do sport at school on Tuesdays and Fridays with our teacher Mr Sykes. He tells us to run round and round the school field. Running is really boring exercise and I'm always last. I hate losing.

K: I like playing tennis so much that currently I'm working with a tennis coach to improve my game. I've got my first competition in a month. I'm very excited about competing because one day I'd like to become a professional player and this is an opportunity to see how good I really am against other players.

1.11

Well, here we are in a place called Banner Elk. Yes, I'd never heard of it either. Anyway, it's in the mountains of North Carolina, USA and it is cold! But that doesn't stop hundreds of competitors coming here every October for the town's annual Woolly Worm Race. The rules for the competition are easy. Anyone of any age can enter but you must have a woolly worm. You can bring your own or you can buy one before the race. Each race has twenty people and twenty woolly worms. You have to put your worm on a piece of string at the start. Then they're off! The only rule is that you mustn't touch your worm during the race. During the day, there are lots of races and if your woolly worm beats the others in the race, you take part in the grand final in the afternoon. And the prize money is one thousand dollars! Well worth it I'd say …

1.12

A: Hey! Have you seen this?

B: What?

A: This advert. You're really good at doing that.

B: Yes, but I have so much work at the moment, I don't have time.

A: So this is a good way to relax.

B: I can take a good one of friends and family but I'm not very creative with it.

A: Alright. Well, what about joining something else? Er, this one! Are you interested in acting?

B: You're joking. I hate standing up in front of people. You're more of a performer than me.

A: Yes, but it's a musical. I'm not very good at singing.

B: Let's have a look at that. But it says here enthusiasm is more important than talent. Go on. I think you'd enjoy it.

A: Emm, well maybe but I think I'd prefer to join this on Wednesday evenings.

B: What? You? Do exercise?

A: What do you mean? Me? Anyway, it looks fun. Why don't you come too?

B: Me? But I can't even walk twenty kilometres, never mind run it.

A: No, but that's the point. Look, there's even a beginner's group. You should do it with me.

Unit 3

1.14

This photo is on a train in Bangladesh. It was the end of Ramadan and lots of people travel home at that time of year. Train tickets sell out quickly so you often see people riding on top of the trains and the carriages. In this picture the woman is sitting between the carriages because there isn't space on top of the train. It looks a bit dangerous but she doesn't look very worried.

1.15

A: One day I'd like to buy an electric car. They're much cleaner than petrol cars. But I'm not sure if I'll see many on the road in the near future.

B: But you can already buy them.

A: Really?

B: Sure, and they have the most efficient type of engine. Unfortunately they're much more expensive than petrol cars. When they're cheaper, more people will buy them.

A: I'm not sure if that's better or worse! With more people on the road, we'll have more traffic jams.

B: Especially at eight in the morning. It's the worst time of the day.

A: Yes. I try to avoid the rush hour now. I leave home before seven.

B: Well, I'd like to leave the car at home but every other type of transport is slower. This town needs better public transport. The buses don't go to the right places. And they are always late. Last week I waited for a number twenty-nine for over an hour …

1.17

Documentary 1

On a beautiful summer morning in Thailand, guests are arriving for a wedding. Some are arriving in cars but the most special guests are riding, in traditional style, on the backs of elephants. Elephants are as heavy as cars but they aren't as fast, and most people also think elephants aren't as comfortable as cars. However, in Thailand these animals have great importance. The Asian elephant became a domestic animal 5,000 years ago. In the past they transported soldiers to wars and worked in the forests pulling up trees and carrying wood. Nowadays, it's more common to see them transporting tourists and people on special occasions, but they are as important as ever in Thai society.

Documentary 2

Lester Courtney and his wife spend a lot of time with their horses, not for leisure but for work. They are traditional tree loggers who cut trees in traditional ways. They also transport the trees traditionally – with horses. Once the trees are down, Dan and Maddy pull them away. They're Lester's two horses. Lester has always used horses. Horses aren't the fastest form of transportation but Lester doesn't believe modern machines are as good. It's true that horses aren't as strong as lorries, or as fast, but Lester prefers working with animals. For one thing a horse isn't as heavy as modern machinery so it doesn't damage the old forests. Lester also prefers horses because horses aren't as noisy.

 1.19

1 J = Javier, D = Driver

J: Hello? Are you the next taxi?
D: Yes, that's right.
J: I'd like to go to the station, please.
D: Bus or train?
J: Oh sorry. The train station.
D: OK. Get in then.

2 D = Driver, J = Javier

D: There are road works up by the entrance.
J: You can drop me off here. It's fine. How much is that?
D: Six pounds thirty.
J: Sorry, I only have a twenty-pound note. Do you have change?
D: Sure. So, that's thirteen pounds seventy. Do you want a receipt?
J: No, it's OK thanks. Bye.

3 S = Shelley, D = Driver

S: Hi. Do you stop at the airport?
D: Yeah, I do. Which terminal is it? North or south?
S: Err. I need to get to the … north terminal.
D: OK. A single or return ticket?
S: Single, please.
D: That's two pounds.

4 J = Javier, T = Ticket office clerk

J: A return ticket to the airport, please.
T: OK. The next train goes in five minutes.
J: Right. That one, please.
T: First or second class?
J: Second.
T: OK. That's fourteen pounds fifty.
J: Wow! Can I pay by cheque?
T: Sorry. Cash or credit card.
J: Oh no … Oh, one moment. Maybe I have enough left.
T: OK. Here you are.
J: Which platform is it?
T: Err, platform six.

5 A = Attendant, S = Shelley, J = Javier

A: Hello. Can I see your passport?
S: Here you are. I don't have a ticket because I booked online.
A: That's OK. How many bags are you checking in?
S: None. I only have this carry on.
A: OK. Window or aisle?
S: Err, I don't mind but can I have a seat next to my friend?
A: Has he already checked in?
S: No, I'm waiting for him.
A: Well, I can't …
J: Shelley!
S: Shelley!
S: Where have you been?
J: It's a long story.

Unit 4

 1.21

My name's Vic and I live in the state of Tennessee. During the week I work in a bank but at the weekends I go caving. Colleagues at work think I'm a bit crazy because it's dangerous and sometimes you have to take risks, but I like the challenge. Every cave is a new adventure. I think my biggest achievement so far was reaching Rumbling Falls Cave. It's a really challenging cave because you climb down a hole that's about twenty metres into the ground. Then you go up two waterfalls and through a cave on your hands and knees for nearly a mile so you need to be physically fit. But at the end, you suddenly come to what we call the Rumble Room. It's an incredible place. It's a gigantic room – and it's like a different world.

 1.23

1 Where did Edurne Pasaban live? In the mountainous Basque region of Spain.
2 When did she climb her first mountain? When she was fourteen.
3 What did she study at university? Engineering.
4 When did Steven Shoppman and Stephen Bouey drive round the world? From 2007 to 2010.
5 What did they go across? A minefield.
6 What did they find? That the world wasn't as dangerous as they thought.

 1.24

I = Interviewer, W = Sandy Weisz

I: Normally we only hear bad news so it's good to have some good news from time to time. For example, did you hear in the news about Maria Garza? She was sitting on an aeroplane in Denver airport with her one-year-old child when she saw a fire from the window. It was coming from one of the engines. Did you read that? No? It was amazing. While the other passengers were running to the exits, Maria climbed out of the window and onto the wing of the plane. She saved her daughter's life and she was pregnant at the time! So, in fact she saved three lives.
In today's programme we're talking about why some people are survivors. We want to know what makes these people so special. For example, what are their personal qualities? Here to help us answer that question is Doctor Sandy Weisz. Sandy is a doctor of psychology and an expert in survival skills. So Sandy, what kind of person is a survivor?
W: Well, the story of Maria Garza is a good one because she showed a personal quality that all survivors have.
I: Which is?

W: They are always decisive. They always think and move very quickly and so she saved three lives. It's an important quality in a difficult situation. Another important quality they need is determination. For example, did you read about thirteen-year-old Bethany Hamilton? She showed real determination. One day when she was surfing a shark attacked her and she lost an arm. It was an incredible story. With one arm, she swam back to the beach.
I: Incredible, and there was another recent similar story … err that couple … the Carlsons.
W: Sorry, what were they doing?
I: They were sailing their boat when a wave hit them. The boat sank and they were at sea for thirty-one days.
W: Oh yes, I remember that story. But they were experienced with boats so skill and knowledge probably saved them more than anything else.
I: Right. So, what if I don't have special personal qualities or skills? Is there anything I can do?
W: Yes, there is. Most survivors don't normally take risks.
I: What do you mean?
W: Well, on an aeroplane, the survivors usually wear seat belts. At sea, you take extra food and water. On a mountain, a climber always wears warm clothes …
I: Right. I suppose we normally think survivors are risk-takers but in fact most of them are quite careful.
W: Exactly. We all take risks – even when we walk across the road – but most survivors don't take unnecessary risks.

 1.26

A: Hi Mark. How was your camping trip?
B: It was great in the end but we had a terrible time at the beginning.
A: Why?
B: First, we left the house early on Saturday morning but after only half an hour the car broke down.
A: Oh no!
B: Fortunately, there was a garage nearby and the mechanic fixed the problem. But when we arrived at the forest, it was getting dark. After we drove around for about an hour, we finally found the campsite but it was completely dark by then. Unfortunately, it started raining so we found a nice hotel down the road!
A: That was lucky!
B: Yes, it was a great hotel and in the end we stayed there for the whole weekend.
A: Sounds great!

Unit 5

1.28

Every day we use objects like computers, mobile phones and household appliances such as washing machines and cookers without thinking. So, when you see a sculpture by the artist George Sabra, it's surprising because he uses these objects in new ways. Take the sculpture in the photo, for example. It looks like a strange animal and it's made of wood, metal and plastic. The body is wood from a beach. The round head is made of metal and the hair is made of metal and plastic computer parts. George makes these sculptures because he wants people to think about the environment and about recycling and reusing everyday objects.

1.29

P = Presenter, R = Reg, S = Sandra

P: OK. So, this week on Radio Talk, we're talking about recycling. We want to know: How much do you recycle? And do you think it's important? The phone lines are open … and our first caller this morning is Reg from Cambridgeshire. Reg, you're on Radio Talk. Go ahead. Reg? Are you there?

R: Hello? Can you hear me?

P: Yes, Reg, I can hear you and so can about half a million other people. What did you want to say, Reg?

R: Well. A lot of people talk about recycling these days and they say it's good for the environment, but I'm not so sure. Take where I live, for example. There aren't any recycling centres in my town.

P: Really, Reg? But what about at your local supermarket? Are there any recycling bins there?

R: OK, yes there are some recycling bins I admit and a lot of people take their rubbish there. But listen to this. A lorry comes every single week to take it all away. I ask you! How is that good for the environment? Think about all the fuel it uses. No, I'm not convinced. And another thing …

P: Actually Reg. I'm going to stop you there because on line two I have another caller. Line two? Are you there?

S: Hello, yes I'm here.

P: And what's your name?

S: Sandra.

P: OK Sandra. You are live on Radio Talk.

S: Well, I'm really angry with the man who was just on.

P: You mean Reg?

S: Yes. He's just like all the people who live round me. They don't recycle much stuff either.

P: What? None of them?

S: Well, not many people on my street recycle. I don't know about other parts of the town. Every week I see them. They throw away a lot of bags. I suppose some people recycle a little rubbish every week. They don't think they have time for recycling.

P: And do you ever say anything to them?

S: Yes, I do! I tell them. You only need a few minutes every day to separate your glass, plastic and paper. And there are a lot of places where you can take recycling. There's no excuse at all.

P: That's an interesting opinion Sandra and so what I want to do is bring back Reg who's waiting on line one … Reg?

R: Hello?

P: Reg, I'd like to you reply to Sandra because she says it's easy to recycle. What do you say to that?

R: Well, she might be right but where I live you can't …

1.32

V = recorded voice, C = Customer care assistant, J = Jane

V: Thank you for calling Teco Art dot com. Your call is important to us. For information about our latest products, press one. For orders, press two. For problems with your order, press three. … All our customer service assistants are busy. We apologise for the delay. Your call is important to us. One of our customer service assistants will be with you as soon as possible.

C: Good morning. Can I help you?

J: Hi, I'm calling about an order for a Computer Circuit Board Clock from your website but I received an email saying I have to wait seven more days.

C: One moment … Do you have the order number?

J: Yes, it's 8-0-5-3-1-A.

C: Is that A as in Alpha?

J: That's right.

C: Is that Ms Jane Powell of 90 North Lane?

J: Yes, it is.

C: Hmm. Can I put you on hold for a moment?

J: Sure.

C: Hello?

J: Yes, hello.

C: I'm very sorry but this product isn't in stock at the moment. We'll have it in seven days.

J: I already know that. But it's my husband's birthday tomorrow.

C: I see. Well, would you like to order a similar clock? We have an Apple iPod one for thirty-five pounds.

J: Hmm. I really liked the one I ordered.

C: Oh, I'm sorry about that. Would you like to cancel the order?

J: Yes, I think so. How does that work?

C: Well, we'll refund the amount of thirty-nine pounds to your credit card.

J: OK. Thanks.

C: And would you like confirmation by email?

J: Yes, please.

C: Let me check. Your email is J – powell at S-mail dot com.

J: That's right.

C: Is there anything else I can help you with?

J: No, thanks. That's everything.

C: OK. Goodbye.

J: Bye.

Unit 6

1.35

In the story of the Sphinx, the answer to the question is 'man'. This is because, a baby moves using two hands and two feet. An adult walks on two legs and an old person walks on two legs but also needs a walking stick. In the question the Sphinx also talks about three different parts of the day: morning, noon and evening. These parts of the day represent the different stages of our life. Morning is childhood. Noon is the middle of our life. Evening is old-age. In the original Greek story, the Sphinx killed many travellers because they didn't know the answer. Finally, one man answered the question correctly. He was Oedipus and when he answered 'man', the Sphinx killed itself.

1.36

Speaker 1

One day I plan to go to university but first I want to take a year off to get some work experience abroad. So, at the moment I'm working at a local supermarket and I'm going to save all my money. Then I'd like to travel to somewhere like Australia if I can afford it.

Speaker 2

People seem to think this stage in life means looking after grandchildren and playing golf. Well forget that! I intend to do all the things I wanted to do but never had time. And as for work! Well, I'll be happy to leave my job, I can tell you.

Speaker 3

We hope to get a place of our own but these days it's really difficult to buy a house. House prices are so high so we're still living with my husband's parents. It's hard not to feel sad about it.

1.38

R = Reporter, L = Lorette

R: It's about six o'clock in the morning here in New Orleans and the streets are very quiet. But in about six hours the city is going to have the biggest party in the world and thousands of visitors from all over are going to fill the streets. However, Mardi Gras is really about the local communities in the city. So, I've come to the traditional Tremé neighbourhood of New Orleans where there are already some people preparing for the big day. So, I'll try to speak to some of them … Hello? Hello?

L: Hello?

R: Hello. What's your name?

L: Lorette.

R: Hi Lorette. You're wearing a fantastic costume. Are you going to be in the parade this afternoon?

L: That's right. I'm meeting everyone at the float in a few minutes and then we're riding through the city.

R: As I say your dress looks amazing. Did you make it?

L: Yes, we all make our own costumes for Mardi Gras.

R: And do you have a mask?

L: Sure. Here it is. I'll put it on.

R: Wow. That's perfect. So tell me. How important is Mardi Gras for the people in Tremé?

L: It's the most important part of the year. It brings people together.

R: Well, good luck this afternoon. You're going to have a great time, I'm sure!

1.40

Conversation 1

I = Ian, A = Abdullah

I: Hi Abdullah. How's it going?

A: Good. I finished all my courses today so I can relax.

I: Great. Maybe you'll have time for some travelling and sightseeing now.

A: Maybe. But I think I'll take it easy this weekend.

I: Oh! Well, why don't you come to my house? My family is coming over. We're having a barbecue in the back garden. It'll be fun.

A: Thanks, but I have a few things to do at home and it's with your family so you probably don't want other people there …

I: No, really. Don't worry because I'm inviting a few people from our class as well. So you'll know people. I'd really like you to come.

A: OK. Thanks, that would be great. Is it a special occasion?

I: Well, my oldest sister has a new baby girl so it's a bit of a celebration for that.

A: Oh! So I should bring something.

I: No, please don't. It isn't like that. There's no need …

Conversation 2

J = Joanna, S = Sally

J: Hello Sally. How are you?

S: Fine, thanks. It's been a busy week.

J: Yes, I imagine. When do you finish?

S: Tomorrow.

J: Oh, really. I didn't realise it was so soon.

S: Well actually, my flight home is on Saturday.

J: But you're staying for another week?

S: No.

J: Oh. Well, what are doing tonight?

S: Nothing at the moment. I'll be at my hotel.

J: Well, would you like to come out for dinner? Let's go somewhere this evening.

S: Really? I'd love to.

J: Of course. I'd like to take you to my favourite restaurant.

S: That would be wonderful. I'd like that very much.

J: Great. Let's go straight after work. I'll meet you downstairs in reception.

S: OK. What time?

J: I finish at six. Is that OK for you?

S: Sure. I'll see you then. Bye.

Unit 7

2.1

People often say twins and triplets have similar emotions and feelings as well as the same appearance. Well, these triplets also have the same job. They are the Koralja brothers. That's Andrew on the left, Joseph in the middle and Robert on the right. They all became police officers fourteen years ago so if you add up their total years of service, that's about forty-two years. And they all work for the New Jersey State Police so they deal with everything from serious crime to traffic accidents across the state of New Jersey.

2.2

Nick Veasey takes photographs of ordinary people, places and objects but no one could describe the final photographs as ordinary. In fact, they are very creative. Nick uses X-ray photography and, as a result, you see inside the object. The final images are often beautiful, strange or surprising. Working with X-rays can be dangerous because of the radiation. So safety always comes first for Nick. His well-equipped studio is a large black building. It has thick concrete walls to stop the radiation. Inside he has different X-ray machines for different sizes and types of images. But not everything he photographs will fit in the studio so sometimes he has to travel to them. For example, he has photographed an aeroplane, a bus and an office building with people working inside. These kinds of projects take many days and many different X-rays. Then, he takes the best image back to his studio and spends a lot of his working day improving the image on his computer until it is ready for an exhibition. You can see his photos in galleries all over the world and many companies also use his images in their advertisements.

2.5

I = Interviewer, E = Engineer

I: How long have you worked for your company?

E: For twenty-five years. Since I left college.

I: So, when did you study engineering?

E I started college when I was nineteen and I qualified as an engineer about four years later.

I: And have you always lived in Pennsylvania?

E: No. I've lived in lots of different places. In the energy business, you live where the work is.

I: So, when did you move here?

E: In 2007. Just after they found the gas here.

I: So, how many different places have you lived in, do you think?

E: I'd say about fifteen, maybe sixteen places.

I: Have you ever lived abroad?

E: Yes, but only for about three months.

I: And how does Pennsylvania compare with other places? Has it been easy living here?

E: Yes, it has, overall.

I: Have the local people been friendly?

E: Yes, they have. Well, most people anyway.

I: Ah, but not everyone?

E: Some people didn't want us here in the beginning because they were worried about the environment. But the changes have been good for this region. It's brought

jobs back to Pennsylvania. So, I think most people have understood how important this is …

2.6

I = Interviewer, C = Candidate

I: Right. Have a seat, Ruby.

C: Thanks.

I: So, I've received your CV and your letter of application. And I see your current job is as a sales assistant at Raystone's Bookshop. So, how long have you worked there?

C: I've been there for about eighteen months.

I: Oh, yes, I see now. So, in that case, why have you applied for this position?

C: Well, I've really enjoyed my work at Raystone's. I've always been interested in books and usually the customers are really nice. And I like trying to find books for them. Especially the rare copies of books.

I: So, why do you want to leave them?

C: Because it's quite a small independent bookshop whereas E.I. Books is a much bigger company. I read on your website you have over fifty branches now and you're still growing. And I see you also have a website where people can order books. So, I think there are probably lots of opportunities for me in the future.

I: Well, it's true that we've grown quickly in recent years. And it's nice to see you've found out about the company. So would you describe yourself as ambitious?

C: Um, I don't know. Not especially but I'd like to have a successful career.

I: And what are some of your main strengths?

C: Err, I work hard and I enjoy working with other people. And, er, I can solve problems.

I: So, I can ask you to do something and you can do it on your own?

C: Yes, I think so.

I: Well, I've asked you a lot of questions. Do you have any questions for me?

C: Yes, I have. I've applied for the post of sales assistant here but earlier I said I was interested in developing a career. Are there often opportunities in the company for promotion?

I: Yes, we're growing all the time and if you are prepared to move, there are jobs at other branches.

C: OK. Great. And in the job description, it says you offer flexible hours. Can you tell me more about that?

I: Sure. Because we open our bookshops in the evenings as well as during the day, we ask staff when they prefer to work. We have one member of staff who likes to work a few hours in the morning and then a few hours in the evening.

C: I see.

Unit 8

2.7

It's difficult to remember what life was like before technology. It solves mathematical problems for us. It sends messages to friends in a second. It even cooks dinner for us. When technology makes a mistake, it's only because it's following instructions from a human. So, what's the next big step in technology? Robots are common in industry such as car manufacturing and recently NASA sent the first humanoid robot into space where it works on the International Space Station. It's called Robotnaut 2 or R2 and it does all the simple or repetitive jobs so the astronauts can spend more time doing experiments. Perhaps in a few years' time every home will have their own R2.

2.8

More than one billion people in the world don't have glasses but need them. These

people live in parts of the world where there aren't many opticians. For example, in parts of Africa there is only one optician per million people. But now, there is a scientist who has found a solution to the problem. Joshua Silver has invented glasses which don't need an optician.

They look like a pair of normal glasses but there is a pump on each side with silicone oil. First, you turn a wheel which controls the pump. The pump pushes the silicone oil through the pipe and it moves into the lenses. The shape of the lens changes and you turn the wheel until you can see correctly.

Silver had the idea a few years ago and he did many experiments before he got it right. The first person who used the new glasses was a man in Ghana. The man made clothes but he had bad eyesight and found it difficult to work. But when the man put on the glasses, he could start working again. Silver says, 'I will not forget that moment.'

As a result, Silver started an organisation which is called the 'Centre for Vision in the Developing World'. The glasses are cheap to produce and so far the organisation has worked in Africa, Asia and Eastern Europe where over thirty thousand people now wear the glasses. Joshua hopes a billion people across the whole world will have them by 2020.

2.11

A: So, what are we going to take with us?

B: Well, I don't know what the weather's going to be like. If it rains, we'll need all this waterproof clothing.

A: Yes, but if we take all that, there won't be space for anything else. Anyway, when I go canoeing I always get wet. Why are you packing that?

B: If we don't have a map, we'll probably get lost.

A: Don't worry. If I bring my GPS, we'll know exactly where we are at all times. What about food?

B: I normally take tins and packets of food when I go on a trip like this.

A: Good idea. If you carry the food in your canoe, I'll pack both the tents in mine.

B: Maybe that's not such a good idea. If something happens to one of us, then the other person either won't have any food or won't have a tent.

A: Well, hopefully that won't happen if we're careful.

2.14

A: OK. All packed?

B: Nearly. I've got the tent. I've got my walking boots.

A: Have you got a good coat? They say it's going to rain.

B: Err, I only have this one.

A: Yeah, it'll be OK. Hey, what's that?

B: Oh yeah, my brother gave it to me.

A: Wow. That is cool! Where do I switch it on?

B: Here. But you press this if you want different types of light.

A: What do you mean?

B: Press here if you want normal lighting. But you need to press here for long distances.

A: Wow! That's amazing.

B: It can light objects sixty metres way. And press it again and you get a flashing red light for emergencies.

A: Aaah, I want one!

B: And listen to this.

A: How did you do that?

B: I pressed this button. It's a sound for emergencies. You know, if you get lost during the day and you need help.

A: Brilliant! What is this for?

B: Plugging it into your laptop.

A: Why do you need to do that?

B: To recharge the battery.

A: But what if you don't have your laptop?

B: Well, the battery lasts for a hundred and sixty hours so you shouldn't need it.

A: Fantastic. Where can I get one?

Unit 9

2.15

While I was working as an English teacher in Japan, I tried to learn the language but it was hard. Even the kids found their own language hard. This photo is of a second grade class at the school. They were all practising writing some of the different letters for the sound 'shou' in Japanese. A lot of Japanese words are homophones so they have the same sound but different meanings. Japanese has so many letters and symbols to learn. There are several thousand, most of which have come from Chinese. It's similar to English in the sense that it has also taken words in the past from other languages. For example, you can find lots of English words which have come from the languages of German and French.

2.17

1

Every day, the ancient Shaolin temple is visited by hundreds of tourists. They come from all over China and from every type of background. There are soldiers, business people, retired people and young couples. In particular, there are parents with excited children who are punching and kicking. Most people have learnt about Kung Fu from films and TV and so they all come to the Shaolin Temple – the place where Kung Fu began. According to history, people started learning Kung Fu at the Shaolin Temple in the fifth century. Since then, Kung Fu teachers have taught generations of students.

2

Nowadays, the name of Shaolin is known across the Kung Fu world. It is a brand and a multi-million dollar business. Shaolin products are sold from the website. There are film and TV projects and Kung Fu demonstrations are given by groups of Shaolin performers. As a result, the Shaolin Temple has started a new interest in Kung Fu and it is taught in hundreds of new schools in China. In the city of Dengfend, for example, ten kilometres from the Shaolin Temple, more than 50,000 students are enrolled at one of the sixty martial arts schools.

3

For six days a week, eleven months a year, the school timetable starts early and finishes late. Male and female students as young as five get up early for their first class. They always wear red uniforms and stand in rows, practising Kung Fu. Many of these students have seen Kung Fu at the cinema and they dream of becoming a Kung Fu film star or a famous kickboxer. Others want to learn the skills they will need for a good job in the military or police force. Some students are sent by their parents because the schools are well-known for their hard work and discipline. At night, the students sleep in unheated rooms. They train outside even when the weather is below zero degrees. They hit trees to make their hands stronger and the movements are repeated again and again for hours on end.

2.19

H = College helpdesk, C = Caller

H: Hello, Corfield College. This is Melanie speaking.

C: Oh hello. I'm calling about your evening classes starting this term. Are there any places left?

H: Er, one moment. Let me take a look. I know one of them is full …

C: It's called *Preparing more effective PowerPoint presentations.*

H: Oh yes. That is a popular course … there is one place but I suggest you enrol soon.

C: Well, can I do it today?

H: Yes, it's all online so you need to go to the website. When you click on the 'ENROL NOW' button, the first thing you're asked to do is to fill in an enrolment form.

C: Right.

H: Have you seen the website?

C: Yes, but I didn't know if I had to fill in the form for a short course. There isn't an interview, is there?

H: No, no. Nothing like that. But when you've completed the online enrolment form, a copy is sent to us here at the office and also to the course trainer.

C: And do I pay when I send you the form?

H: It's up to you. Payment is accepted either when you enrol or no later than six weeks before the course starts. But you must pay a deposit so a place is reserved for you.

C: Well, I can pay it all straight away because my employer is paying.

H: Fine. After we've received payment, a receipt is emailed to your employer.

C: And then what happens?

H: Before the course starts, you mean?

C: Yes.

H: Once you've enrolled, you're sent a list of books to buy or any course materials. But actually … for your course … I don't think … no, all the materials are provided by the trainer. He'll provide those on the first day.

C: OK. Well, I'll book it now in that case. Thanks for your help.

H: You're welcome.

Unit 10

2.20

I = Interviewer, Z = Zoltan

I: Zoltan, you're a herpetologist which means you study snakes all around the world. So you have to travel a lot. Do you ever take holidays?

Z: No, not often. My work is also my hobby so I've been to Paris, to Rome, to the Pyramids and I went sightseeing there but it was always because my work took me there. For my last trip I was in the Sudan and I went looking for snakes.

I: But you must take a holiday sometimes?

Z: Well, once or twice I have travelled to places not connected to snakes. For example, I spent a holiday in the Seychelles with some friends. They enjoyed the beach and the markets while I went diving with my underwater camera.

I: Is that your most important item when you travel – your camera?

Z: Yes, my camera and my sleeping bag. With a sleeping bag, you can sleep anywhere you want.

I: So, do you ever stay in hotels?

Z: If I go with friends, I might stay at a luxury hotel or a resort but normally I'm on my own so I rarely book a hotel in advance.

I: What about when you were a child? Did your family take holidays?

Z: Yes, but I have been interested in snakes since the age of four. So, when we travelled, I looked for snakes and took them home. For me, a holiday has always been about exploration – about finding beauty and the unknown.

2.22

Story 1

A: So, where did you go exactly?

B: On the River Nile from Aswan to Luxor.

A: Wow! How long did it take?

B: Well, the cruise took about four days in the end but we stopped in lots of places. But on the first day, just after we'd left Aswan, the boat's engine stopped working.

A: Oh no! What happened next?

B: Well, eventually they fixed the problem but we spent an extra day on the ship which was fine. It was relaxing watching day-to-day life on the river.

Story 2

A: Where did you stay?

B: In a hotel near the train station. But it was a mistake. My bag was stolen from hotel reception!

A: Oh no! When did it happen?

B: Just after we'd arrived.

A: Who took it?

B: A man outside the hotel. He'd followed us into the hotel. Fortunately, the hotel receptionist ran after him and got it back. After that it was fine. We went sightseeing, visited a couple of museums. You know, all the usual things. But then, on the very last night, there was no electricity at the hotel.

A: So, what did you all do?

B: Well, first I went to look for the manager but she'd already left. The person at the front desk had some candles and all the guests sat together in the bar area and sang songs. Actually, it was a lot of fun in the end. That was probably the best part of the holiday …

2.23

I = Interviewer, M = Madelaine

I: So, Madelaine. We've talked about some of your photography and your travel writing with *National Geographic* magazine but I know that you're also very excited about your new job.

M: That's right. Recently, I've also started working as a tour guide with *National Geographic Adventures.*

I: Is that strange for you? I mean, you're someone who is fascinated by travel and experiencing new places so what is it like taking groups of people around on tour buses and showing them famous cities? It sounds a bit boring for someone like you.

M: Actually, it's fascinating because it isn't anything like what you've just described. These are *National Geographic Adventure* holidays so they're special types of holidays for people who love adventure and, on my tours, they are especially interested in photography.

I: So, this isn't your traditional package tour holiday by the beach with a bit of sightseeing.

M: No, not at all. It's for people who are bored with that kind of experience. This is something quite different. For example, my next job is in the famous Galápagos Archipelago.

I: Wow!

M: Exactly. This tour is very exciting because I've never been there before and it's such a legendary part of the world.

I: So, give us a basic idea of the type of people who go on the tour. How big is the group, for example?

M: Well, it's a small group of us, about nine or ten usually. Sometimes it's couples, but often they're independent travellers and you make new friends.

I: But don't independent travellers get annoyed with other people in the group. I mean, after all, they normally travel on their own.

M: Well, of course, everyone has the same interests so quite a few people come on their own and then make friends with everyone in the group. But if someone wants to go and walk up the side of a volcano on their own or spend the day in a canoe out on the sea, that's fine. The itinerary is very flexible. But there are also scheduled events. For example, I give some talks about taking photographs and in the evenings we usually cook our meals together on a barbecue – it's a lot of fun.

I: One last question. Some of our listeners are probably thinking it all sounds amazing but they're worried about the physical requirements for this kind of holiday. How physically fit do you need to be?

M: You don't have to be an athlete or anything, but you should be an active person and we tell people that before they come. This is an adventure holiday after all. But there's also plenty of time for relaxing by the beach in the evenings. And you never get tired of the views. It must be the best job in the world …

2.25

TI = Tourist information, T = Tourist

TI: Bonjour Monsieur.

T: Ah, bonjour. Sorry, do you speak English?

TI: Yes, I do. How can I help?

T: I'm interested in the catacombs museum. Can you tell me if it's open today?

TI: Err, let me check. I don't think so. A lot of places are closed on a Monday in Paris. No. Every day except Monday.

T: Oh, well. That's OK. What time does it open?

TI: At ten and it closes at five. … Would you like to book a ticket for tomorrow? I can do it for you here. There's usually a long queue for the catacombs but if you book it here you don't need to queue.

T: Oh right. That sounds like a good idea. But err … I'd like to know how long it lasts?

TI: The tour through the tunnels is forty-five minutes long and you might have to wait a few minutes at the beginning. So, about an hour in total.

T: Fine. Is there much walking? I can't walk very far you see.

TI: Well, the tour is about two kilometres long. And there are some steps down under the ground at the beginning and then at the end.

T: Do you have any idea how many steps there are? Is it far?

TI: Over a hundred I think. Yes, a hundred and thirty.

T: Oh dear. Perhaps I'd better choose something else.

TI: Have you been on the sightseeing bus? It takes you all round Paris …

Unit 11

2.27

Just over one hundred years ago, the British explorer, Captain Robert Falcon Scott died with his team of men in the snow and ice of Antarctica. He had reached the South Pole but never returned to this hut which was the base for his expedition. Now the hut is falling down under the snow but we would like to save it. Not just because of its connection to Scott, though this of course is important, but actually, we are more interested in what you find inside the hut. Because of the freezing temperatures in this part of the world, the hut has become a time capsule – a place where nothing has changed. So for example, inside the hut there is butter and other items of food which are one hundred years old. The ice has preserved them all. There are even some of Scott's old possessions and equipment. When you go inside, it's almost as if Scott has only just left the hut. It's important to look after this hut because you can't find anything else like it in Antarctica or anywhere else in the world.

2.28

R = Reporter, A = Archaeologist

R: I believe archaeologists discovered this pyramid in 1978.

A: That's right. But we haven't excavated everything yet. There's still a lot to do.

R: Where are we standing now?

A: We're near the north wall of the pyramid.

R: And why have you brought me here?

A: Well, recently we discovered this box in the ground which tells us a lot about the Aztecs.

R: Yes, I can see that it's full of objects. What are they?

A: Some of them are pots or plates. They used to make them for cooking.

R: I see. And what else is in there?

A: There were some small pieces of gold and a precious blue stone called jade but we've taken them out now. The Aztecs used to do a lot of business and so these types of stones were important. We also found some small statues which had religious importance. And also there were knives. The Aztecs used to sacrifice animals – and even other humans – to their gods. So the knives are probably for sacrifices.

R: Did you find any bodies?

A: Actually, yes. The skeleton of a dog but it wasn't from a sacrifice. It wore a beautiful collar so it was obviously an important animal.

R: Did the Aztecs use to keep dogs as pets?

A: No, they didn't use to have pets. Well, we don't think they did. But obviously this dog was important in some way. Maybe the owner used him for hunting.

2.30

1 Did the ancient Egyptians use to build pyramids and castles?
   They used to build pyramids but they didn't use to build castles.

2 Did the ancient Greeks use to watch theatre and sport?
   Yes, they did.

3 Did the Celts use to live in South America and Asia?
   No, they didn't. They used to live in parts of western Europe.

4 Did the North American Indians use to grow corn and potatoes?
   Yes, they did.

2.31

Good morning and thank you all for coming. Today I'd like to talk about my holiday in Peru and in particular, about my journey to Machu Picchu. It's also called 'The Lost City of the Incas'. Let me begin by telling you about the history of Machu Picchu. It was discovered by the explorer Hiram Bingham in 1911 …

So, that's everything I wanted to say about Hiram Bingham. Now, let's move onto the history of the Incas and why they built Machu Picchu. The first Incas lived in the region of Peru around the thirteenth century …

OK. Now, the next part of my presentation is about my own journey through Peru and up to Machu Picchu. For this, I'd like to show you some of my photos. So, this first one is a picture of me in the town of Aguas Calientes. You have to catch the bus from here to Machu Picchu …

OK. That's the end of my talk. So, to sum up, Peru, and especially Machu Picchu is a magical place and anyone who's interested in history should go there. Are there any questions?

Unit 12

2.33

I'm standing in the middle of some trees on the quiet Barro Colorado Islands in Panama.

It's nine o'clock in the evening so it's difficult to see. But if you wait and look really closely you start to see the ground move. And what looks like leaves is starting to move. But they aren't leaves, they are toads and during the day they hide from other animals. On the side of the tree, there are two eyes looking at me. In fact, they are the wings of a butterfly. These animals are experts at using plants to hide themselves. And not only when they are hiding but also when they go hunting. Take snakes, for example. I can't see any in the long grass I'm walking in but I know that there are hundreds of them living here so I have to be really careful …

2.34

Everyone looks at nature differently. Maybe you're somebody who has no interest in nature and if you go anywhere green, you don't notice anything. Or maybe you can name a few different plants and animals in your local park. But for people like David Liittschwager, nowhere in the world is without natural beauty. He sees plants and animals everywhere he looks. David is a photographer for *National Geographic* magazine and he wanted to show how much nature there is around us all the time. So, he took a green metal frame measuring one cubic foot to different locations around the world. For example, to the middle of a forest, on the side of a mountain, in the ocean and in a river. Nowhere was too far away or too difficult for David. Then, he spent three weeks in each place and he photographed everything alive inside the green metal frame. This included photographing living things as small as one millimetre in size. The result was a series of photos showing over a thousand individual organisms in each cubic foot and a new view of our world and its ecosystem.

2.35

A: Would you move to another country if the weather became much hotter in your country?

B: No, I'd love it if the weather became hotter.

A: I'd go and live somewhere else.

B: Would you?

A: Yes, I wouldn't want to stay. I'd find a country with a colder climate.

B: Oh, I wouldn't. I'd spend every day outside by the pool.

2.37

Z = Zoo manager, C = City Council

Z: What about giving us more money?

C: I'm sorry, but the council doesn't have any more money for the zoo.

Z: But if we don't find a solution soon, then we'll have to close it. And the zoo is part of the city. It's a tourist attraction.

C: Yes, but that's the point. It simply isn't attracting enough tourists. You're going to have to find the money from somewhere else.

Z: It's also an important place for animal conservation. Some of these animals are close to extinction. If we didn't have zoos, they wouldn't survive.

C: I understand that but we need to find a different solution. What if you advertised the zoo more? In the newspaper or on the radio, for example.

Z: But if we don't have any money, we can't advertise.

C: Well, why don't you try sponsorship? You know, ask a company to support the zoo.

Z: Actually, that isn't a bad idea. You might be right!

C: I have the names of some company bosses you could contact …

Life Pre-intermediate Student's Book
John Hughes
Helen Stephenson
Paul Dummett

Publisher: Jason Mann

Publishing Consultant: Karen Spiller

Editorial Project Manager: Karen Spiller

Development Editor: Shona Rodger

Project Editor: Amy Smith

Production Controller: Tom Relf

Head of Marketing Communications:
 Ruth McAleavey

National Geographic Liaison: Leila Hishmeh

Art Director: Natasa Arsenidou

Cover Designers: Sofia Fourtouni
 and Vasiliki Christoforidou

Text Designer: Keith Shaw

Compositor: eMC Design Ltd.

Audio: Prolingua Productions

Contributing Writers: Mike Downie, David Gray
(video lessons) and David A. Hill (grammar
reference)

Contributing Editors: Clare Nielsen-Marsh,
Jessica Rackham

The Publishers would like to thank the following
for their advisory roles in the preparation of the
material: Lobat Asadi (Middle East) and
John Evans (Teacher, UK language school)

For permission to use material from this text or product, submit all
requests online at **www.cengage.com/permissions**.

Further permissions questions can be emailed to
permissionrequest@cengage.com.

ISBN: 978-1-133-31570-4

National Geographic Learning
Cheriton House, North Way, Andover, Hampshire
SP10 5BE United Kingdom

Cengage Learning is a leading provider of customised learning
solutions with office locations around the globe, including Singapore,
the United Kingdom, Australia, Mexico, Brazil and Japan. Locate our
local office at **international.cengage.com/region**

Cengage Learning products are represented in Canada
by Nelson Education, Ltd.

Visit National Geographic Learning online at **ngl.cengage.com**

Visit our corporate website at **www.cengage.com**

CREDITS
Although every effort has been made to contact copyright holders before publication, this has not always been possible.
If notified, the publisher will undertake to rectify any errors or omissions at the earliest opportunity.

Photos
The publishers would like to thank the following sources for permission to reproduce their copyright protected photographs:
Cover: George Steinmetz/National Geographic Image Collection
Inside: pp 5 (Barry Bishop/National Geographic Image Collection), 6 (Daniel Munoz/Reuters/Corbis), 8 (Maria
6 (t) (Kristin Piljay/Alamy), 6 (b) (Danita Delimont/Alamy), 7 (tl) (John Woodworth/Alamy), 7 (tr) (dbimages/Alamy),
7 (cr) (Nadia Isakova/Alamy), 7 (bl) (Jeremy Fahringer), 8 (tl) (Brendan McCarthy/The Bendigo Advertiser), 8 (tc) (Patrick
McFeeley/National Geographic Society/Corbis), 8 (tr) (Amy Johansson), 8 (tcl) (Stephen Alvarez/National Geographic Image
Collection), 8 (tcc) (Peter Essick/National Geographic Image Collection), 8 (tcr) (Bill Ellzey/National Geographic Image
Collection), 8 (bcl) (Michael S. Yamashita/National Geographic Image Collection), 8 (bcc) (NASA), 8 (bcr) (Cary Wolinsky/
National Geographic Image Collection), 8 (bl) (Zoltan Takacs), 8 (bc) (Barcroft/Fame Pictures), 8 (br) (Christian Ziegler/
National Geographic Image Collection), 9 (Brendan McCarthy/The Bendigo Advertiser), 11 (Shutterstock), 12 (David McLain/
National Geographic Image Collection), 13 (Max Power/Corbis), 15 (Pete McBride/National Geographic Image Collection),
17 (Dr Joe) (theboone/iStockphoto), 17 (Petra) (Shutterstock), 17 (Sabine) (megamix/iStockphoto), 18 (Peter Horree/Alamy),
20 (Cesare Naldi/National Geographic Image Collection), 21 (Patrick Mcfeeley/National Geographic Society/Corbis),
22 (Bettmann/Corbis), 24 (t) (Ric Thayer/Reuters/Corbis), 24 (c) (Jim Cole/AP/Press Association Images), 24 (b) (All Canada
Photos/SuperStock), 25 (Ross McDermott), 26 (Ivan Kashinsky/National Geographic Image Collection), 27 (t) (Ivan Kashinsky/
National Geographic Image Collection), 27 (bl) (Ivan Kashinsky/National Geographic Image Collection), 28 (Shutterstock),
29 (Blickwinkel/Alamy), 30 (Peter Macdiarmid/Getty Images News), 32 (Ross McDermott), 33 (Amy Johansson), 36 (tl) (Patricio
Robles Gil/Sierra Madre/Minden Pictures), 36 (tr) (Joe Petersburger/National Geographic Image Collection), 37 (Alison
Wright/National Geographic Image Collection), 39 (Ami Vitale/Getty Images), 40 (bl) (Shutterstock), 40 (bcl) (Shutterstock),
40 (bcr) (Shutterstock), 40 (br) (Shutterstock), 42 (dbimages/Alamy), 44 (Li Huang/ColorChinaPhoto/AP/Press Association
Images), 45 (Stephen Alvarez/National Geographic Image Collection), 46 (bl) (AFP/Getty Images), 46 (br) (Steve Bouey),

Printed in China by RR Donnelley
2 3 4 5 6 7 8 9 10 – 17 16 15 14 13

47 (Reza/National Geographic Image Collection), 48 (Bryce Milton), 50 (tl) (AF archive/Alamy), 50 (tr) (Jim McKnight/AP/Press Association Images), 51 (Buz Groshong), 52 (Robert Houser/Photolibrary), 53 (Shutterstock), 54 (Kristin Piljay/Alamy), 56 (Pacific Stock/Photolibrary), 57 (Peter Essick/National Geographic Image Collection), 59 (t) (Peter Essick/National Geographic Image Collection), 59 (r) (Peter Essick/National Geographic Image Collection), 62 (Paul Miller/epa/Corbis), 63 (Luca Babini), 64 (l) (TEcoArt), 64 (r) (TEcoArt), 65 (Jeremy Sutton-Hibbert/Alamy), 66 (aberCPC/Alamy), 68 (Shutterstock), 69 (Bill Ellzey/ National Geographic Image Collection), 70 (Richard Ligato), 72 (Nathan Benn/Alamy), 73 (Krista Rossow/National Geographic Image Collection), 74 (Louise Gubb/Corbis Saba), 75 (Peter Adams/Photolibrary/Getty Images), 76 (Superstock/Photolibrary), 77 (Shutterstock), 78 (Sean Drakes/LatinContent/Getty Images), 80 (Justin Kase z01z/Alamy), 81 (Michael S. Yamashita/National Geographic Image Collection), 82 (Nick Veasey), 84 (tc) (Scott Goldsmith), 84 (bl) (Scott Goldsmith), 84 (br) (Scott Goldsmith), 85 (tl) (Scott Goldsmith), 85 (bl) (Scott Goldsmith), 87 (Robb Kendrick/National Geographic Image Collection), 89 (Shutterstock), 90 (Jiri Rezac/Alamy), 92 (Shutterstock), 93 (NASA), 94 (t) (Centre for Vision in the Developing World), 94 (bl) (Joshua Silver/ National Geographic Image Collection), 95 (Vestergaard Frandsen), 96 (cr) (Bryan Smith), 96 (br) (Iridium Communications), 97 (Iridium Communications), 98 (bl) (Robert Clark/National Geographic Image Collection), 98 (bcl) (Annie Griffiths/National Geographic Image Collection), 98 (bcr) (Flip Nicklin/Minden Pictures), 98 (br) (Robert Clark/National Geographic Image Collection), 99 (tl) (Robert Clark/National Geographic Image Collection), 99 (tr) (Robert Clark/National Geographic Image Collection), 99 (bl) (Greg Dale/National Geographic Image Collection), 99 (bcl) (Robert Clark/National Geographic Image Collection), 99 (bcr) (Robert Clark/National Geographic Image Collection), 99 (br) (Robert Clark/National Geographic Image Collection), 100 (t) (Christine Whitehead/Alamy), 100 (b/g) (Shutterstock), 101 (mathieukorview/iStockphoto), 102 (Toshiaki Ono/Age Fotostock), 104 (NASA/Bill Ingalls), 105 (Cary Wolinsky/National Geographic Image Collection), 106 (Fritz Hoffmann/ National Geographic Image Collection), 107 (Corbis Cusp/Alamy), 109 (c) (Shutterstock), 109 (r) (Shutterstock), 109 (br) (David Robertson/Alamy), 111 (David Boyer/National Geographic Image Collection), 112 (jsmith/iStockphoto), 114 (Jeremy Fahringer), 116 (Chris Rainier), 117 (Zoltan Takacs), 118 (billyfotoview/iStockphoto), 120 (thinair28view/iStockphoto), 121 (bl) (Pete Ryan/ National Geographic Image Collection), 121 (bc) (Frans Lanting/National Geographic Image Collection), 121 (br) (Walleyelj/ Dreamstime), 123 (Stephen Alvarez/National Geographic Image Collection), 124 (Stephen Alvarez/National Geographic Image Collection), 125 (Ralph Lee Hopkins/National Geographic Image Collection), 126 (John Woodworth/Alamy), 128 (ArtBoyMBview/iStockphoto), 129 (Barcroft/Fame Pictures), 130 (Andrew Rakoczy/Photo Researchers/Getty Images), 131 (Ancient Art & Architecture Collection Ltd/Alamy), 132 (NASA Headquarters – GReatest Images of NASA (NASA-HQ-GRIN)), 134 (Martin Schoeller/National Geographic Image Collection), 135 (Michael Nichols/National Geographic Image Collection), 136 (Shutterstock), 137 (Reinhold Messner/National Geographic Image Collection), 138 (Danita Delimont/Alamy), 140 (American Museum of Natural History, New York, USA/The Bridgeman Art Library), 141 (Christian Ziegler/National Geographic Image Collection), 142 (tl) (David Liittschwager/National Geographic Image Collection), 142 (tcl) (David Liittschwager/National Geographic Image Collection), 142 (tcr) (David Liittschwager/National Geographic Image Collection), 142 (tr) (David Liittschwager/National Geographic Image Collection), 143 (t) (David Liittschwager/National Geographic Image Collection), 143 (ct) (David Liittschwager/National Geographic Image Collection), 143 (bc) (David Liittschwager/National Geographic Image Collection), 143 (b) (David Liittschwager/National Geographic Image Collection), 144 (b) (Carsten Peter/National Geographic Image Collection), 144 (inset) (Robert Clark/National Geographic Image Collection), 147 (t) (Peter Essick/National Geographic Image Collection), 147 (c) (Peter Essick/National Geographic Image Collection), 148 (David Cheskin/PA Archive/Press Association Images), 150 (b/g) (Nadia Isakova/Alamy), 150 (cr) (Peter Arnold/Photolibrary), 150 (cr) (National Geographic Image Collection/Alamy), 152 (Michael Roberts/National Geographic Image Collection), 153 (bl) (Shutterstock), 153 (bcl) (Shutterstock), 153 (bc) (DonNicholsview/iStockphoto), 153 (bcr) (Shutterstock), 153 (br) (Shutterstock), 154 (cl) (The Art Archive/Alamy), 154 (tr) (redhumview/iStockphoto), 155 (cl) (The Art Archive/Alamy), 155 (tr) (redhumvview/iStockphoto)

Text
We are grateful to the following for permission to reproduce their copyright material:
National Geographic for extracts adapted from "Quiz: Need more sleep?", http://ngm.nationalgeographic.com/; "Longevity, The Secret to Long Life", http://ngm.nationalgeographic.com/; "The Big Idea", 15 October 2009, http://ngm.nationalgeographic. com/; "Kamchatka Project", 15 July 2010, http://newswatch.nationalgeographic.com/; "Preserving Native America's vanishing languages" by David Braun, 15 November 2009, http://newswatch.nationalgeographic.com/; and "Introducing National Geographic Adventures!" http://www.nationalgeographicexpeditions.com/, copyright © National Geographic, reproduced with permission; and Zoltan Takacs for an interview, used with kind permission.

Illustrations by Matthew Hams pp 10, 144, 162; Kevin Hopgood pp 23, 56; Dave Russell pp 53, 60, 72, 145; Martin Sanders pp 50, 58; Mark Turner p 72; Eric Olsen p 16; Laszlo Veres pp 108–109; Graham White p 34; National Geographic Maps pp 6–7